I come from a land that was nobody's land
and anybody's. I come from a war
of accents and blood, from heather
taking root in the bones of clans,
while the wind whispers
the old names. I come from a land
where villages are crumbled and sunk, where stories
disturb the bottoms of lakes.

KATIE HALE

'Offcomer'

NORTH
COUNTRY

An anthology of landscape and nature

Edited and with an introduction by

KAREN LLOYD

and SARA HUNT, coeditor

Saraband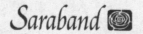

Published by Saraband
1801 Lightbox,
MediaCityUK, Salford,
Greater Manchester, M30 9AF

Registered office:
3 Clairmont Gardens
Glasgow, G3 7LW
www.saraband.net

ISBN: 9781913393403

Printed and bound in Great Britain by Clays Ltd, Elcograf S.p.A.

1 2 3 4 5 6 7 8 9 10

CONTENTS

ENDNOTES

CONTRIBUTORS

ACKNOWLEDGEMENTS

INTRODUCTION

The North is 'the backbone of Britain', writes poet Lemn Sissay in 'Anthem of the North,' the brilliantly assertive poem that opens *North Country*. This anthology came into being because we believe that Northern writers deserve specific attention; that they are indeed worthy of anthems. And attention is long overdue. *North Country* is therefore both a survey and a celebration of the North's landscapes and nature – and the writers whose work is collected here – a set of voices that provides a much-needed addition to our literary and place-specific culture.

As Paul Morley writes in *The North*, 'north' is a word 'that says so much and leaves plenty to the imagination.' Part of the anthology's job, therefore, was to explode preconceived notions of what the North is – or isn't. We needed to locate writers whose specific approaches take the reader into the heart of a new North; somewhere we're invited to look closer, or to look again; to encounter landscapes and nature in new and reinvigorated ways.

Through *North Country* we are witness to the ways in which literature has flowed through place *and* time, scoping a field from Wordsworth to Harriet Martineau and from Ted Hughes to Jenn Ashworth and Andrew Michael Hurley. Poets like Jason Allen-Paisant bring us bang up to date, his 'Those Who Can Afford Time' questioning exactly whose literature our education system represents and how that reflects the way we experience the world around us. Our aim was to assemble a diverse cohort of writers, which is necessary not only in the light of the Black Lives Matter movement but also through issues of access and mobility. *North Country* is therefore not only inclusive and representative of a broad geographic spread, but also reflects how society, politics, culture and personal experience change and develop over time. Some are household names – the Brontë sisters, Thomas Bewick,

Sarah Hall and Ted Hughes, but we also wanted to include new and emerging voices, a number of whom are published for the first time. Most writers are native to the region, though not all; we have also given a truly Northern welcome to a small number of writers from other part of the country, including Ghanaian-born Maxwell Ayamba, because of how their writing reframes, or reinterprets, significant aspects of northern experience.

North Country is made up of four sections, beginning with **Inflorescence**, in which we're delighted to bring some of the region's most exciting new and emerging literary voices to the page. There's no doubt that they will be the subject of much further attention. Secondly, **Retrospection,** in which we have gathered some of the most iconic literary voices – those whose movements and legacies continue to influence new generations, but others whose involvement in Northern landscapes is more surprising. Thirdly, in **Resistance** we bring together work that refuses – either through its subject matter or literary approach (or sometimes both) – more outmoded ways of looking at landscape and nature and instead makes new arguments or explorations; the kinds that resist ecocide, social stereotyping or pejorative ways of thinking about our natural and urban environments. **Restoration** brings together the kinds of celebratory work that shows how literature is a potent force for engagement with the world around us. Here are extraordinary examples of the written word that allow us to see exactly what can be achieved when the demands of humans are balanced against the simple prerequisites of nature and land.

Bringing new and emerging voices to a wide readership has been a joy and a privilege. Inflorescence celebrates their work. Take Stephen Dunstan, who is exemplary of the sort of new writing we set out to find. In 'Rezzarection,' Dunstan takes us on a journey into the ex-industrial outskirts of Barrow in Furness, a place frequently (not to say, lazily) characterised in the press as just another 'crap' town. But forget all that. Look at how the

worlds of football and birding are spliced together in a lockdown
Barrow FC game watched on-screen at home, where Dunstan
simultaneously reflects on the birds that have made their home
on an adjacent reservoir. When an away fan comments online that
the area surrounding the football ground was 'a dump,' Dunstan
retorts, 'to quote Basil Fawlty, what were they expecting to see
on the outskirts of a Cumbrian shipbuilding town? Herds of
wildebeest sweeping majestically across the plain?' In contrast,
Anne Taylor's essay (or cultural ramble) titled 'Wild Greens and
Golden Lads' unravels the life and uses of the humble dandelion. Who'd have thought that a roadside weed had this much to
offer? Taylor's insights are a joy to behold. In Walking to Spurn:
A Line Between Sea and River, Alison Armstrong walks the restless shore of Spurn Point, unravelling layers of human histories in
this loneliest northern outpost. Jules Carter's experimental essay
'A Place of Highest Honour' explores the Lake District's highest
mountain, Scafell Pike, and what it means to this time-served
fell-runner and climber, a writer whose sustaining narrative pur-
sues a series of unexpected twists and diversions.

Amongst the usual suspects in **Retrospection** (William and
Dorothy Wordsworth, Southey, Harriet Martineau and Elizabeth
Gaskell) we also include some literary surprises. For example, the
joint 1857 expedition of Charles Dickens and his co-conspira-
tor, Wilkie Collins. From Dicken's initial letter to his friend: 'I
am open to any proposal to go anywhere any day or days this
week....If I could only find an idle man (this is a general observation), he would find the warmest recognition in this direction,'
and the resulting journey north from which Dickens produced
The Lazy Tour of Two Idle Apprentices, a humorous interpretation of the pair's adventures in deepest Cumberland, and which
must be one of the greatest instances of self-effacing and gently
rollicking storytelling in the English language. 'Thomas Idle'
is Collins, and 'Francis Goodchild,' Dickens. After a series of

misadventures, Thomas concludes that activity is the root of all evil; that the only way forward, therefore, is to do absolutely nothing. But then, there's a mountain to climb, and it's raining. As the terrain steepens, Collins, aka Thomas Idle, asks, 'Was it for this that Thomas had left London? London, where there are nice short walks in level public gardens, with benches of repose set up at convenient distances for weary travellers...'

Poet Kathleen Raine's intense and formative experiences as a child growing up in the village of Great Bavington in rural Northumberland provides a deeply affecting set of images and reflections. Taken from her memoir of 1973, *Farewell Happy Fields*, Raine memorialises those early years with great facility, recording what existed and what was soon lost in this place of deep 'ancestral continuity.' Raine's world view however, offers no pastoral idyll; the village is a centre of hard living, a place where brutality and joy exist together with lives lived 'inwoven with the land.'

The North was also home to that disciple of nature and language, the Jesuit priest, poet and diarist Gerard Manley Hopkins, who taught for some years at Lancashire's Stonyhurst College. In one diary entry Hopkins notes, 'What you look hard at seems to look hard at you,' and nowhere is this more clear than in his observations of the Northern Lights seen from deepest rural Lancashire, a place where dark skies would then have been taken for granted. Dorothy Wordsworth reflected in her journals the daily joys she took in her surroundings near her Grasmere home: 'Walked to Ambleside in the evening round the lake, the prospect exceeding beautiful from Loughrigg Fell. It was so green that no eye could weary of reposing upon it.' And through our increasingly urbanised culture most of us have become what is called 'plant blind;' no longer able to identify common species of wildflower. It's rewarding then, not to say sobering, to read from the diaries of John Gough of Kendal, the 'blind botanist,' who, having lost his sight at the age of three from smallpox, went on to identify every single plant species in the Lake District through touch and scent.

In **Resistance**, we bring together writers whose work refuses conventional sentiments about place and nature, or that invite us to reconsider aspects of our cultural heritage. Maxwell Ayamba investigates notions of culture and race in our cultural institutions in the post-Colston landscape, and in 'The Rose Experts' Kate Davis explores identity, belonging and perceptions of wealth and poverty in her home town of Barrow. William Atkins takes a walk through Northumberland's Otterburn military training territories, the bogs and hills holding memories of occupation from Roman times. It was also important to locate writing that addresses our urban landscapes, and nowhere is this more successfully accomplished than in David Cooper's essay on Manchester's street trees, in particular the Manchester poplar, and in Michael Symmons Roberts circuitry and 'motherboard' of 'Great Northern Diver,' which in one momentous sentence observes the city at night from high above.

Sarah Hall's novel *The Electric Michelangelo* opens in the seaside town of Morecambe. In the selected passage, a fire engulfs the town pier in 'an almost biblical vision.' Caroline Gilfillan's 'Eagle Owl' considers a captive owl through the expedient of rural 'wildlife' entertainment. Norman Nicholson's 'Windscale' scrutinises the UK's major nuclear waste storage through the infamous 1957 fire and subsequent poisoning of adjacent land and water courses and beyond.

Much contemporary nature writing seems to be preoccupied with nature as the background to stories of personal recovery. At this juncture in the history of the planet, though, our aim was to navigate towards writing that brings urgent news from the environmental frontline. We know only too well that humans continue to destroy habitats and ecosystems, but we are also the only species capable of attaching meaning to experience. This is the theme at work in **Restoration.**

NORTH COUNTRY

Lee Schofield's 'Northern Hay Meadows' is an eloquent reminder of the disaster of industrialised farming, but then moves forwards through the changes taking place on the farms Schofield manages in the eastern Lake District. Hay meadows were once everywhere, places where invertebrates pollinated, where bees harvested the bounty of wildflowers and ground-nesting birds bred and thrived. And they can thrive again; even here in the harsh landscapes of the Lakes, Schofield shows that regeneration of plants and pollinators is entirely achievable. Here too are poems from Simon Armitage's Stanza Stones project, reimagining rain and puddles as visions of transformation, and Dani Cole explores the history and ecology of an urban woodland between Wigan and Bolton.

Linda France writes with great care and attention about a Newcastle city-centre walled garden in a piece that allows us to question the kinds of value placed on such hidden civic gems, and Mark Carson's 'think-poem' on the osprey has this assiduous fisher-bird manoeuvre its latest catch as 'a heavy bastard and I need the lift.' We travel deep underground with Peter Davidson on the miners' tradition of fashioning spar boxes – 'glass-fronted cases filled with assemblages of ... minerals ... sometimes an abstract arrangement, sometimes representations of street scenes or fantastical parks or caverns of crystals and shards of coloured minerals' in the high villages of the Wear and Tyne valleys.

Think of *North Country* not as just another nature anthology, but as a place to be at home with old friends and to make new acquaintances. Stay for a while or for the duration. Tune in as these distinctive voices from across and beyond the North invite us all to look more closely, more imaginatively, at some of the landscapes that we think of as home or our refuge, that give us hope, and that we think we know.

Karen Lloyd
Cumbria, 2022

Anthem of the North
LEMN SISSAY

The North Star leads the way
To the mountain top in awe
That, my friend, is why they say
Up up up... North

And so we build year after year
And we rise tide after time
We bring light to darkness
And we shine

Welcome to our future
And all she endows
This is our dream, our vision
This is our power, our house

This is the backbone of Britain
And they say it is cold
But there is nothing warmer
Than a Northern Soul

Even the tides of oceans speak of you
Upon their chosen course
"Bring as many waves as you can" they say
"for we are heading North"

And they come in waves to kiss our coast -
Urged on by the North Wind
The surge of river greets the Sea
"Come in" it says "come in"

The A's the E's the I's the O's the U's
Flocks of vowels fill the night with song
Great they are and migrate they do
The North is where they belong

Daughters of suffragettes sons of mines
The digital revolution – the creation
True North you North
You heart of our nation

And our children grow wings
And soar across this earth
But home they are assured
Is the greatest place on earth

Oh North North I love you
You made me the best I could be
You waited with open arms
And took in a stranger like me

We are the beautiful North
The darkness of night bows
We are a waterfall of light
This is our power, our house

One

INFLORESCENCE

*New and Emerging Voices
from the North*

Wild Greens and Golden Lads
ANNE TAYLOR

(i) We turn the corner of the lane at Sandwath Bridge and suddenly, filling the verge with a dazzling yellow, there are dandelions, hundreds of them, faces turned to the sun. The colour is almost shocking in its intensity. Oil-seed rape is not grown in my part of east Cumbria – this is sheep country – but I remember that sharp, bright colour from living further south. What I'm looking at today is a warmer yellow, strikingly vivid against the dull grey tarmac of the road. It is a moment of joy on an early spring morning.

(ii) There is a scattering of dandelions in our lawn, and a persistent one at the front door step, but they are poor, weedy specimens compared with these gloriously rounded golden buttons. Should I be nurturing the dandelions in my garden? Are they the first flowers to bloom in the spring, an important early source of nectar for bees? Surely not. I had snowdrops in the borders and lesser celandines in the lawn, long before the first dandelions. What about trees, shrubs and hedgerows? Place-names such as Whingill, from 'whin' meaning gorse, and The Ellers, from 'eller' for alder, tell of our local vegetation. Gorse flowers and alder catkins both produce early pollen and nectar.

(iii) The Old English name for dandelion was *aegwyrt* – eggwort – because of the rich egg-yolk colour. I love that word *wyrt* or *wort*, as in butterwort and toothwort, *wort* being a general term for a plant, vegetable or herb. So a pottage or *briw* was a porridge or one-pot meal made from cereals (such as barley or wheat), pulses (such as peas or beans), with onions of various kinds and *worts*. Have you eaten Easter Ledge Pudding, a north country survivor of the Old English pottage? It was made in parts of Westmorland,

Yorkshire and Lancashire to accompany roast lamb for Easter Sunday dinner. Boiled barley was mixed with beaten eggs and fresh hedgerow *worts* such as nettle tops, dandelion leaves, ramsons and sorrel, then baked in the oven or boiled in a pudding cloth. But the extra special ingredient was *Bistorta officinalis* – known by various country names such as Easter Ledges, Easter Mangiants or Poor Man's Cabbage. Every family had its own recipe. Sometimes the cereal would be oatmeal, sometimes the eggs were first hard boiled and chopped, but the most important element was always the freshly picked spring greenery, such as dandelion and bistort.

(iv) *Dandelion*, from the Greek, Latin and then French *dent-de-lion* or lion's tooth. The dark green leaves have 'teeth' that are unevenly jagged, teeth of varying lengths that curve out in many different directions. A bite from such a jaw would be painful indeed. Had the ancient Greeks seen lions? I was surprised to find the answer is yes. Lions appear in many stories and images from ancient Greece, in Homer's poetry for example, and as marble statues and painted on Greek vases. Sufficient lion bones have now been excavated to suggest that small packs of native lions still roamed much of southern Europe until around AD 100. But by then they had been hunted to extinction.

(v) 'Agrimony and Lyons Tooth, that children call Pysbed'. A sixteenth-century quote in the *Oxford English Dictionary*. How interesting that *dent-de-lion* has been translated back into English. And *pysbed* or *piss-a-bed*? Variations of this name are found all over Europe, *pissenlit* in France for example, because the plant is supposed to have diuretic qualities. A green salad served in a Parisian restaurant with little cubes of fried bacon is not ashamed to proclaim that *pissenlit* is the main ingredient. You will find 'salade de pissenlits' listed in French, Belgian and Swiss recipe books, but would you serve or eat 'piss-a-bed salad with bacon' in London?

(vi) You are more likely to have drunk dandelion, probably combined with burdock. The cordial is made from the fermented roots of both plants, and naturally caffeine-free dandelion coffee is made from roots that have been roasted and ground. When my parents moved to Suffolk in the 1970s there were still women in their village who gathered cowslips and dandelions to make wine, elderflowers for 'champagne' and crab-apples for jelly. Perhaps they also made dandelion honey. Not a true honey but dandelion flower heads slowly cooked in water, steeped overnight, strained and simmered with sugar. The syrup is delicious on porridge or ice-cream. Today there are not enough cowslips for a posy let alone for wine – Mrs Beeton's recipe requires one gallon of cowslip flowers. Crab-apples fall to the ground unused, and dandelions are strimmed from the roadside verges.

(vii) Are dandelions the seagulls of the plant world? We don't mind them as long as they don't disturb our lives; that we can enjoy and marvel at them at the edge of the road or in a field, but not in our neatly trimmed garden lawns or allotments.

(viii) In Britain we make daisy chains, a fiddly picnic occupation, trying to split the slender stem so the stem of another daisy can be inserted – and so on until you have a coronet or necklace. In other parts of Europe it was more usual to use dandelions, surely much easier with their thicker stems. But then of course you release the bitter milky sap: sap that gives the plant another country name, Devil's Milk Plant. And a variety known as the Russian dandelion, first found in Kazakhstan, exudes enough milky sap to be used as a source of rubber.

(ix) Perhaps you call dandelions 'Fairy Clocks', 'Time-tellers' or 'Clocks and Watches'? Blow the seed head to tell the time; the number of puffs needed to blow away all the seeds gives you the hour. You are left with a bald head on the stalk, the Priest's Crown, a name that Geoffrey Grigson tells us goes back to the fourteenth century. His book, *The Englishman's Flora,* included as many local names for our wild flowers as could be found, listing them by county, including of course the names for dandelion. This was compiled in the days before computers, so the names were all written down on slips of paper which then had to be physically sorted for the index. In the foreword to the 1987 edition Jane, his wife, describes how Grigson's children were enticed to assist in this process; they were given a point for every rude name they found. The dandelion would have been a rewarding plant for them to document, with names such as pee-a-bed, pittle bed and wet-weed.

(x) We'd completely forgotten about the dandelions until a week or so later, walking the same footpaths again, heading towards Waitby. Past Kirkby Stephen Cemetery, down Middlegate and into Greensike Lane. A cold still day, our heads down, striding out to keep warm, scarves pulled tight. As we turned the corner after Sandwath Bridge I thought, 'Oh, it's been snowing.' It was certainly cold enough. But no, it wasn't snow. A drift of white dandelion clocks – the seed heads – perfect spheres of feathery parachutes ready to float away on the breeze. And wherever the seed lands on a patch of suitable soil it can germinate immediately, so perhaps there will soon be more dandelions on the opposite bank. I pulled up a clock and studied its structure; the dense cluster of seeds, the intricate pattern of hairs, each one a fairy brush. I remembered then that in Shakespeare's time, in his home county of Warwickshire, 'golden lads' were the dandelion flowers and 'chimney sweepers' were the seed heads.

> *Golden lads and girls all must,*
> *As chimney-sweepers, come to dust.*

The Posy Is a Poem
CLAIRE BURNETT

I picked a posy as I walked the towpath so as not to forget the
way meadowsweet frothed the neck of tall red clover

how I had never seen magenta and cobalt vetch flowers in such
abundance, or their green tendrils scramble quite so high

walking with a stick I feel clumsy, while balancing me, it affects
my gait. I chose to leave my things in the car

be without distraction from my mobile phone, unencumbered
by my bag swinging against the momentum of my stick

which is why this poem is a posy. I would prefer to walk in
wilderness, but injury no longer allows this, so I am learning

about edgelands, where habitat exists alongside diesel fumed
narrowboats and farmland

I picked just one of everything to remind me of the walk, which
makes the posy become a poem

Queen Anne's Lace, blue geranium, a yellow flower I have
never seen before, one of everything except two bullrush stems

so as not to forget their rustling into susurration, as I pondered
the windowless liveaboard moored on the other bank

at home as I unpack wilted blooms into water, I can feel the
wooden gate I leaned on to admire the small herd of brown
and black cattle

the stately bull standing in the stream, surrounded by cows and
calves, appreciating the rarity of the scene

of anything less than a few hundred head of milkers or beef bulls, compacting the land, nameless except for numbered ear tags

I think of my father, wonder what he would have made of the industrialisation of bovines since he hung up his farming coat in 1973

the thornless thistle reminds me of the stone still heron, mirrored by the water, eyes fixed on dinner, until a woman threw a ball for her dog

the poem rehydrates in the miniature cut glass chalice, to survive on the kitchen table for a week

Firelight, Family and the Legacy of Place
GEOFF COX

There's a final rise, it's about half a mile beyond an owl-haunted, ruined farmhouse, a place where anticipation always builds, just before the ancient plantation comes into view. The steepening slope offers an excuse to slow the pace, especially as we're both carrying heavy winter packs, but I know that it's a sense of trepidation that slows me. I fear what damage may have been done up here; we're close to the end of a long winter and a succession of violent storms. From my home in the valley I've listened to high winds shrieking around these hills, driving heavy snowfall and keeping me from venturing out to assess damage to fences, trees and buildings. The snow is still banked along the sinuous wall-lines that map the route my son and I have chosen, but the parched yellow grass of the open fell is clear.

As we breast the rise the shallow valley opens in front of us. I scan the trees, stark against the pale pasture but all seemingly intact, the occasional fallen limbs are from other storms, other winters. In the last light of this short Spring day we gather dead-fall around the exposed roots of Scots Pines, a sparse legacy of the plantation that once fed the gunpowder works, now long abandoned in the valley below. This wood will burn well and the resinous tang of its smoke will live with us, and on us, long after Adam and I have returned to our different lives. Over the years I've watched how the outlines of these trees have changed, becoming ever more angular with age. They resist, forgotten up here, rarely visited. Yet soon their rough bark will animate in the shifting flare of the fire we will build.

We scrape away the orange carpet of pine needles to expose the dark stain of our last fire. I nod to myself, acknowledging how well we'd disguised it, leaving the barest of traces here despite repeated visits. Further up the hill, along the line of a drystone boundary wall, there will be even less trace of our original camping place, established more than two decades ago. We abandoned it when a kestrel came to occupy the tree overhanging our then customary fireplace. Like us, the nesting predator must have appreciated the open prospect on offer.

It's silent now. Smoke rises vertically. The wind that died with nightfall has left no echoes, no trees creaking and whispering as they did when light faded. The hollow excludes the sounds of outside, a circle of solitude that calls for low voices.

Once we talked of the home we shared, now we talk of two homes, as Adam has grown our lives have grown apart. We both feel secure in this bowl between the trees, as we always have, a place to share thoughts and concerns about the little-frictions of family life. He was young, around five or six, when I first brought him here to sleep under trees and stars. Now we have two families to talk about, though the conversations are in essence the same.

"Moving to a new school is always a challenge"

"Have you thought about asking Mum...?"

"Weekends are hectic now that we've signed up to..."

"It would be good if we could make time... Maybe in the summer...?"

Slowly the conversation fades, we have said what needs to be shared.

It's quiet now....

I think of re-lighting the stove and brewing more coffee, but that would disturb the companionable silence. I offer a wry smile, thinking that to any observer this scene would represent a degree of privilege; a white, male, middle-class man sharing a comfortable and well-equipped experience of 'the great outdoors' with his fair-haired, handsome son, keeping watch at a campfire while he settles to sleep below winter trees and bright stars, and yes, there's a grain of truth in this - but I've come to love this place, and these infrequent opportunities to spend time with my son. The combination of the two is one of the great pleasures in my life. I care deeply that this place remains unspoilt, hence my deep-seated fear that one day I'll enter the valley and find it changed in some way. Irrational I know, this is low-value land, remote and rough; it will never again see life as a commercial plantation or anything more than grazing for hardy sheep and the ponies ridden by the farmer's daughters. Yet what is a love of place other than a reaction to the fear of its despoilment? Yes I would fight to protect it, but is that commitment both empty and safe, made in the knowledge that I probably won't ever have to?

A deep yawn brings me back to the present, I want to sleep. Sliding into my sleeping bag I shiver. The sudden cold of man-made fibre is unwelcome after the warmth of the fireside. I tuck my hands into my armpits, searching for pockets of comfort. As I lie on my back and look up at the stars, a deeper cold settles on my face. It will fall below freezing tonight, no doubt we will wake to a frost-transformed world and getting up will be a challenge.

INFLORESCENCE

I'm beginning to warm inside the sleeping bag and I wonder now if I've overdone the layers I'm wearing, but I'm too close to sleep to worry about it now. Yet sleep eludes me and I fumble in the pocket of my bivvy-bag, lifting out the waterproofed paper that I know will be there, a small ritual that's part of these blessed occasions, a crumpled copy of Mary Oliver's poem 'Sleeping in the Forest'. For years I was reluctant to allow anyone else to see it, preferring to read the poem deep in the confines of my sleeping bag, like a naughty, book-loving child reading under the bedcovers. Now I'm careless of who might observe me reading poetry; anybody sharing the intimate experience of sleeping under the stars must, by now, know that this is only one of my eccentricities?

What has Mary got to say to me tonight? The words will be the same; I can recite them from memory, but there will always be new meaning.

"*I thought the earth remembered me...*'

Yes; this place is familiar to me and to Adam. We find our favoured sides of the fire, stones moved by the current to settle in this riverbed.

Tonight I give thanks that this is my resting place. Glancing up at the crystal-pointed sky, clearer from here than city lights would ever allow it to be, low clouds are edged with the filigree silver of a setting moon. A night for clear thinking and the white fire of stars.

As ever, Oliver's words allow me to understand the imperative to be a better guardian of what is to be passed down to the next generation, a better parent of children and planet. In this I feel a dragging weight of responsibility and the fear that I will never be strong enough to succeed. I fold away poem and paper, hoping only to wake as those words suggest, to have vanished a dozen times into something better.

Sometime later I open my eyes. I'm not sure how long I've slept; these cold spring nights are long. The skies remain clear and the pale light of stars detail the crystal-edged stems of dead bracken and grass. The silence is absolute. What woke me is knowing that I have to piss. I wonder if it can be ignored? I sigh and begin to wriggle out of my warm cocoon, stepping onto grass made brittle with frost. The fire is just a vague glow of orange in the darkness. It could be revived I reflect as I tiptoe around it, stepping to the edge of the clearing, avoiding treading on anything that would make going barefoot a mistake. By now the moon is far below the horizon and the almost-darkness seems to draw the stars closer. I am tempted to stay here and watch for the passage of satellites and shooting stars, but a shiver drives me back to my sleeping bag.

Passing the fire, I convince myself that there's a better use of this time than the likely fruitless attempt to return to sleep. I can't resist the urge to build-up the fire, to make the flames dance again. Memories stir unbidden, of the fire grate in the Victorian tenement where I was born, hard against a dirty, industrial river. Blighted by the slum-clearance order which excused the landlord from any improvements it was no place to raise children, yet there we were, and there we grew. We called it home for the first three years of my life, until the day the bulldozers moved in, delighting my parents but bringing me to tears when I wasn't allowed to watch our house being torn down. Post-war Sunderland was being redeveloped, new council housing estates were eating into the farmland around the town and we were rehoused to a red brick box among a thousand, near-identical, red brick boxes.

The new estate was a paradise for us kids, large green spaces filled with the things we hardly ever saw in the East End – bees, flowers, healthy mature trees; and things that we had never seen, ladybirds, hedgehogs, birds that weren't the predatory gulls we had shared the river with. A paradise for kids, we didn't know words like 'environment' then; it was all just space to run free. Yet it must have been a nightmare for our parents. The move hadn't alleviated their poverty, it had simply moved it miles away from workplace and where wider family still lived; miles that cost bus-fares that simply could not be afforded. We grew strong legs and a deep sense of territory, walking everywhere, always conscious of the invisible boundaries that define working-class towns. That's how it was. Small children rarely recognise the poverty they are born into. Maya Angelou knew this in her line from *I Know Why the Caged Bird Sings*:

"Children's talent to endure stems from their ignorance of the alternatives."

The warm embers need little kindling. I lie close, low to the fire and blow until orange grows to red and small flames appear against the bark of larger logs. I sit up, slightly dizzy from blowing life into ash. The light in the clearing comes to life once more, dark trunks moving in the dim light of new flames, jerky as the fire takes hold, then slowing to the colour of gathering heat. My face grows warm, but my back feels the chill of a Spring that has yet to summon its strength.

Memory tells me that cold was a constant feature of the anonymous house where I grew into a teenager. A coal fire in one room and no other heating meant that winter nights had too many people crowded into too small a space. And from this I learned that being outside offered freedom and space, even if the cost was some discomfort. There were always friends to play with on the new estate, small gangs of semi-feral children with a happy knack of creating opportunities for adventure. The narrow belts of sycamore trees that had been spared by the developers as 'landscaping' became our forest playground, a disused sand quarry offered the chance to test our nerve by jumping off crumbling cliffs or tunnelling deep into its friable depths. The weather never stopped us and our parents seemed happy not to know the risks we were taking as we roamed across the territory we claimed as our own. I have never lost the belief that, in most times and most places, it is better to be out beneath an open sky. Eventually I grew to make a career out of introducing people to the outdoors and it's a source of pride that Adam has, in turn, grown to appreciate what wild places have to offer.

An involuntary shudder makes me zip myself deeper into my jacket and lean closer to the fire. I have to acknowledge that staying warm isn't as easy as when I was younger. There's no wind but I sense faint movement around me. Smoke rises slowly and gathers in the branches above. Small noises speak of the passage of nocturnal animals. Time passes.

It is a privilege of ageing to contemplate the passage of our lives, and night-time is the space that gives this reflection its deepest substance. I am closer to seventy than sixty, though I hope my lifestyle lessens the weight of those years. I once read a study of Hadza hunter-gatherers in Tanzania that suggested that older people may have patterns of sleep that echo the need for them to be the 'night-watch', allowing the active-young to rest before the next day's hunting and gathering. Adam's sleeping now but I know that he'll certainly be ready for anything that tomorrow brings. I look over to where he lies stretched out and still. He's half a head taller than me and strong, a man in his prime. I hope he thinks that he got a good deal from *his* start in life.

It's not often I take time to consider my early years, the years before I loaded my life into a backpack and walked away from a city that had given me little but memories. It's a part of my past that belongs in an album of tarnished images which, these days, I can easily choose not to open. I'm not sure that I have the courage to ask Adam to tell me how he thinks about his growing-up? He'd answer with honesty and I'm not sure that I'd want to hear all that he has to say. I know that my career meant too much time away working, too little time there when he might have needed me. He left home as a teenager too, following his passion for the mountains to work as a ski-instructor, rejecting any thought of university to live the dream he'd had since he was a child, and from there into an enviable job designing outdoor equipment, a role that seems to have been tailor-made for his interests. It's clear that his decisions about his life have generally been positive ones, moving towards the things he wanted to make happen: a contrast to mine which were so often about turning my back on people and situations that no longer gave me what I needed. I rarely knew what I wanted. I just knew when I didn't have it.

I stand, kick the spilling embers back into the heart of the fire, raising smoke that catches my eyes and throat. I wipe away the grit and tears. I'm no apologist for how we have mistreated the world, though sometimes I wonder if caring for the planet is just another of those luxuries that can be afforded when a person has food in their stomach and a roof over their head?

The sky has lost its uniform deep blue, stars are disappearing from its eastern arc and trees are recovering form and silhouette, their angular shapes now static after a night of dancing in our firelight. Another half-hour and I'll light the stove, start the ritual of brewing morning coffee. Then it will be time to pack up and return to our other worlds, mine at home in the valley below us, Adam's back on the South Coast and the tenuous contact of occasional video calls. As ever I will be reluctant to leave; reluctant to re-engage with a world where my family only demands infrequent consideration, once again wondering when my son's busy life will afford him the time to come here with me again. When I walked away from Sunderland I walked away from everything that that place meant, rarely again seeing the family and friends that were so closely associated with a town that, for me, held no future. I have to believe that Adam's willingness to share these nights with me is a sign that he has better memories of the place where he was born and raised. Some day we will douse this fire and never again return to these trees, though this will only be recognised in hindsight.

He Taught Me to Skim
SHIRLEY NICHOLSON

An ebony pool as the Irthing pauses
its dash through the ravine with pebbles

as various in shape, texture, colour as words,
gathered in folds of sand under

pine, sweet chestnut, rowan. On the far side
a rise of rock, its crannies tucked

with fern, moss; its dark river nooks
pockets for froth that collects like skeins

of white wool. To reach the river edge,
more deer track than path, is a drop

through trees that stand on tiptoe to reach
the light, keep the pool hidden until found.

This was his childhood place where the glance
of light revealed the right stones.

He showed me how to choose them,
feel the stone's smooth flatness in my hand,

bend by the water among the pebbles,
my fingers twisted to bring about those arcs

of bounce, radiant splashes, distance;
my hand's flick sending them across the surface.

He would come year after year to this
unwritten page, this black pool.

Caravan of Love
TARA VALLENTE

When we bought our family home, we'd no idea that we were moving in with a colony of house martins. Yet now, fifteen years later, we are all literally nestled under one roof.

I feel quite protective of them, even though there is a permanent pile of droppings on the conservatory roof. If I was one of those house-proud women who made everything sparkle, then there wouldn't be a pile of house martin poo. If I was one of those women, I would never have time to write a word, but my windows would shine.

When our neighbours had their roof done, they boxed off their eaves, and their little caravan returned the following spring to find themselves homeless. So, given that house martins always return from Africa to live within a mile of where they fledged; they moved in with us instead.

Our collection of nests has grown to eight. Three of them are beside each other, a little terrace dangling like a string of beads below the roof line. Not surprisingly, the filthiest bit of conservatory is below that spot. There's at least one nest above each bedroom window and our morning silence is broken by the growing brood.

Last week, I saw the familiar swooping above Tewet Tarn and I heard their call. I thought, Great! They're on their way. But they must have been someone else's birds, because when I got home, our nests were silent.

Yesterday, I saw a bird inspecting the nests and I wondered if that was one of our house martins? Or was it a cheeky house sparrow claiming the nest for its own? They say house martins make the entrance hole to the nest too small for the sparrows to squeeze in. We'll see.

If I was a house martin, I'd be pretty upset to find a squatter in my house. Those fantastic ball-shaped nests take up to a thousand hours to build. Each mouthful of muddy puddle is collected in the beak, mixed with spittle and shaped to protect up to five eggs and two adult birds.

You can tell the difference between a swallow and a house martin if you can catch sight of its underbelly, because it's creamy white. I never get close enough or have eyesight good enough to make out its feathered blue muddied lace wings. They fly so fast!

You'll find me at sunset sitting on the top step holding my breath as they head towards the fascia boards at breakneck speed. Except they never break their neck, they simply slip inside the house martin shaped hole in the nest.

So what do the house martins think every April when they land? Do they peer through the conservatory and comment on how much we've changed?

Last year, there'd have been plenty to talk about. Firstly, why was everyone at home all the time? Why was Dominic pottering in the vegetable garden? Didn't he have a job to go to?

Why were the boys at home all the time? Don't they go to school? Don't they have any friends?

And why was the road silent? Where was everyone?

And me. They would have wondered about me. Why had I planted hundreds of seeds in the conservatory and why was I gradually disappearing into a self-made inner oasis? Did they notice I was locked inside my thoughts?

Just as the house martins once lived wild and free on cliffs, they now stay close to houses and bridges. Close to humans. Close to us. And we, in 2020, close to them.

From my green-glazed sanctuary, I wake with them, I sip coffee as they fire out of the nest, feeding on the wing. I watch as they sit for weeks on their eggs. Then I lie on the floor among my green beans and tomatoes and see them zipping back and forth with food for their young. If the weather is good, as it was in lockdown, the house martins will have another brood. They're almost unique as a species because the older siblings help to feed the next batch of babies.

One afternoon, the baby house martins threw themselves out of the nest onto the slates above the kitchen. It was like watching a series of aborted attempts to fly. One by one they jumped, flapped and landed a metre or so down the slates.

And then as the afternoon light faded, I watched the moon rising over Clough Head, and the whole house martin colony darted back and forth across the sky. Swooping and perfecting their new-found skill. They had learnt to fly. They had survived another year. So had we.

To Weed
(After Elizabeth-Jane Burnett)
CLARE PROCTOR

To remove unwanted plants from an area of ground. To eliminate as unsuitable or unwanted. To untether them from their moorings. To unthread from the earth. To understand persistence.

To care about the outward appearance of things. To value one plant/leaf/bloom/petal/shade more than another. To rate properties of beauty or nutrition or seasonal interest. To label something as common. To consider society's expectations.

To make a decision. To unwind time. To understand that mark making is temporary. To know you can never reach deep enough. To understand that the job is never finished.

To leave your mind at the door. To be at peace. To follow in your mother's footsteps.

To be connected to a fork, paint fading under your hands. To be the sun watching your body from afar. To understand distance.

To be aware of small movements. To uncover pink-brown bodies, full of earth. To identify larvae. To be in service to a Robin. To be in awe of ants.

To work on your knees. To wear gloves and use a mat. To accept that still, your skin will be imprinted by stone, that soil will dig its way into the curve of your fingernails.

To be willing to kill. To kill without thinking. To be meticulous. To be merciless. To feel nothing for the heap of bodies wilting in a bucket. To decide that some lives are less important than others.

To think of nothing. To see movement as meditation. To know patience is prayer. To face the earth. To know your time will come.

The Magic Cattle Grid
LOREN CAFFERTY

I have christened it the magic cattle grid. I visit it so often that my friends and family now accept, and even on occasion use, that ludicrous name. In truth there is nothing remarkable about the grid itself, it rattles and rumbles under cars and tractors in the usual way and crossing it on foot requires the customary and vaguely embarrassing, dainty steps for coping with that mild peril.

As a destination 'cattle grid' might sound a little underwhelming for the foot-weary traveller, particularly as no matter from where they have arrived there is no doubt they have undertaken a walk of some effort. If from Slaidburn then they have traced for almost fifteen miles the footsteps of the famous Pendle witches, if from the edges of Lancaster then acres of endlessly yielding grouse moor and if from either of the villages of Hornby or Wray then a steep, unrelenting upward slope.

My own, personal, walk, is the least hard fought of all the routes. I live in the heart of Wray; opposite my house begins the incline of a lane that climbs up and out of the village. It is a matter of seconds for me to be beyond the tiny village school with its 'gift of £200 for ever' from a local boy made good, and who was sold by his drunken father and returned to wreak his revenge years later – that revenge being to educate the village children beyond the reach of the grinding poverty and cruelty that afflicted his family. The lane is narrow – a single car width – meaning that while traffic is quite rare, if I do meet any vehicles, I must meld myself into the hedgerows, prickly and sparse in winter, greener and softer in spring and full of plump, staining fruit in late summer and autumn.

There is a push upwards, tarmac threading through a patchwork of cattle and sheep grazing land where the warp and weft are a mixture of lush pasture, low drystone walls and field bottoms that dip to rush-covered wetland. This varied landscape means the air is rich and thick with noise; skylarks, lapwings, cuckoos, curlews, ducks, geese, oyster catchers, owls and buzzards push their songs and cries into cacophonous, glorious competition. The Forest of Bowland is a strange place, an undiscovered country into whose bourn few venture. It sits on a map, like a disappointing sandwich filling, between the fresh and familiar slices of the Yorkshire Dales and Lake District National Parks. The acquired taste of reality is far more satisfying.

When the road finally flattens – if only temporarily – I am exactly one mile from my front door but, turning onto the final upwards section of my walk, I could be hundreds of miles from anywhere. Fell ponies tug insistently at the grass in the field ahead, half hidden by huge blooming gorse bushes. Largely unused to people they ignore me as I resist the temptation to pause there, allow my heart rate to slow to normal and my vision to adjust to the widening of the landscape. For me, walking this route, that moment must always be deferred until I have crossed the magic cattle grid and rested my arms on the stout wall that supports the bars. It's like opening the hot, wrapped paper round chips in the car after visiting the chippy, the gratification is instant but the payoff is awkward, greasy and unfulfilling. These are pleasures best savoured stationary where all the senses can appreciate the experience.

I grew up by the Irish Sea, watching the sunset when the tide was out was a wonder that never lost its thrill. The burning embers of the day streaking the sky with pinks and oranges above the apparently endless sands gave me a true sense of the vast that has only been matched when driving through middle eastern deserts. Landscape, however remote, rarely creates the same sense of limitless space. There is always a mountain or valley just over the next lip with an idea – however vainglorious – that with a little sustained effort you could get there relatively easily.

INFLORESCENCE

At the magic cattle grid two opposing sensations merge within me. The same awe-inspiring, humbling recognition of my own insignificance that the coast creates and the hugely comforting sensation of being right in the centre of something, of the world wrapping itself around me, of my sinking as if into a hug.

Ingleborough as the nearest and most prominent mountain demands attention first; it stills the feet. There is no more walking until it has been appreciated. On a fine day the contrast between the cornflower-blue skies and Ingleborough's striking geology is at its most noticeable. Ask a child to draw a mountain and you expect rising, triangular peaks – here the peak is more of the flat cap variety, fitting perhaps for a hill in Yorkshire. The dark grasslands of the base narrow into limestone pavement, the grey streaks of grit stone sit on top and its weathered surface provides the unusual effect of a level summit.

From my position, at the cattle-grid, across the valley where the Yorkshire Dales bleed into the Forest of Bowland, Ingleborough is flanked by a Praetorian guard. To the right sits Pen-y-Ghent, its own odd shape disguised from this angle, leaning its shoulder towards its bigger brother. To the left, half hidden, is Whernside, a purple shadow tapering away towards Ribblehead. I rarely see anybody at all exploring Roeburndale and it is strange to think of the hundreds of people on those nearby mountains undertaking the Yorkshire Three Peaks challenge.

The thing that strikes me every single time I visit the magic cattle grid is the variety in the landscape that spills out from this single point. Across the great bowl of grazing land, flecked with farms, woods and even castles, the Howgills rise in distant grassy mounds, silky smooth grass in undulating waves before they give way to the dark edges of the Lake District which ripples and rolls west in lead coloured dips and peaks to the coast. On the brightest day, I have discovered, you can lean and peer into just the right spot to see a triangle of Morecambe Bay, splinters of fractured light the only real clue to this hidden watery surprise.

The immediately adjacent moorland in which this special place sits might seem prosaic as if set in opposition to the poetry of the green, sweeping vista. But as the months and years have passed since I first began to walk here, slipping through the kissing gate beside the cattle grid, I can properly appreciate the unique personality of such land. It is where the curlews scream and the lapwings fight with the buzzards. It is where in the springtime the leverets sunbathe on the little lumpen islands of green that float above the wetter, boggy heather. It is where the grouse scratch and graze, hidden, until my presence sends them fleeing and flying in a panicked escape. There is a vaguely unloved feel to this moor; the grouse butts are almost comedically rudimentary – several posts stuck haphazardly into the ground with wire strung between them and the tracks leading from one to another no more defined than sheep trods. Where the ground is criss-crossed with streams, planks have been jammed into the banks - but the flaking wood has taken on a sponge-like appearance and standing on them feels like a move in a primitive video game where the player might find themselves tumbling downwards to wet feet and sodden calves.

At various times of the year I find myself bathed in a kaleidoscopic range of colours. I have discovered that the muted browns and greens generally associated with grouse moors are, in fact, just camouflage for the reds, blues, purples and pinks that tip the sprawling heather. Though often a soft brown, the peaty ground is an ever-changing carpet underfoot that bakes into a firm black, cake-like volcanic rock or becomes saturated with the iron-orange sheen of the water so common in this area.

Before walking this landscape had become something comforting and familiar, I was slightly afraid of grouse moors; there are so few landmarks, the rise and fall of the ground is often hidden by the twisting, hardy wood and blooms of the heather.

Crossing such areas can be slow and hard-won. Now I have learnt that with close acquaintance this land has a character of its own. Natural paths open between rambling roots. I can measure the easiest places to move through the ankle-twisting maze in relation to the leaning dry stone walls and the places where the fell ponies usually gather. I can ascertain the distance to the trig point that overlooks the last villages in the Lune Valley by the wetness underfoot and know the precise moment at which the rise of the hill allows the sweeping majesty of Morecambe Bay to suddenly appear. The fact that I have never met a single other person on this moor (unless I was with a walking buddy) has led to a strange feeling of possession; as if the landscape is mine; as if I can supply the love that it lacks.

I decide that today, as on many days, the climb upwards to the top of Caton Moor to the futuristic fingers of the windfarm feels like a pointless endeavour. The ground can be so full of water here there's the danger that I might end up swallowed by the ground, stuck as fast as if I was navigating the treacherous sinking sands so far below in the bay. Instead, I stick to the tarmac beyond the cattle grid and walk to the end of the valley. There are five or six farms – ending at the surprising cluster of a tiny Methodist chapel and Lower, Middle and High Salter, their names proclaiming their position on the historically important salt path between Hornby and Slaidburn. Nowadays the ribbon of tarmac reaches High Salter before fraying into the state it seems likely to have had when the traders drove their prized cargo on the winding road between the Tatham and Mallowdale hills.

I have walked the path all the way to the pretty riverside cottages and welcoming sight of the pub, the Hark to Bounty in the Ribble Valley, but most often I stop at the final fell gate and gaze at the summits of the evocatively named local hills with their echoes of darkness and magic; Gallows Hill, Blanch Fell, Hell Crag, Wolfhole, the Ward Stone. There is something distinctly other worldly up here, perhaps it's the way that on those frequent days of inclement weather the wind drives the rain horizontally across the ground so that it never seems to land, or perhaps it's the sheer isolation of the place, but I frequently feel as if the chill of history is creeping inch by inch across my flesh. It is hard not to conjure the image of the Pendle Witches slogging their way towards me as I stand at the gate.

For me the clang of the gate's rod driving home is the signal that I am about to walk back to warmth and comfort, a hot shower or a cup of tea but it serves as a brutal reminder that those pitiable, victimised women passed through the site of that very gate just over four hundred years ago. They were heading towards the crashing bolts of the Lancaster Castle dungeons and, ultimately, a death sentence. For me the ability to walk alone and comfortably on this path is a daily expression of my personal freedom, my fierce sense of independence while for Old Demdike and her co-accused, walking this path was part of a punishment for expressing a degree of independence from the norms of their day by practising healing and midwifery; practices that attracted notice and the hysterical accusations of witchcraft. Their presence in my consciousness only heightens my sense of gratitude.

This feeling has been one that has taken on a greater importance for me in the last few months. I am ashamed to admit the truth, I have spent my life taking good health, and my ability to largely do as I pleased, for granted. Then last November my body seriously let me down. I slipped two discs in my lower back. This was not the comedy clutching the spine, of being bent double and yelping for two minutes on television; this was, for me, catastrophic incapacitation.

'Walk,' said the doctor as he wrote me a sheaf of prescriptions. My silence on the other end of the phone was lengthy and sceptical. He was insistent. 'Walking will help.'

INFLORESCENCE

And so began a whole new regime built entirely around following that advice. Sitting down was impossible and sciatica pulsed through my legs like an electric fence had been wired across my pelvis whenever I tried to lie down. I lived to walk; my doctor was right; the only relief I ever experienced was as my hips loosened and there was a brief, glorious pain free moment at the top of every shallow leg swing. Time took on a strange, elastic quality as I visited the magic cattle grid through the storms of January and February and into the odd, lonely months of early Coronavirus lockdown – irrespective of the time of day or night. Walking became something utterly integral. It was the only thing I could do. I felt more connected to this landscape and the birds and animals in it than I did the life on hold back in the valley floor, at work or with friends.

I no longer cared about weather conditions; any escape from the pain was a price worth paying no matter how wet, cold or sunburnt I might get. I quickly dispensed with a head torch at night, the curves and dips of the walls so familiar now that I needed no artificial light. When, in April, the pink super moon made its appearance, I discovered a whole new delight in my walking.

Just before midnight on the night of the full moon, I strolled up to the magic cattle grid. As I crossed the bars and rested my arms on the wall the sight that met me struck me to the core. The light was an ethereal burnished steel but oddly bright so that the Lakes, the Howgills, the Dales and the shallow stirrings of the Pennines behind me were all traced out as if in the shadow and light of a charcoal sketch. It seemed there was no other person or creature awake. Every light in every farm and hamlet was extinguished. A tractor hitched to a slurry tank lay waiting for daybreak in the next field. The birds were silent. I could see for tens of miles and name and claim everything in the milky vista spread out before me. I felt a sense of belonging so strong it surged through me like adrenaline.

I was not born here. My accent is slightly 'off' with its fractionally longer Cumbrian vowels. When I walk, I walk up on the 'moo-er', not the 'more' as those with a greater birthright claim might. But this walk has become mine – and it feels like home.

The Whitecoal Makers
SALLY GOLDSMITH

They lived like gypsies in shifty shelters
of propped hazel and turf, working
for loppings, rammel and broom brash
but never wrote it down –
their precise alchemy of oak, owler, flame.

No record of their names, forgotten men,
unlike their masters, flash yeomen turned
lead smelters – the Eyres, Strelleys, Mowers –
still whiffing of the farm but newly fat in their halls,
or the sixth Earl with his *most commodious milne.*

Their *kylnses* pock the wood,
brambled hollows over which we stumble,
our tools a tape, a camera, GPS, two metre pole,
their tools just axe and froe, tinder for *coalinge*
the coppicings in Smeekley and Brindwood.

We guess at humble lives, the way they stacked
oak wavers, warm draughts to dry them,
made the fuel to fire the bellowed mills
that smoked and blighted families and fields,
their woodland poverty where now we walk our dogs.

INFLORESCENCE

We map each kiln, each Q shaped spout sketched
and questioned as to how it funnelled air.
Or not. The Qs are questions too, this trade unwritten,
these men, their skills rubbed out by unimportance,
their lack of letters, the plenteousness of coke.

*Whitecoal kilns – small pits – have been discovered all over
woods in parts of south-west Sheffield. Until the 1980s, no one
knew what they were.*

For the Vernon Oak, Sheffield
SALLY GOLDSMITH

Under the tarmac your roots snout out
water, clay, a once-upon-a-time Derbyshire field,

above you are unfurling into green, heedless,
of the slashers who'd have you, chip you.

He brakes, the guy in the Tesco van.
Oh not this one too! Save it if you can.

You just stretch, embrace the street,
its windows, roofs, this blue sky day,

catch at the sun with crabbed arms,
filtering light through your new spring dress.

You wear our bright hearts and ribbons.
Who knew such love, in spready middle age?

Hard not to love, your heart-wood
beating to spring's rhythm, limbs akimbo.

They'd have you, severed from this street –
your anarchy upsets their frantic measuring.

Acorn, green sprout, hedge shrub, maiden,
field tree, street tree, nuisance, stump.

The Vernon Oak is a 200-year-old street tree in Sheffield, threatened with felling during the long protracted guerilla campaign by Sheffield Trees Action Group (STAG) against Sheffield City Council and their contractors Amey. This tree was one of many finally saved in 2018, and the Council now works with STAG, Amey, the Woodland Trust and the Sheffield and Rotherham Wildlife Trust in the Street Tree Partnership under a new strategy. A real victory for people power.

Rezzarection
STEPHEN DUNSTAN

Barrow AFC's return to the Football League after a 48-year exile has been watched on desktops, laptops and iPads rather than on the terraces of the Holker Street ground. I am a season ticket holder, and whilst watching often unattractive long ball tactics and generally disappointing results, I have taken solace in glimpses of the mute swans on the reservoir beyond the ground seen through the gaps between the stands. I was rather affronted by an away fan comment on the internet that the backdrop to the game was a dump. To quote Basil Fawlty, what were they expecting to see on the outskirts of a Cumbrian shipbuilding town – herds of wildebeest sweeping majestically across the plain?

But then I am probably too attached to Ormsgill Reservoir, or the 'rezza', as it's almost universally known by the folk who fish, walk dogs, jog or take in nature there. It's obviously manmade with a correspondingly angular footprint, and in keeping with the town's industrial heritage was created to provide a source of water for the steelworks that used to stand imposingly to the west. A local birdwatcher dismissed the rezza on Facebook because it wasn't kept tidy and didn't have the diversity of Leighton Moss RSPB reserve. The fact that he could help keep it tidy didn't seem to have registered, and if the football team and nature of urban Barrow is League Two, that doesn't stop either having value and being worthy of appreciation.

I don't want to paint over the cracks and tell it like it isn't; of course there are challenges for the wildlife in a site like this. Some years the feral supermarket trolleys seem to breed better than many of the birds. There are usually simmering tensions between some of the anglers and the professionals who have evolved to do it more efficiently. Handsome goosander and red-breasted merganser ducks both winter here, white bellies hiding them from fish prey and serrated bills gripping tight when they inevitably get a 'bite'. Above all there are the boy racers, for they generally are male, who deliberately plough through the goose creches for sport when the inexperienced birds venture onto the adjoining road. It would be easy to write this off to accidents, but on more than one occasion drivers have been seen to accelerate to ensure collisions.

Part of the appeal of watching a site like Ormsgill Reservoir is the predictability of it. The two islands provide undisturbed refuge for several species of waterfowl to raise their young. A couple of years ago seven pairs of tufted duck had flotillas of ducklings on the water simultaneously, the best productivity in Cumbria outshining several major nature reserves elsewhere. Some of the certainty and predictability of what I might expect to see here has gone though. Chestnut and black pochard ducks were staples of my rezza-watching youth, but as elsewhere in South Cumbria and in line with national trends, they no longer occur here on migration stopovers. Sleek great crested grebes used to slip silently out of sight, then they disappeared from view for good.

But of course it's partly about the unexpected encounters too. One of my earliest birding memories here was of a black swan, resplendent on the water. The 50-year-old me would briefly appreciate it and move on to something that hadn't escaped, but back then this visitor oozed exotic demeanour, and I was trans-fixed. Turning out to a WATCH (junior Wildlife Trust) group wildfowl count, I was the only one whose 'binoculars' weren't two toilet-roll cardboard tubes glued together, which happened to be useful as I picked out a rare red-necked grebe. Scaup, black tern, sabine's gull and gannet are other highlights hard earned over the intervening three decades.

The old Cemetery Cottages Club on the reservoir's east shore was recently demolished and now a new estate is going up in its place. It includes a line of dormer bungalows with amazing views over the Rezza and I want one; my wife points out that we live 70 miles away in Blackpool and she may be onto something there. But there is something about going back to where it all began, and in carbon conscious times, to be able to enjoy nature literally on the doorstep. That's kind of what's happened during Covid. With few realistic alternatives for many people in Barrow the reservoir has become their refuge and focus. Pre-Covid, I rarely encountered anyone else birding or taking photographs, and certainly not back when I was a kid, but now there's a thriv-ing group of people sharing their nature images from the rezza and learning about the birds that visit. Credit must be given to the local council for undertaking significant improvement works to the path where a quagmire had formed in places along the northern bank. It is heartening to see wheelchair users sharing their pictures of nature at the site now that issues of access have been addressed.

Whilst Barrow AFC were still languishing in the National League, I was made aware that the rezza Wetland Bird Survey counting all waterbirds needed someone to take it on. In fact, the site was considered a priority. I loved the place, and my mum and dad live in nearby Dalton-in-Furness, so I signed up to visit every month from September to March. I recommend it as citizen science that anyone can do if you pick the right water body for your bird identification abilities. And it's not lost on me that when Covid finally relents and the turnstiles reopen I will be travelling to Barrow to kill three birds with one stone.

Technically the first sentence of this essay and the sentence immediately above are inaccurate. As the Covid tiers ebbed briefly in South Cumbria, for a brief window fans were allowed into games. On 5 December 2020 I drove to within half a mile of the ground, adjacent to Laburnum Crescent where I'd lived as a child. It was a day of hope and possibilities, ending nearly half a century of footballing resentment, underachievement and disappointment. Skirting the edge of the rezza on an overlong but carefully chosen route, I joined fellow fans in blue and white excitedly making their socially distanced way to the ground. It was a special moment. But being able to gaze right and see the swan herd in real life, not via lockdown tv watching, was equally life-affirming. Does this part of the world matter to me more than it objectively should? Yes; yes it absolutely does.

Sweetheart
ELSPETH WILSON

I bought you
because there wasn't any
other love in the
house. You were marked

as part of the 'tiny'
category so that
when you arrived
there was so much

brown packaging
that I thought you
were already lost
before you'd been

found. But you were
there, a speck of
green in the beige
of former trees,

ready for your
windowsill. It
wasn't – isn't –
much but you have

some pens for
company, some
filled-up notebooks,
a webcam. And I have

you, a bump in my
peripheral vision
as I write this, a small
hillock in the view

out the window,
when I look
straight ahead,
in the shape of

a friend

Fragments On the Mountains Edge
NICOLA CARTER

The way we see the world shapes the way we treat it. If a mountain is a deity, not a pile of ore; if a river is one of the veins of the land, not potential irrigation water; if a forest is a sacred grove, not timber; if other species are biological kin, not resources; or if the planet is our mother, not an opportunity – then we will treat each other with greater respect. Thus is the challenge, to look at the world from a different perspective.

David Suzuki

I. I enter the adit without a head torch. Without any artificial light. I do this because I am curious to know how the darkness will feel. The first few metres of the mine tunnel receives indirect sunlight, so I can see well enough. This area is referred to as the 'twilight zone' and experiences subdued temperature and humidity fluctuations. These conditions are ideal for small shade tolerant plants, such as liverworts, mosses, and ferns. And here they are, offering the walls and floor a living skin of green. As I enter the adit I feel the temperature drop immediately, cold air rushes towards me – a result of temperature or pressure differentials with the air outside. I walk slowly, cautiously, stepping between the tracks of the old tramway. Puddles of water have formed between the old tracks and are a constant here. I move deeper inside the mountain, leaving the verdant hues behind. As I move I notice the sharp edges of stone decrease in value, become less distinct, and then… disappear into black. I become submerged, engulfed. I loose my edges. I stand quietly in this blackness and listen. Water speaks. It drips from rock – precipitate and leaching. In certain places it has found and formed channels, and it streams down and out. Out to find its own level.

II. A wooden post marks the entrance to the adit. It is overspread with moss. The moss takes support from the wood, takes nutrients from the wood, uses the wood, and a few other essential ingredients, to become more moss. The cavities of the wood are filled with air, swollen with water, packed out with roots of moss, and microscopic things like bacteria… it is filled with plenty of not-wood…

III. The problem with boundaries is that the closer you look at them the less certain they become.

IV. Pigeons navigate using roads; bats fly along hedgerows and treelines; bumblebees way-find using paths and roads. I am a modern human animal: lines excite my eyes and awaken my attention. Lines. Edges. Contours. Boundaries. Thresholds. Peripheries. I wander channels, chutes and troughs carved by fingers of water that chatter and crash down steep fellsides. I dawdle the length of the becks and ghylls that languish and meander across valley bottoms, where many fractal-like fingers of bodies of water connect. I amble paths walked by other human feet and tracks trod by non-human animals. I scramble grooves and gullies gouged by rockfall. I climb cracks and fractures that snake their way up crag-faces. I ramble alongside margins of vegetation: bracken, heather, and grassland.

V. *Black Star*, 634m, summit of Honister Crag.
A stack of silent stories sits atop the crag. Stories of human passage to this place. Each story is represented through selection, through the placement of a single stone. A stone that fit a human hand. A stone placed sensitively onto this precarious pile. A gesture made, an action, a mark left. Left to settle. Left to be joined by others. Form and meaning slowly transform as the wind and rains blows through the spaces between stones.

VI. Carefully, I lift a rock from the cairn. I feel its heft. Take in its blue-grey hue. Run my eyes and fingertips over every crevice, every wrinkle, every imperfection on its otherwise smooth surface. It is the definition of solid. I place the rock back onto the pile and as I do thoughts arise in my mind, thoughts half-remembered from Buddhist teachings. Thoughts around impermanence and insubstantiality and deep, deep time.

VII. I stomp down the incline, legs feeling heavy and sore, feet dragging lazily and lifting small pieces of slaty rock. I listen as the rocks clang against each other, as they tumble and catch in the air. The long resonant ringing noise the stone makes gives it its local terminology, 'metal'. As I walk the landscape it becomes alive with metallic voice.

VIII. Adits have been driven into the sides of this fell – driven inside the mountain following slate veins that, long ago, outcropped at the surface. Humans dug through the outer skins of the mountain, revealed its dense inner core and blasted its hard skeleton. They chiseled away at the bones of the mountain. They created great recesses and channels within the mountain. They created entrances and hollowed out great halls within the mountain. They scooped out tonne after tonne of rock. And as the days rolled into weeks, rolled into months, rolled into years, rolled into centuries, so these dark chambers grew and grew. Where rock once stood there is now a dance of air, water vapour, dust and microbes.

IX. And yes! There is mould in the mine: interconnected networks of hyphae form fuzzy mycelia. Filaments of communication, connections, run deep. What multiplies here that is not visible to the human eye? What pulses and gyrates?

X. It is the emergence from the adit that I enjoy the most – the enrichment of my senses of vision and smell. Objects seem so much sharper. Hues so vibrant. The air feels warm and moist against my skin. I inhale deeply and taste the plants and soil. I inhale the very skin of the mountain as it releases itself into me.

XI. With each journey, the mountain alters me in small but significant ways.

XII. With each journey, I alter the mountain in small but significant ways.

XIII. Later, I think again about the cairn – the pile of rocks and the air and rain that swirled between them. I think again about boundaries. I try to think about them differently, see them differently. I try to consider them on an atomic level. Half-remembered college science lessons tell me that the atoms that form the rock are bound together in a relatively stable state. And that the atoms in the air have different properties – the atoms move rapidly in all different directions. So it would seem that the boundary between the rock and the air would be very distinct. But read a little more, dig a little deeper, zoom in a little further... and what you will find is that on an atomic level, a boundary does not have a fixed or exact location. Zoom in closely and the rock has no definite shape or form. Some of the atoms in the rock are reacting with those in the air. Some are being assimilated into the rock. The edge, the boundary, is fuzzy. Indistinct. As nebulous and hazy as the clouds that billow the flanks of the mountain.

XIV. And I half-remember Buddhist teachings that say that it does not really make sense to talk about 'things'. That the world is not a collection of 'separate things' that occasionally interact with each other. That the world is really a confluence of inter-dependent processes. That nothing has any self-existence. That the greatest delusion is the delusion of a separate self. A delusion of a duality between a separate self and the rest of the world. A world of objects. Rocks. Plants. Animals. Waterways. The Earth, objectified and externalised, is there for me to exploit in any way I want. And I start to wonder if the ecological crisis we face might also be a spiritual crisis?

XV. I realise that I cannot stand on the mountains edge.

XVI. I am descending the steep stone-pitched path when its shining glossy jewel-like violet-blue-black hues pull my attention. A ground beetle is lain on its back. Its legs move slowly, rhythmically, hopelessly, forwards and backwards, over and over. I imagine panic, confusion, shock... but the beetle's only response appears to be this stubborn and useless movement. I stoop, reach down, and allow its legs to hook onto the micro-indentations of my fingerprints and gently I lift it up, off the path, and away from the line of a hundred human feet.

XVII. Morning, late summer. I wake to find the fellsides swathed in fog that conceals and reveals aspects of the landscape that surrounds me. I stand and watch as tiny droplets of water, aerosols suspended, shift and drift from place to place, carried in light breezes. They swirl and whirl. They slide and glide around each other. Sometimes they are tightly packed and sometimes they are more scattered. Sometimes many droplets journey together, moving in the same direction, surging and forming elegant streams, and then, just as quickly, they disperse, become strewn and spin apart. I stand and watch as some collide with rock. Some collide with vegetation. And some collide with my flesh. Here and there. They condense on these surfaces, and where they do I watch droplets develop and pool together, form perfect little spheres of liquid. I look closely and see these drops of water refract and bend the landscape in a thousand rich and subtle ways. These droplets communicate a thousand rich and subtle ways of seeing. And as I stand and watch, the Earth continues in its steady motion and what I see is the star at the centre of the Solar System, our Sun, rise and warm the air. The clouds of fog appear to shrink slowly inwards from their edges, and what was almost tangible now gradually vanishes from my sight. The water droplets return to gas.

As one thing seems to vanish, an other is revealed.

The winner of the Future Places Environmental Essay Prize 2021

Freestyle
J.A. MENSAH

Racing towards the sea in my vest and leggings, I don't stop until the water reaches my belly button. That first touch of it shocks and my skin tightens around me. I wait for a bit, but there's only one way to get used to it: I dive in. Swallowed by cold and dark,

I blow all of my breath out and it bubbles in front of me. I pull wide on a breaststroke, come up for new air, then swim freestyle in the direction of Outer Farne Island.

I notice it then: she's not with me. I stop and tread water, looking out for her. The sea spreads wide, salty and deep, its waves gently rolling and tossing. The movement feels playful, as it rocks me in my position. But I've seen its strength, depth and darkness and I know never to forget what the sea can do. I can't see Amarie anywhere, but before panic sets in she appears, hovering just beneath the surface like the black ink of a cuttlefish. I swim on, stronger with her beside me.

Outer Farne is the only Farne Island that is completely swallowed by the sea at high tide. This keeps other people away. We arrive at low tide and crawl onto the bank. The island is covered in blotches of guano that make me think of Dalmatian spots. We settle on a clean grassy area to catch our breaths. The sun dries my skin and leaves a trail of crystals where the wet's turned to salt, little white specks shimmering along the skinny brown of my arms and legs.

'What are you going to do about the trip?' Amarie asks.

I shrug. 'I guess I could talk to her.'

Amarie sits cross-legged looking at me, 'How?'

'Stop pressurising me. I'll think of something.' I pause. 'Maybe, maybe I'll say something like ... about, how it's the end of the term and the end of the school year ... and how everyone's really excited about the class trip to the Grace Darling Museum. I might say, how they're all talking about it, so I was looking forward to it too – but that Sister Maria told me I might not be allowed to go. I could maybe ask Mother about it, like it's a question, like I'm not sure of the answer.'

'She didn't even have the decency to tell you herself.'

'She'll be trying to protect me.'

'From a museum?'

'She'll be thinking that it's for my own good. And maybe the Grace Darling Museum won't be that special – we don't know... It would be nice to leave the island – the proper way for a change ... and to see the mainland, to actually walk on the mainland.'

Amarie doesn't say anything. I get up and wander away from her, feeling judged by her silence. It is barely the end of June, but it has been so warm that the tips of the grass have started to turn yellow. I brush my toes through strands of blonde grass as I walk, pulling a few out that are practically straw. I stop beside a rock pool, dip my feet in its waters and then settle myself on its incline. I grab at flotsam and seaweed that's trapped there and kick the water up. We should never have started talking about the trip to the museum; it's completely changed the mood of the day.

A dazed-looking mackerel circles the edge of the water, trying to avoid my feet. I lean in to touch it, and it slips along my palm and swims towards the farthest wall, putting as much space between us as it can. Its scales are smooth to the touch, like undersea velvet. Having nowhere else to go, it turns around, trapped. We look at each other. It feels like a challenge. I'm on my feet in the water, but crouching as though I'm about to catch a ball in rounders. The mackerel moves, slowly, away from the wall. I lunge. It tries to escape, but my hands are around it. I tighten my grip. Gotcha! I squeal and jump, nearly lose my balance but manage not to fall. I hold it up to show Amarie. It thrashes between my fingers. Amarie gives me a thumbs-up, then turns away. Deflated by her response, I nearly lose my hold on it. I steady myself, then throw it up and out – momentarily it glides through the air, then splashes into the open water, to freedom.

From the NorthBound Award-winning novel *Castles from Cobwebs*

INFLORESCENCE

In the Calder Valley
Simon Zonenblick

Nature diary notes from canalside walks near Sowerby Bridge, Yorkshire, from summer to autumn.

Summer

I've spent much of the last few weeks in canalside wanders, particularly near my home – the Rochdale Canal between Sowerby Bridge and Luddenden Foot, or, in the opposite direction, the Calder and Hebble towards Elland, Halifax, or Brighouse. In summer, the canal and towpaths burgeon with biodiversity, a far cry from the heave and hustle of their industrial past.

Perhaps most noticeable at this time of year are ducklings and goslings, the latter being either the young of Canada geese or the white, street-strolling Embden geese resident in Sowerby Bridge. It is life-affirming to see ducklings, clumsily clambering in and out of the canal, swimming around mother ducks in search of grass to nibble, or venturing in ones and twos on their first daring escapades beyond parental cover. The Embden goslings appeared almost overnight, like balls of yellow wool brightening undergrowth, or sunbathing on the towpath, guarded by parents who raise elastic-like necks to hiss at passersby veering too close. The Canada goslings are adolescents now – half the size of their black-and-white parents, confidently waddling along the towpath gobbling grass, grey-white feathers as shaggy as ash. Today I watched a dozen Canada geese swimming in triangular formations along the canal at Brearley.

The largest birds are usually herons, who tread treetops in the breeding season like gregarious avian acrobats. These summer evenings they are often seen prowling the towpaths, or on brows of boats, watching for fishes slipping by below – the canal is rich in minnows, tench, carp, and more. Smaller birds are easy to spot too, though – down the towpath near Tuel Lane Lock you have a chance of seeing grebes, with their fancy head feathers and frequent underwater dives. At Siddal, I've watched wagtails swooping over stones at Hebble Brook. On the sandy path at Sowerby Bridge, sparrows snaffle worms, twisting in the drizzle under watchful eyes of grazing geese, crows and blackbirds meander tasselled grass, finches feed on dandelions seeds. Wrens flit branches. Jays and bluetits dip and dive among sycamores. Pigeons dodder through the daisies, navy blue feathers glossed by sun. Many birds are happier amid the berried bushes between the Calder and canal, jewelled with the wings of butterflies, the stripy fizz of honeybees, the small charcoal black of beetles, and the tiny eggs of insects, cropping up on tree trunks.

Despite their human-dominated history and the boats bobbing along their edges, the canals of the Calder Valley are highly rewarding for the wildlife spotter or casual walker.

INSECT SEASON

On a recent walk along the canal, some friends and I noted that this year, insects were greater in number than we'd noticed previously around these parts. Perhaps it's a combination of the gradual development of trees planted in recent years, not to mention the hotter weather – which brings about the imperative of mating – but I have certainly noticed a boon of invertebrates on the leaves and branches flanking the canal, climbing in and out of riverside flowers, and turning up unexpectedly on roadsides, in fields and woods, over the last few months.

Naturally, there is no shortage of the seasonal regulars – if anything the wasps are outnumbering the bees, and seem to be thriving, along with butterflies, beetles, dragonflies and damselflies whipping past like jazzy shafts of jasper, crystalline-sheathed. But in the spring and summer of 2021, I was also introduced to a variety of invertebrates I'd never previously encountered.

INFLORESCENCE

First, the Cinnamon moth caterpillar, a twisting black and orange tube that feasts on ragwort, and develops into a mysterious looking moth of black and red. Seen close up, its coloured ringlets gleam like lacquered shellac, winking in the sunlight. So zealously do these varnished vegetarians gobble the toxic ragwort that its toxicity absorbed into the bargain, making them hazardous for predators to consume.

Although I'd seen evidence of their handiwork many times, I hadn't, until recently, laid eyes on the ashy mining bee – *Ardrena cineraria*, like a little black "cola bottle" sweet, but for its cellophane-like wings, and the woolly white rim circling its face.

Large rose sawflies – *Arge pagana* – have carroty-coloured bellies, and dark, transparent wings, and split the stems of roses by weighing them down with eggs. I saw my first hanging around conspicuously on my windowsill one late spring afternoon. At least the aptly named brown house moth *(Hofmannophila pseudospretella)* seemed more at home within my home – unlike sawflies, brown house moths are almost always found indoors and are known to sample cereals and fruits, as well as having a penchant for furniture, fabrics, bottle corks and wood – though my fluttering 'flatmate' seemed content with browsing the juncture of the wall and ceiling.

Lately it has also been common to spy old favourites, like the weevils, shield bugs and ladybird larvae clambering over foliage or scooting over roadside paths. These last are like flecks of black rubber, dabbed orange, and I've seen them in gardens in large numbers. Recently I caught sight of one patiently ascending a towpath tree, scaling the bark with irrepressible energy. Later that same day though, I noticed one manically exploring an electricity box on a Sowerby Bridge side street.

Closerotomus norvegicus is a creature which happens to go by two of my favourite Latin and common names – the potato capsid. Along with the vegetable its common name suggests, this spud-scoffing bug feeds on nettles, clover, daisies, carrots and chrysanthemums - and is even a connoisseur of cannabis. Fly-shaped, but with two long, arced whiskers that lend the look of an eccentric professor, its sandy brown back tapers to a tiny triangle of green, and I've seen it threading through the long grass at the Copley reserve, stopping atop golden samphire, antennae sticking out inquisitively, fingering the humid air.

Much smaller than these exhibitionist bugs are the tiny velvet mites – around four millimetres long – cropping up in sandstone walls, or thronging on rotting logs like explosions of scarlet stars, speeding in mazy masses this way and that across the wood, each one a squiggle of wriggling ruby, fast-pedalling on the hunt for other small invertebrates. Yet smaller still are the innumerable black grain-like beetles, scrabbling over stems and walls throughout the woods, watersides and reserves. Almost everywhere I go, I see them – jiggling through the weeds, defying identification, and seeming to multiply, until the very ground we walk on has become a superabundance of invertebrate life.

HERONS

Walking along the canal one chilly, early autumn Sunday, I pass waddling throngs of ducks, watch a canal boat pass beneath a bridge, chugging through the dusk towards Sowerby Bridge.

Plodding towards Copley, I'm caught by the glare of a beady eye – black, rounded by sharp yellow, piercing, accusatory. Almost more sinister is the razor beak – angled, dagger-like, towards the water. Almost, but not quite, because for all their predatory glower, there is something of the jester in a heron. Their flappy flights, legs a-dangle, can have a clumsy quality; the jutting neck can give the appearance of some odd, mechanical dance. Grey herons (*Ardea cinerea*) are suited to the watery Calder Valley. I see them sweep through sunsets, wings outstretched, an ashy pterodactyl above the roofs and tree-tops. At Barkisland, I watch them, semi-visible in fields of reeds, stationery under driving rain, in fields outside Brearley, on the prowl for voles or shrews, or combing plumages with "grooming claws." You can see them fishing in the river, stock-still before the sudden plunge of a lethal beak, and the gobbling and gulping of large, fat fish. Occasionally, you might see a mother silhouetted against the bough of a tree, craning her neck, dispatching breakfast to her chicks.

Urban herons are not unheard of, though I've never seen one on the streets – the closest they have come was during the first 2020 Covid Lockdown. Emboldened by our scarcer numbers, herons, like other birds, emerged for longer periods, on canal paths and on the edges of car parks, even residential areas. I saw one most days that spring, along the canalside, by the normally busy Wharf Street, Sowerby Bridge, and sometimes followed it, prodding around locks and milestones like some avian investigator.

Those surreal spring evenings it felt like the birds were the natural citizens of the towpaths. Gone, for a few quieter, less polluted weeks, the cans, the cigarette butts and the fishermen replaced by growing numbers of increasingly confident birds – an eco-system thriving without human influence.

The Scafells—A Place of Highest Honour
JULIE CARTER

I'm walking up England's highest mountain, Scafell Pike, and my footsteps are words, commas, full stops and capital letters. I have come to walk-write. I don't often *just go for a walk*. I am a fell runner and a rock climber. Most of my walks are on the way to climbs, and most of my summits are approached breathlessly, on lactic acid burned legs. Now I am gifting myself the time to assimilate something of what all those intense encounters mean to me, and what this place means. Time to seek words. Each slow step is a walk along a sentence.

Sentence—related to *sentience*—derived from *sentire*—to feel.

A sentence is 'the expression of a complete idea'.[1] In that way it is like a climb or a run. Although climbs and runs are more like essays—requiring my body to have one idea after another.

Opening the gate at the fell bottom; I am opening an idea. In itself a mountain has solidity; for me it is a thing conceived:

Peak—Summit—Achievement—Healer—Artwork—Monument—Remembrance.

The neuroscientist Anil Seth tells of how we create our own worlds, making sense by using seen-before patterns and expectations. 'Our conscious experiences of the world are forms of brain-based prediction – controlled hallucinations – that arise with, through, and *because of* our living bodies'.[2] I catch myself almost making a miss-step here. Expecting the predictable will end only in a pleasant relaxing outing and I will come back from my walk unenlightened. My purpose is to be curious. I will defy the zeitgeist of the athlete's tracking app Strava, and forget about times and goals and grades, and I will walk. And I will write when a sentence entices me along into an adventure, wording me towards somewhere new.

I could tell you how it was I came to love these fells. How since teenage years, in my addicted, personality disordered, anxious, depressed, psychotic wanderings, this place has been my constant, all that is trusty and secure. The fells adopted me and parented me. I'm not suggesting they are constitutionally capable of caregiving; it is just what happened between a physical mass of mountains and the psychology of a girl.

To be parented by ruckles of rocks, lumps of earth.
To be embraced in gullies and lulled by clouds.
To hallucinate a whispered possibility—
'You'll be alright'.

INFLORESCENCE

My manifesto is that everything we do is a creative act—nothing is mundane. The first time I realised that rock climbing is the enactment of poetics was in 1987, when reading *Native Stones* by David Craig, soon after my first awkward flounderings up vertical faces. This from Craig's Chapter Two, 'Into Rock':

> *He chimneyed up the gigantic split*
> *Sitting in air like an ejecting pilot*
> *While the sky out there*
> *Blazed at him and the granite ground his spine.*[3]

I still have the book, given to me by a lover—a man. The last six pages are covered in blackberry stains from a picnic taken with my other lover at the time—a woman. It all seemed beautifully unconflicted. Neither of the lovers were climbers. The man died of a heart attack soon after. I remember the way he and I would laugh conspiratorially; in on life's joke of heart-breaking joy. The woman, whose gaze perfused me at a cellular level, emigrated to a far-off place with her husband, leaving the juice from blackberries we'd picked together on the pages. It has not mouldered. As yet.

The Scafells originating as a fiery belching soup of molten volcanic lava, are now cooled and solid, managed, cultivated, grazed and paved, adorned with dry-stone walls and cairns, photographed, painted and written about. The Lake District is more a curated gallery than a wilderness. But it is not tame. You can get seventy-miles-per-hour winds up here, often stronger, and after fifty I can't stand up.

If a mountain is an object, then where does it begin and end? Where is its perimeter and how deep are its innards? Does the oh-so-well-worn path which meanders up to the Mickledore neck, between Scafell Pike and Scafell, belong to one, or the other, or both?

These fells and their neighbours—
Lingmell—Great End—Esk Pike—Bowfell—Broad Crag—
Ill Crag—Slight Side—   are not discrete.

They are like people in a crowd whose bodies are pressed into
each other so that only the heads are distinct. Except that—they
were never separate. It is only that humans have given them iden-
tities, made them into entities with names. Having created these
individuals, we then have relationships with them. Innumerable
particular unfathomable relationships.

> Icons, conquests, challenges,
> objects of desire, uplifters,
> steadyers, soothers, songs,
> dances, poems. Lovers—
> who bodily pull me in.

Toiling up the well-laid path I look over to the summits of the
Scafells and see their profile as that of a dignitary lying in state.
From the furrowed curve of the Pike's summit brow along to a
pert nose, plump lips, and rounded chin, dipping to the neck of
Mickledore—the isthmus of ridge which joins the two mountains. Then along the rise of sternum, over the rocks of Broad
Stand up to the chest of Scafell. Once seen the person could not
be unseen. A flimsy mist was dabbling the tops. The late-to-rise
sun, halfway between gold and silver, was cupped in the dip of
the neck. A jewel adorning the fell-body.

Then I experienced a horrible writerly invasion of my unfeigned
vision. To see a human form in a hillside—what worn out metaphor; what naive pagan myth. Is this the kind of weakness that
George Eliot described as 'a disease of the retina'?[4] Has my love
got the better of me, to sentimentally humanize the rocks?

Approaching Brown Tongue towards Mickledore, I am walking beside the cleavage made by the streaming water of Lingmell

Ghyll, with the mass of Scafell Pike rising up on the left and Scafell on the right. But neither of these mountains is a simple rounded mound. The Pike has the clean triangle of grey rock, Pikes Crag, which you meet head on. Scafell has its own crag, more complicated, bigger, consisting of different walls each of which is looming and huge. The rock walls are separated by rakes.

// Lord's Rake // Ladies' Rake // Steep Ghyll //
Deep Ghyll // Moss Ghyll //
To the left of Moss Ghyll, on the clean sweep of Central
Buttress there is // The Great Flake. //

My heartbeat bounds with the mention of it. I have never climbed The Great Flake of Central Buttress and I would be at the limit of my ability making an attempt. I'll train this winter. I'll wait for a good hot day next year when the rock is dry. I'll go with Mandy—my wife; the person I have climbed with for thirty years. We'll climb together as we so often do, so able to read each other's movements. We'll be in love up there, up on the Great Flake.

The page in the guidebook is familiar:

'Central Buttress.
E1 5b. 124m. 6 pitches.
A route of immense historical significance.'[5]

The climber Mabel Barker was born on the Cumbrian coast in 1885. She fell in love with the Lake District as a teenager, and in the early 1920s she fell in with rock climbers and was powerfully magnetised by the crags. She led the Great Flake section of Central Buttress in 1925. This was only the fourth time it had been climbed but the three previous leaders had the help of shoving hands under their feet from their companions tied onto the chockstone lodged behind the flake. Mabel was too quick for that.

'Moments of tense excitement and rapid action passed quickly [...] being slimmer than former climbers, I got further into the crack and chimneyed it. I faced out and think there was a small hold far up on the inside wall. Almost at once I felt the top of the Flake with the left hand. "I've got it!" [...] there was probably not a happier woman living at that moment.'[6]

I too have been the happiest of women on that same rock face, leading the long slab on Moss Ghyll Grooves. Delicate, balanced, exposed, and thrilling. Two grades easier than Central Buttress and first climbed in 1926 by Blanche Eden Smith and three others.[7]

Both Mabel and Blanche were members of the woman only Pinnacle Club founded in 1921. I too am a member of the family that is the Pinnacle Club and this year I am, humbly and proudly, the editor of our *Centenary Journal*.[8] A tangible connection with my climbing ancestry and the adoption papers which make me legitimate.

Mabel's ascent of the Great Flake caused outrage. Her male climbing partner was accused of gross irresponsibility because she had been *allowed* to lead. Mabel responded that 'at no point did I find myself having any serious difficulty with the climbing,'[9] which must have been a crushing disappointment to several egos.

Climbing is a craft—an act of synthesis. Mabel Barker was a creative genius.

The local shepherd Joss Naylor once ran the up and down Scafell Pike, in forty-seven minutes. Born in Wasdale eighty-five years ago, Joss is a blazing pioneer of fell running; he is an icon of that sport. Recalling his run up the Pike decades later, Joss talks about it in fine detail, describing his exact route from Wasdale, up Little Brown Tongue and a short-cut under Pikes Crag across to the summit.[10] Then it had been a case of 'legging it down there pretty fast', which was something he described as 'pretty special'. For Joss this was a super-short run. His other records were mainly set over several hours and some, like all the Wainwrights and the Pennine Way, over days.[11] All this was done naturally, out of curiosity, in the way an artist works. Joss works as an artist in his fell running and in the building of drystone walls, which sometimes merge into sculptures. Walling is one of the shepherd's arts. Not just an enclosure of territory but a necessity for sheep sheltering, and piecemeal farming of land. Each stone is carefully chosen, handled, and fitted into its place. Joss has a great pride in his walling and he has incorporated seats and monuments into his walls around the lower fells of Wasdale. Each one is like himself, fitting its place perfectly, robust and pleasing, and a complete one-off.

Recently I went exploring with Joss on a hillside above Wastwater. I followed his bandy trackster-clad legs, matching his surefooted strides up steep tussocky fell, as he pointed out which walls he'd built, and which were the devotions of his father and grandfather. He said a good wall depends on good cobbles. Close to a sheepfold that Joss has restored were vague outlines of ancient walls. Some university men had told him they were Bronze Age remnants, but he wasn't sure. We both stood quiet for a minute, wanting to pull ourselves into the past, to see what it was like. There was a fleeting sensation, seeing the valley from this lookout, as if we were scanning for wolves.

Joss the shepherd—Joss the world-class athlete—honorary
MA graduate of Lancaster University—Joss the artist-
sculptor-waller—Joss Naylor MBE.

— — — — -- — — — — — — - - - — — — — — — —

— — — — — — — — — Joss — — — — — — — —   — — —

— —

NORTH COUNTRY

I asked him—if fell running was art, then what was his greatest masterpiece? It was on a certain spring morning, on his own, flying round the hills above his farm, in his boots, before he owned trainers. It was during the small window in his life when he was free of the back pain that has plagued him since boyhood. 'It was magic; it just felt great; running free.'

Now, walking alone up the Pike, I find words strewn all over the place. I examine each word, handle it like Joss would handle a wall stone, and put them down, into two piles.

The pile of cobbles to build from:

Flow / touch
/ dance / alive / into / open / adventure / habitat
/ commitment / attempt / sing / breathe / share
/ mysterious / practice / stretch / erosion / compete / relate
/ body / see / stand / rubbish /move / ecology /bare
/ navigate / howl / retreat / intrigue / experience
/ destruction / love / embraced

The suspiciously cracked pile to leave be:

Nature / selfie / use
/ lost / ownership / mental / resource / conquest
/ do-it, done, did-it / magical / recreation
/ mindful / World-Heritage / right-of-way / rite-of-passage /
wilderness / heavenly / tick
/ National-Park-Authority / hellish / itinerary / pastime /
eternal / brave / spiritual / smash-it.

One word is an odd shape and I can't decide where to put it—

DANGER!

INFLORESCENCE

Once, approaching the top of Scafell Pike provoked memories of competing in the Wasdale Fell Race. One year as I'd stumbled over the jumble of boulders to the summit cairn, going gingerly, trying to avoid both injury and an agony of cramp, I'd been thinking about Joss. Sometimes I think about heroes when I'm absolutely knackered but need to keep going. Like Joss I was born with a badly made spine. 'Keep running' Joss says, 'that's the main thing'. On the drive to that race, I'd seen Joss where the route crosses a road near his farm. He was setting up a drinks table, ready to dole out life-saving liquids to passing competitors. It was a sweltering thirty-degree July day. During the race I'd had to swim in Sprinkling Tarn, to cool my blood, just to be able to keep going. On the ascent of the Pike, the last of the race's many grinding uphill slogs, I passed a friend and rival. Turning to the final descent, I tried to pretend I was a bit like Joss. My legs got wheeling—everything went beyond my conscious control. I was consumed in a wild trust, in running and in the fell, and in my rival. Without each other's competition neither of us could have found the commitment. I am grateful for that fast legged friend on my tail who was pushing me towards my limit, towards a place where I existed only as movement.

When foot and fell meet, a lot of things have to happen. Land on the front of the foot, weight forward, bend legs, soft legs absorb the forces, and release them. Ankle angle is very precise. Arms are active but not like wings, stabilisers, that's all. Eyes see three steps ahead, then fully ahead. Long sight for fraction of a second, then back to short. Chest open, shoulders down, air drawn in through nose as well as mouth. My cerebellum, so called *little brain*, is situated at the back of my head above the spinal cord, under the knuckles of the skull. A subconscious nerve centre, the conductor of the piece, receiving proprioceptive information from every joint and sinew and responding in micro-time. A bit more angle right ankle, a little forward lean in the torso, a shorter step, left a bit. Neurones transmitting electrical impulses up to 120 metres per second. That's over forty return journeys per second between my cerebellum and my ankles. My decades of practicing and studying medicine don't make these things less astonishing. If I had to consciously think about everything that got me down that hill I'd be there for days. How long do you think a conscious thought takes? Two seconds is quick. Oh intellect, oh cerebral cortex! Seat of all that's meant to be clever, office of *executive functions*. What a slow sluggish lump of jelly you are compared to innervated quadriceps, the skill and knowledge of the leg, the wisdom of the foot.

Thoughts are a futile energetic drain, until I'm over the line. Then my friend comes in and we go for a cup of tea while covered in dirt and sweat and snot. Middle-aged English ladies do like taking tea.

Racing is a deeply cooperative act.

The physicist and philosopher Carlo Rovelli explains that everything 'exists only in relation to everything else'.[12] Our relationship, our experience, is as real as our fell shoes and the salt on our skin. The *hard problem* of consciousness remains ineffable, except for those who believe in spirit, or mind, as an entity separate from body. I find this Self, this feeling of I, peculiar. Science points to it being an illusion. A few moments before the end of the race there was no I, only body and breath and fell. Once back across the finish line, *I* returned.

In 1817 John Keats described 'negative capability': 'Capable of being in uncertainties, mysteries and doubts without any irritable reaching after fact or reason'.[13]

Almost two hundred years later the psychologist Mihaly Csikszentmihalyi described 'flow': 'A psychological state of complete absorption in the current experience.'[14]

INFLORESCENCE

Keats's description seems passive. Csikszentmihalyi requires active engagement to reach further towards a loss of self. Both writers describe in detail what is to be gained by such loss. There are other methods of escaping the straightjackets of ego and identity but none I have personally found as effective as climbing and fell running, where the walls between the self and the world dissolve.

There is a state of existence where experience moves beyond words, and time, and kudos. There are no symbolic figments, only earth and rock, water and wind, and the beat of pulsing warm blood.

I have climbed on the Scafells in all seasons. In summer I have laboured up to the crags with Mandy, carrying a rucksack full of ropes and equipment, setting it down, putting on my harness, gearing-up and tying-on. Then one of us leading up a crack, a slab or a steep face. Smearing rubber-soled rock shoes onto tiny dimples; balancing and moving, responding to the rock. In winter we climb wearing big cramponed boots, arms extended by ice axes, getting purchase in frozen water, thankful for the flask of hot coffee. Each fresh time I set out, there is a moment when none of those previous days have ever happened. When the morning is new and I have never in my life seen anything like this. When the world imposes itself on me, and I make no effort to retaliate by thinking or remembering.

The physicality of walking was essential to how the sibling poets Dorothy and William Wordsworth perceived the world, and it was fundamental to their creative process. I understand this walking-writing as a way of opening oneself up, of becoming an instrument orchestrated by the habitat. I wouldn't imagine it was like taking dictation, since it involved them in so much strenuous commitment of muscle and brain, but neither do I think it was a process of composition by an internal intellect. Perhaps writing is neither a process of reporting nor composing. It is engagement, involvement, curation—a way of doing love.

Perversely, the Wordsworths' ground-breaking poetry, which idealised these fells, has been co-opted into an ingredient of the *Lake District Brand*. Those ten thousand daffodils are now reflowering as a marketing tool.[15] In his sonnet 'The World is Too Much with Us', William Wordsworth referred to commodification of human experience as 'a sordid boon'.[16] Now here we are with impossibly jammed-up roads, desperately eroded fells, polluted lakes and litter strewn on the Pike by the skip-load. The Lake District is buckling under the weight of humanity. But we can't blame love-struck poets and their sensibilities towards the fells. And are they not asking us if this place is something more than a leisure park?

Dorothy's description of her expedition up Scafell Pike is exceptional in that it is the first known written account of an ascent of England's highest mountain.[17] It was an adventurous act, going with a female friend and three employed staff, at a time when women hardly ever ventured up mountains. Dorothy described standing on the summit as being at 'the point of highest honour'. Does she mean her own honour or the Pike's honour? Or were they both honoured by each other's presence?

And what about the view from the summit now? The way Sellafield's nuclear repository draws the eye; the largest dump of nuclear waste in the world. That issue of danger is left hanging on the idea of safety being guaranteed – for thousands of years.

In 1802 Samuel Taylor Coleridge walked straight up Scafell's flank from Wasdale, sat on the summit, and wrote a letter to his love, Sarah Hutchinson.[18] He then set off down towards Mickledore, and his antics became the stuff of legend. According to The Fell and Rock Climbing Club it was 'the first recorded recreational rock climb in England'. Coleridge climbed alone, down a route now known as 'Broad Stand', graded as 'Difficult' in climbing guide books.[19] Many a walker comes across Broad Stand, as Coleridge did, not realising the difficulty of what they are undertaking. And to add to their problem the rock is now a gallery sculpture, polished smooth by the millions of hands and feet that have passed over it in the two hundred years since. Coleridge made it safely down, but there is a place under the crag which the mountain rescue teams are now too familiar with. The place where the bodies land.

I have an image of Coleridge climbing down from Scafell and I think of him like a wolf. The gentleman who has gone feral. I imagine his howl echoing around in the mists of Mickledore. The prickling of his skin at hearing his own voice sung out by the mountain. I had a dream about meeting him as he emerged, squeezing himself from between the rock walls which form the tight cleft of *Fat Man's Agony* at the bottom of Broad Stand.

And standing on Mickledore, with Eskdale to the south and Wasdale to the north he instructed me to throw back my neck and howl. And we howled, Coleridge and I, because both of us are addicted to animal excitements.

Howl is the first and longest word.

Howl for the last wolf—speared at Humphrey Head
Howl for Coleridge, and for all who climb
Howl for the need to escape the zoo
Howl—to know danger and not be dangerous
Howl while you have breath.

to the south of Mickledore, there is a bowl with a huge flat bottom.

NORTH COUNTRY

The Great Moss

The Great sponge, great absorber, the soak-away, carbon-sink, the great stink, the great sphagnum wound dressing, antiseptic, healer, cleaner of pus.

The great soft bed, the great flat bottom, the great red carpet laid out, the fiery flamey breaker of fire, quagmire, sprawling sunshine drinker.

The great rain-butt, the great reservoir, bog, peat, the great preserver, the great wobbly-body, the fragile moss, the fragile ground, not ground but moss.

The Great Moss, splat, suck, sink-down, sink-in, feet, legs, torso, head, brain, mind, come into moss-mind, clean-mind, sweet-mind. The Great Moss—please don't worry, you are not alone, the Moss will take you in.

On the way back down Scafell Pike I met my friend Lindsay Buck on her one-hundred-and-fourth ascent this year. She takes disposable gloves, bin-bags and an empty rucksack. She has returned from these walks with an assortment of things:

many sorts of many wrappers / empty cans / a can with a dead mouse inside / bottles – both broken and intact / an empty bottle of expensive champagne accompanied by lipstick-marked stemmed glasses / a used male catheter / a drone in working order / half a meat pie in polystyrene tray / half a kebab / a half-full foil packet of delicious roast chicken bites / various single gloves mostly right hands / a pair of trousers / ready-bagged dog shit / human turds bagged by herself / dog leads / hats / plastic red poppies / a sweatshirt / a small square of matting / many plastic bottles / drinks cartons with straws / a pair of underpants with shit inside / blood stained tampons / used sanitary towels / used alcohol wipes / walking poles – both broken and intact / face masks / a headtorch / an unopened bar of milk chocolate.

She says it's about education. She says people don't understand how to behave. We need to talk to them and help them. It's the kids who are capable of caring. We need to teach the kids, and the kids will teach the parents.

I come to fell races in cars, and I park up early on summer mornings to get to the crags for climbing. It's what we do; it's the norm to drive a diesel car up Wasdale, along the shore of England's deepest Lake, consuming the vision that was voted 'the UK's best view' in 2007. I love you / I destroy you / I love you / I destroy you.

I've bought an electric bike. I'll try harder. But there aren't many buses and I am addicted to the places and experiences the car allows me into. This is a problem. The lichens don't like it. These founders of ecosystem need clean air. The mycologist and lichenologist Beatrix Potter was thwarted in her science by her gender, and by the fact she championed the symbiotic hypothesis of lichens. Victorian British scientists were scathing, but Beatrix Potter knew the mutualism of lichens was real.[20] They are two things, a fungus and an algae or bacteria. Two things—working as one species.

The Scafells make rain by pushing water-laden westerly winds skywards. Where the rain falls at their eastern feet in Borrowdale, there are remnants of temperate rainforests sheltering lichens I barely know—but help to poison. The lichens are gas victims of another holocaust. We don't know how they came to live, but we know how they came to die.

Dog lichens,
Elf's ears,
Satin lichen,
Kidney lichens,
Barnacle lichens,
Lungworts,
Srobs,
Shingle lichen,
Dimple and Felt lichens,
Jelly-skins,
Grey crottle,
Wart lichen,
Sea-storm,
Desperate Dan,
Heather rags,
Horsehairs,
Beards,
Cudbears,
Shaggy straps
and Bleeding hearts.

Borrowdale is my home too. Dirty-filthy lichen murderer that I am. And the moss needs the lichen, and the ferns need the moss, the trees need them all and I need the trees. I choke on my own words.

After my walk I sit in the carpark drinking coffee with Lyndsey and the National Trust warden and we bask in the outrage of autumn colour. Behind me the fells lie in state. The point of highest honour? What should I do?

Should I change my surname to Mickledore?
Mickledore, from old English, meaning—'great door'.

Which would not be appropriate
as I am not interested in openings—
I am attending to happenings,
correspondence between feet and fells,
stretched hands reaching for holds of rock,
the physical consummation of love.
Here, and now—what constitutes consent?

Mallerstang and the Source of the Eden
DICK CAPEL

In the south-eastern corner of Cumbria, two springs of crystal-clear water called Red Gill and Slate Gutter ooze out of Black Fell Moss, a remote bog high up on the eastern side of the spectacular Mallerstang valley. Liberated from the saturated peat, they scamper over the brow of the hill and converge to form Hell Gill Beck, the boisterous adolescent stream that runs south-west down into the valley bottom and swings abruptly north to become the River Eden.

For many years, as the curlews returned to greet the arrival of spring with their plaintive, bubbling cry, I have visited the source of the River Eden; a personal annual pilgrimage after the long, cold paralysis of winter to celebrate both the awakening of the new year and the embryonic rise of the river. On one late-March visit, it didn't feel at all like spring up there; lines of thick snow lay across the moor, and grey sheets of ice glazed the pools of water skulking inside its dark peat hollows. The bleak fell was still comatose under a leaden sky, frozen in the tenacious grip of winter's spell. There was no sound of the curlew that had earlier greeted my arrival in the valley below, and I listened in vain for skylarks or meadow pipits or the distant fluting of golden plovers. The moor was unrelentingly silent, and a screen of smoke rising on the horizon, where gamekeepers were burning the heather, partially concealed the stark outline of Ingleborough, lending emphasis to the melancholy of a lost wilderness.

I didn't stay long. My pilgrimage on that occasion was also the start of a journey along the entire length of the River Eden, which had to begin at the top of the hill known as Hugh Seat. There, at a height of 689 metres above the valley bottom, I could attain a real sense of the watershed where, as documents relating to the old boundary inspections, or 'perambulations', describe it, 'Heaven water deals and Heaven water divides'. With Mallerstang Edge to the east and Wild Boar Fell to the west, virtually identical heights of just over 700 metres, Mallerstang belongs, geologically, to the limestone country of the Yorkshire Dales. Dominated by horizontal layers of carboniferous lime-stone, capped with gritstone escarpments, it represents more than 350 million years of geological history. Derived from sed-iment deposited and compressed by shallow tropical seas and primeval rivers, lifted by tumultuous upheavals in the Earth's crust, they were cut into shape by the interminable passage of Ice Age glaciers and the manic meltwater in their wake.

Surrounded by that vast, ancient landscape, I always feel acutely aware of the fleeting and minuscule time span of human history; a mere two million years. A very small stone cairn on top of Hugh Seat, inscribed faintly with the initials AP and the date 1664, puts this neatly into perspective. The cairn is Lady's Pillar, erected at the request of an extraordinary seventeenth-century landowner called Lady Anne Clifford, the Countess of Pembroke, who owned vast tracts of old Westmorland stretching between Mallerstang and Penrith. It marks the source of the river and commemorates her notorious predecessor, the Norman knight Sir Hugh de Morville, who owned the same estates five hun-dred years earlier and was one of the four knights who murdered Thomas Becket, the Archbishop of Canterbury.

INFLORESCENCE

My plan was to travel the route in stages, short sections at a time, sometimes walking, sometimes by car, over the course of the proceeding seasons. I descended from Hugh Seat feeling disappointed that there were no stirrings of spring at the source of the river. But I still had the warmer embrace of the green valley below to look forward to, with its promise of skydiving lapwing, their sharp *pee-wit* call complementing the curlews' refrain, and perhaps the sight of a few early spring flowers on sheltered grassy banks.

*

Hell Gill divides Cumbria from Yorkshire and was the northern boundary of the Yorkshire Dales National Park until 2015 when the park was extended further north to include an extra 417 square kilometres in Cumbria, now called the Westmorland Dales. The River Ure starts its journey in the opposite direction just a short distance from here on the Yorkshire side.

The nascent River Eden snakes its way across level ground before plunging into the narrow, hidden cavity of Hell Gill, the limestone gorge that gives the beck its name. More than a thousand years ago Mallerstang was occupied by Viking farmers, so Hell Gill may well have been Hel's Gill, an entrance to the Viking underworld of the dead.

Hell Gill is 30 metres deep and 365 metres long, yet, in places, little more than a metre wide. Most of the time it tumbles gently in a series of hidden waterfalls and pools. Braver people than me venture down there in the drier summer months, coming in from the top end, sliding and slipping from pool to pool in the half light and emerging at the bottom to dry themselves on exposed rocky ledges in the brightness and warmth of the sun. In spate the beck fills the ravine with a raging, plunging, crashing torrent. In his book *Waterlog*, the late Roger Deakin describes how he attempted to scramble down the Gill in more running water than was reasonably safe and halfway down found himself beneath an overhanging rock, staring into a terrifying "gothic emptiness". Sensibly, he retreated and climbed back to the top, despite the full strength of the water being against him. I was happy to give the experience a miss and, skirting to one side, came down onto the wide green track still known as Lady Anne's Highway.

From *The Stream Invites Us to Follow*

Walking to Spurn – A Line Between Sea and River

ALISON ARMSTRONG

I have been drawn back to the changing shape of the East Yorkshire coastline over recent years. More of it is lost to the sea each year, as the boulder clay, which makes up much of the land, breaks up and is vulnerable to erosion. In Roman times, the coastline lay five miles out to sea. Towns, villages, hamlets topple from the edge as the ground on which they stand gives way. There is a fascination to these places as they quietly await their fate. In some places stand half-abandoned farmsteads with dilapidated outbuildings and obsolete machinery, overgrown with grass and nettles. Rusted tin shacks and the shells of old cars litter the area. In others, like Mappleton, there is an orderly neatness about the place. A business-as-usual sense to the pretty geranium-filled window boxes and neat-curtained windows. I am drawn to the unfinished nature of their narratives, that a place, the location of a community with all its history and ties, can just fall into the sea, disappear.

This is a falling-away world. A fringe of land already adjusted to loss. Roads come to a sudden jagged end. And the spaces in between have returned to wildness. Between Bridlington and Kilnsea the coastline is one of the fastest eroding in the world. The boulder clay of the cliffs is prone to slippage and collapse and is constantly changing, fraying at the edge. The speed of land loss seems to be increasing, up to ten metres per year. The loss leaves behind the names, the memories of names. There is a sense in which, when the land erodes, it forgets. Contributes to forgetting. No longer does it hold memory to account. When something disappears physically the obligation to remember it goes with it. A name holds something in place. Is a fixative against forgetting.

When Owthorne Church fell to the sea in 1816 the bell was moved to Rimswell Church. The bells from Kilnsea are at Easington Church and Aldborough, near Hornsea. But for most of these places all that remains is the name. I am reminded of a line from Annie Dillard's *Teaching a Stone to Talk:* 'All those things for which we have no words are lost.' Like lots of the place names in the area, they carry the presence of old languages, the people who have settled there. The Old Norse between the Anglo-Saxon names of earlier settlers reflects the Viking habit of settling in the space between Anglo-Saxon settlements. The past surfaces through these names. Clings to the tongue. Ringborough. Monkwell. Monkwike. Waxholme. Owthorne. Newsham. Old Withernsea. Out Newton. Dimlington. Turmarr. Northorp. Hoton. Old Kilnsea. Ravenspurn. Ravenser Odd. Their locations on old maps are scattered points like a broken string of beads, lying now beneath the sea. The undoing of a landscape.

When I was eighteen I couldn't wait to leave this area and my home town of Withernsea. Literally, to go west. Trashy amusement arcades, grab machines filled with faded soft toys, the stale metallic air billowing with cigarette smoke. Cut-price food shops long before they became normalised. In the dull half-light of adolescence, I did the place a disservice. Now I find myself pulled back – stirrings of nostalgia, loss, absence, grief, have grown into a deep hankering for the whole landscape.

Two million years ago, much of Holderness was still a tropical ocean, evidenced by the glut of fossil relics of crinoids and corals, brachiopods and ammonites found in the area. The bay was filled in with boulder clay, gravel and rocks carried by retreating ice at the end of the last glaciation, around 11,000–12,000 years ago. In contrast to the relatively stable, and more slowly formed, chalk cliffs of Flamborough and Bempton further north, this stuff is all fracture and fissure, collapsing at an alarming rate and accelerated by the combination of storms, westerly gales and high spring tides that can cause surges that can take out several metres of land in one go. On the beaches, pillboxes from WWII are upended, fallen from the clifftops. Sections of brick wall, part chimney stacks and corroded artefacts of domesticity sink into the sand. Near Mappleton, land mines buried in the mud as defence regularly turn up on the beach. Concrete posts, with rusted steel wires jutting out, stand strangely in their new positions. The sharp edges of broken tiles are eroded to smoothness. It feels, as a place, not only at the literal edge of the country, but at the end of the line, economically, culturally, politically. The whole area has long had the air of a backwater, though this itself has also been part of its identity; part of the local pride and resistance to being like elsewhere.

Walking the lonely stretches I have become used to not seeing anyone, but here among the scattered buildings it is disconcerting. Behind a gate a dog barks in indolent schemes like a maniac coming to the end of its energy. A chicken scrabbles on the ground by a post. They are the only signs of habitation. A rusted weathercock on a roof with missing tiles. A weathered St George's flag hangs limply from a metal post. Absurdly, near Hollym, fifty yards from the cliff edge, there is a llama, ragged and unkempt in a field behind farm buildings. It is so still and badly formed that at first I think it is a home-made statue. It watches me retreat, malevolent-looking. From a safe distance, we continue to watch each other, a strange ambivalence between us.

The continual presence of the North Sea is reassuring. I have none of my usual map-related worries of having wandered off the path, lost, my walks veering off and having, like I suspect all maps to ultimately have, no actual relation to the route/landscape. Walking south to Spurn Point is easy: just keep the sea to the left; no danger of getting lost. And in a deeper way too, its vast grey indifference is calming, it reassures my irrelevance to the grand scheme of things. All my mistakes and wrong turns have no significance here. There is no better reminder of the relentless movement of time than the rhythmic persistence of tides.

It is like a poultice drawing out the melancholy. Hope worn away by wind, leaving only fatigue and a grey sense of fate, sprung into relief by the sight of a bird. A group of ringed plover run back and forth by the shoreline, held to the rhythm of the waves. A grey heron flies in an exaggerated straight line with slow, prehistoric grace.

Arriving at Spurn, there is a change of potential in the narrative, to see it not as diminishing, but shifting. Over three miles long, Spurn Point is a spit of land forming a sweeping curve which continues the line of coast into the Humber estuary. Debris from further up the coast is transported here by longshore drift; a process known as deposition. The energy in the waves carrying the material reduces where the North Sea meets the Humber Estuary. Ada W Phillips said in 1962, 'It is out of the ruins of Holderness that the Spurn is constituted and maintained.' Erosion provides the material and pattern of its evolution, as it grows southwards and westwards, before being demolished by severe storms that recur every 250 years or so. Records show that there have been at least six different Spurn Points. A rough, fragile outcrop terminating in a wider, rounded end, the Point houses a lifeboat crew and residential buildings, with bunkers and tunnels and gun emplacements hidden under the sand and gravel. In other parts, it is a strip as thin as 50 metres, with dunes at this narrowest part, just beyond the Washover, reaching 30 feet high, structured on the extended root systems of marram grass and sea buckthorn.

The Point's isolation and exposure to the elements has attracted its share of hermits in search of solitude, from Wilgils at the end of the seventh century, who fathered Saint Willibrord, saviour of the souls of Dutch pagans, to Richard Reedbarrow who petitioned parliament in 1427 for the right to build a beacon to guide sailors. The locals still take pride in the mavericks attracted to the place. Sue Wells of Westmere Farm bed and breakfast told me of a chalet on Beacon Lane, 'Mad Mick's place is named after a lifeboat man who became increasingly eccentric and at odds with everything. After he died, it was sold to a man named Gary who named it Mad Gary's. New people have bought it now, done it up, but they don't share the same sense of humour and have renamed the house.'

Spurn Point has existed in some form for more than 10,000 years, in a constant flux, continuing despite its precariousness, its various stages of growth and destruction chronicled in texts from early Christian texts to the tenth-century Icelandic saga Egil's Saga, it is twice mentioned in Shakespeare's historical plays as 'Ravenspurg'. Circa 1235, Ravenser Odd, thought in the majority of chronicles to have been an island east of the Point, was 'one of the most wealthy and flourishing ports in the kingdom,' according to William Shelford, boasting a merchant class, royal charter and returning two members to parliament. But by 1355 the graveyard was washed away so that bodies 'horribly appeared' and had to be reinterred in the churchyard of Easington, foreshadowing what would happen in 1843 to the dead in Kilnsea graveyard. By 1360 the Point and the old town of Ravenser Odd were destroyed by floods. The remains, hidden by the tide, were the cause of frequent shipwrecks. It was common for centuries for the crew on these trapped vessels to drown within sight of land, at the behest of sea captains whose traditions were rooted in the dishonour of accepting assistance.

It is hard to imagine this rich history, this flux of fortunes, looking out towards the calm, grey-brown flats of Kilnsea Clays.

The weather is constantly changing; a single day can come with an onslaught of hail, baking sunshine, gales, mist and fog. I have known fog here so thick that your own outstretched hand becomes invisible, and the water vapour, hung on minute particles of dust, is so dense it hurts the lungs to breathe. It brings with it too a claustrophobic eeriness, broken only by the low bark of a foghorn as a ship enters the mouth of the Humber. And even on fogless days, walking the lonely, windswept interior of the spit, the visual field is limited by the height of dunes and scrub, which increases the feeling of being apart from everything else.

Andy Mason of the Yorkshire Wildlife Trust, a practical man attracted to the precarious nature of the Point, and self-confessed storm chaser, told me when I visited him at the Trust about the early spring storm of 2018, which took 20 feet off the top of most of the dunes and revealed parts of shipwrecks and a hidden bunker from WWII. And in 2013 a storm surge, coinciding with a high spring tide and westerly gale, caused a breach ripping out the road and temporarily making the tip of Spurn Point a designated island. Rising sea levels and an increase in the frequency of storms are a growing threat here, and there is a respect for the weather more acute than I have seen in any other place.

I stay the night at the Crown and Anchor, on the very edge of the land, facing the mudflats of the Humber. It is low tide at dawn and I watch a flock of some 60 dunlin in their dark-bibbed summer plumage perform their quick walk over the mud, occasionally pecking for food. From a single loud call, they run at full speed and take off, flying in a straight line little more than a foot above the mud and land again further down the estuary. A whimbrel has found a small crab, which is huge in its slender beak – and it keeps on going at it, dropping and picking it up again. The roe deer I have seen at the same spot in winter feel like a distant dream, out on the mudflat in their first year of antlers, before night had properly begun to recede, licking salt from the wet sheen of mud, light growing in pools around them.

I set out to the Point before the grasshoppers have woken and walk by the canal scrape – the small canal located between the Point and the mainland – breakfasting from a vagrant apple tree midway across the scrape. At the end of the scrape the controversial Yorkshire Wildlife Trust visitor centre stands, structured atop a wired ballast foundation, out of reach, it is hoped, of flood waters. Turning onto the old path of Spurn Road, bordered by clumps of red fescue and stunted hawthorns, the wind has died down and I look out for summer visitors. Towards the Warren, I hear the throaty clicking of a stonechat before I locate it on the arched branch of an elder. Whitethroat flit about the scrub appearing, for an instant, to throw a darted look before disappearing again in a flash of wing. The song of a wren detonates close by, trilling among the thickets, and just beyond I can hear the soft-fluted repeats of a willow warbler. During spring and autumn migrations birds fall here in their hundreds, thousands, exhausted and flapping into the dust and sand, but I have been here on days of high westerly wind and failed to see a single bird – other than the crows which seem to take some pleasure in flying into the wind. The locals are fond of saying that no two days are the same on Spurn.

This is a place that always has that dishevelled look about it, that, after a day out on the peninsula, you can't help but share, covered gradually with the grease of salt carried in on the wind. There is a wildness about the place, a vulnerable hold on existence, though it is, in reality, more durable than the rest of the coastline. And although, for a small area of land, it defies the flatness of the rest of the region, the landscape is dominated by water and sky, and given over to the surrounding textures of grey, so that the details of the land come into sharp relief; the brittle architecture of sea holly held towards the light, the flick and tremor of a bird. The dunes and stretches of grass carry a late-in-the-season look, whatever the season; the grasses sere and bleached by the weather. Marram grass and sea buckthorn dominate;. their roots and rhizomes spread deep and wide giving structure to the dunes, trapping sand and other debris as they continually evolve. Scurvy grass grows in white flowering clumps – so called because it was dried and taken aboard ships as a cure for scurvy. At the edge of the paths sea bindweed prostrates itself, throwing up trumpets of pink flowers and providing cover for a large and bewildering variety of beetles, which scurry beneath the vegetation as I walk past.

On the estuary side of Spurn, large wintering flocks of knot and oystercatchers jostle at the shoreline above the water's edge and wheel in practised displays, their shrill whistles rising above the tumult, as group by group they reposition in huddles among the stalks of sea blite and lyme grass, an ongoing negotiation of space, the low winter light reflected from the mud flats. Brent geese, shelduck, redshank, curlew, a seemingly endless stream of birds come and go, shifting position, dabbling in the shallows, their ululating calls and shrieks rising with them as they regroup further down the spit in a continuous ripple of movement. At high tide the birds move off to nearby grassland, scrapes, lagoons, ditches, flooded corners of fields where they begin the ritual all over again.

It is this continual passing through of birds that pulls me to this ragged Point, rather than the precarious exposure of land with its capricious shifts of weather. That shared fact of transitory existence we share with all living things, but with birds in particular: they seem always to live on the very edge of survival in the spin of seasons. The rhythms of nature on this fragile spit of land, perhaps that's the pull – existence pared to the bone.

Being in the North Sea
ADAM FARRER

While my parents were busy sifting through cardboard boxes and unpacking essentials, I slipped away to the cliffs with our dog, Daisy, a gangly Labrador/whippet cross. We headed down the weathered concrete steps that led to the sands, my steps hurried, keen to acquaint myself with the place where I planned to spend most of my time. I let Daisy off her lead and watched as she gambolled away across the wet sands, her long legs making her look coltish and uncoordinated at first. But when she reached the sea, she looked as if she belonged in it, becoming giddy and joyous. She hurled herself around in the shallows, biting at the waves and spume, running in wild circles as arcs of water whipped from her tail. I wondered if this was how I looked to other people when I encountered water. Not graceful or amusing, but wild and demented. It didn't bother me in any case, my overriding feeling as I watched her being one of envy.

Before we'd made the move to Withernsea, our whole family had taken a trip there to get the measure of the place and we stopped for a snack in a seafront café, where my mother soon got chatting to a talkative, elderly woman. She'd been sitting at the table next to ours and became too intrigued by our jarringly out-of-town voices to let us enter her orbit without investigation. After some small talk about where we were from and why we were in town, the two of them got on to the topic of the sea.

'People are funny about swimming here,' the older woman had said, explaining that not many people looked at the coast of Withernsea with a sense of longing. The water closest to the coastline is coloured by the eroding clay cliffs, giving it the murky quality of under-milked tea. 'They worry about sewage,' she said, adding that some holidaymakers tended to look at the sea and picture the source of its colour to be a huge undersea soil pipe, belching a continuous stream of sewage into the waters. So, inevitably, they shied away, fearing they'd emerge as filthy as a seabird caught up in an oil disaster.

'It isn't dirty though,' the woman assured us. 'It's just full of clay.'

I thought this sounded like a pretty neat definition of dirty water, but for someone wired like me this was never going to be a problem. The fact that no one else was swimming was part of its charm. What could be more of a luxury than your own private sea? This was how I'd seen it on that first day, this expanse of water, no one in it but my dog. And shortly thereafter, my dog and me. I took off my trainers and socks then ran into the water. Clothed in jeans and a t-shirt but still shocked by the jolting cold of the North Sea, which even in July tends to greet bathers with more of a slap than a kiss.

My mother had always taught me to acclimatise to the sea in stages. First to put my feet in, then my hands, before wading in at intervals. Knees, hips, chest, shoulders, pausing at each step to centre my breathing and swat at my body with handfuls of water, dowsing myself. Adjusting. I dunked my hands, filtering the water through my fingers and watching it fall like bands of fogged, amber glass. When I looked down though, I couldn't see through it at all, my legs appearing as if they'd been severed at the knee and that I was miraculously walking the rust-coloured surface on stumps. Everything below that point was a mystery. I could have been entirely safe or millimetres away from being savaged by flesh-snipping crabs. But I felt no threat or concern. Being in the North Sea had given way to something I'd felt in rivers before, but never so strongly: an even deeper sense of cradling comfort. I absorbed the smell and the grit, the way it made my body bristle with activity, the saltwater shimmying into my pores, thrilled at the knowledge that I'd later get to enjoy the sensation of it crisping and tightening on my skin as it dried. Even though, to the sea, I was insignificant, *I* felt like I fully existed. I was alive in a way I never felt on land. I wanted more of that and before long I was up to my chest, my pockets filling with sand and seaweed. I knew that I was in too deep but also that, for me, there had become no such thing.

When Daisy and I arrived home a couple of hours later, soaked and guilty, my mother just looked at us and sighed, no longer bothering to ask what was wrong with me. Knowing that what I'd done had been inevitable.

'Dry the dog off and get changed,' she'd said, turning to fill a drawer with cutlery. 'There's a box of clothes in your room.'

For the rest of that summer, I repeated this pattern, exploring the coastline and testing my mother's patience. Never fully dry, always leaving a trail of sand and damp footprints behind me. So, it was a relief to her when September rolled around; it was time for me to move on; college in Hull beckoned.

From the NorthBound Award-winning Cold Fish Soup

Place-Names and Poets—
the Makings of a Cultural Landscape
JACK HARTLEY

Skarð Old Norse 'notch, chink, mountain pass' | *Gap* Modern English 'break or opening in a range of mountains, col, pass' from Old Norse *gap* 'gap, chasm' | *Pass* Modern English 'a narrow route through mountains' from French *pas* | Scarth Gap Pass, mountain pass, Cumbria (OS: NY 189 133), 54° 30' 31.7"N, 03° 15' 13.8"W | 'Scarf Gap, Buttermere,' poem by Norman Nicholson, from *The Pot Geranium* (1954).

As a cultural historian and student of philology, I study the ways languages interact and evolve through time. For me, place-names are exhilarating evidence of the entanglement of life and land, and the stories that words contain. To experience a place is not just to feel with the feet or look with the eyes, but to engage with its embodied memory. In so doing, one can traverse time, language and cultural distance as naturally as the migration of birds. The following essay will narrate something of how this can work by looking closely at one place, a particular location within the modern administrative county of 'Cumbria'—which still exists, just—and is the county in which I grew up.[1]

THE NAME

Between the Lakeland valleys of Buttermere and Ennerdale lies a mountain track, Scarth Gap Pass. The route runs over a notch in the ridge between the fells of Haystacks and High Crag; and the notch itself is known simply as Scarth Gap. Pronunciation has varied over time and spelling has varied with it. Known previously as the two-part Scarf Gapp, the name acquired 'pass' at some point in the twentieth century. Whether 'Scarf' or 'Scarth', its etymology is Old Norse *skarð* 'notch'—as in a notch on wood—but also 'mountain pass'.[2]

Scarth Gap Pass, as it is labelled on modern Ordinance Survey (OS) maps, would originally have been made up of just one component, Old Norse *skarð*. We know this because the place-name now contains three elements that all mean the same thing; one or several of them had lost their descriptive capacity over time and therefore needed an additional element to help the name make sense.

To explore the historical linguistic significance of a name like this can provide a window into the past, but it also reveals *landscape as process*. Names are not some abstract phenomenon but tools we use, constantly being adapted and manipulated, and always telling a story. To use a word is to place yourself on an etymological continuum, to enter into its evolved and evolving linguistic context with all of the past interactions and influences implied by that.

Place-names colour and inflect how we interact with a place, not as some abstract geographical form but as somewhere that has human significance. For those living in valleys divided from their neighbours by steep craggy ridges, the easiest throughways—Scarth Gap Pass for instance—become worn with the feet of generations. More than that, these places inflect the world view of the valleys' inhabitants, so that to think of the next valley is to walk the pass in the mind, its trod scored into fell and its name scored into the psyche.[3]

THE PEOPLE

The people who named Scarth Gap Pass 'Skarð' spoke a form of Old Norse. To them, the route between Buttermere and Ennerdale was simply, well, Pass. The details of how these speakers of Old Norse came to inhabit Lakeland's dale-heads are debated. Originating in Norway, their sailing route took them via the Orkney and Shetland Isles, rounding Cape Wrath, traversing Scotland's western seaboard, and entering the Irish

Sea before landing on Cumbria's shores and gradually making their way inland to find what unsettled land there was, mainly the largely uninhabited further reaches of the mountain valleys.

How many of these settlers were from Norway? And how many speakers of other languages did they interact with along the way, feeling the influence of and absorbing 'foreign' elements from the cultural melting pot that was the Viking-Age Irish Sea? We may never know the precise answers to these questions—a question, really, of *who were they*? What we do know is that we feel their presence more strongly than Lakeland's other previous inhabitants, such as the Romans or Brythonic speaking tribes, because of the pronounced mark they left in our place-names and regional vocabulary.

In time, these Old Norse speakers mixed with other local populations. Grammatical Old Norse ceased to be spoken and the regional language became a heavily Old Norse-inflected dialect of Middle English, retaining many words of Old Norse etymology and of course leaving behind a rich topographical language that still colours the landscape.

The passes between the Lakeland valleys had an essential function, joining up communities separated by fell and ridge, layering the landscape with a history of movement, use and collaboration between those who inhabited it. Scarth Gap Pass has long been used as a major route connecting the Buttermere and Ennerdale valleys. In the past, male Herdwick sheep—known as tups—from Buttermere, were walked over the pass into Ennerdale where they were met by the Ennerdale tups. From there, they went over Black Sail Pass and on to Wasdale Head. There they met the Wasdale and Borrowdale tups, which in turn had come over Sty Head, the most direct route between Wasdale and Borrowdale. Sheep and shepherds then stayed the night at Wasdale Head before all walking the next morning to the Woolpack Inn in Eskdale for the Fell Dales Show where all of the best tups were shown and judged.[4]

The Poet

We now have the place, and we know something of its significance through time and the historical picture its etymology opens up. But how does this linguistic artefact lying dormant in the landscape—its precise etymology unknown by the vast majority—continue to mean something? We can find an example in Millom-born poet Norman Nicholson's 'Scarf Gap, Buttermere'.[5] Nicholson uses the significance of this mountain track and what its name can reveal, as a metaphor for the cultural memory preserved in a place. Memory, in Nicholson's vision, is not a faculty that any one of us possesses alone, but a thread joining generations through enduring linguistic resonance, memorialised in physical locations through the historical significance of the words.

The fells that insulate Buttermere valley from the rest of the world—High Stile, Melbreak, Robinson, Grasmoor and Hobcarton Fell—become in Nicholson's poem 'the wrack and backwash / Of the geological tides'. A landscape is not a given, not a stable unchanging thing, but, over time, as mutable as the tide. This is true for all its components, geological and cultural; in this stony landscape, memory

> return[s] with the wheatear,
> [to] find the name scratched on the same stone.

The word *skarð* has been metaphorically gouged into rock and to discover it with all of its etymological significance is to comprehend the memory of the landscape—as it existed in the past, as it exists now—and to comprehend that it exists as a changed, changing thing.

Physical objects can vastly improve the capacity of our minds to remember things. The idea of the memory palace—popularised by Arthur Conan Doyle's stories of Sherlock Holmes though attested in classical Latin dialogues from the first century BC—makes use of this; memories can be attached to a physical object or location and stored within an architectural space for far easier recall than if they were disembodied, abstract entities. The same is true of cultural memory. This can be witnessed in place-names. As a place enters into human significance through an act of naming, language becomes welded to topography, ensuring each can endure as they would not be able to do individually. If a name or word was not attached to a place, if *skarð* was not to the pass between Buttermere and Ennerdale, for example, and it did not continue to be referred to as the place was used and moved through, then the name would not survive.

Nicholson's motif of names scratched into rock evokes this the importance of a physical location in the survival of place-names. It is a motif that he uses several times throughout his work. In 'Cornthwaite', from *Sea to the West* (1981),[6] the memory of a Norwegian landscape is also scratched on rock; and in 'For the Grieg Centenary' from *Five Rivers* (1944),[7]

> the Norsemen foraged down the dales,
> Crossing the sea with the migrant redwing,
> Thieving heifer and yow and teg,
> Leaving their names *scotched on the flanks of hills*.[8]

Each of these poems conjures a notion of cultural memory, evoking the presence of the past in the landscape of the present. Name and place function together as linguistic memorial, a touchstone for memory, a reminder of the ongoing presence of the landscape's previous inhabitants and the words they used.

Another indication of human interaction with place, as well as connections across time, is the motif of migrating birds. In 'Scarf Gap, Buttermere', it is the wheatear that finds the words scratched on stone. In 'Cornthwaite', it is the migrant fieldfare;

and in 'For the Grieg Centenary', it is the redwing crossing the
sea with the Norsemen. The birds in these poems ground the
words in the seasonal movements that characterise a place—its
year-round fluctuations—bringing nature into the cultural landscape as well as offering a metaphor for migration and memory.

Scarth Gap Pass does not mean 'Pass Pass Pass' to the Modern
English speakers who traverse it; its original components have
lost their significance. But the name still has the capacity to tran-
scend historical distance through Nicholson's poem. In 'Scarf
Gap, Buttermere', the pass is defined by the feet of those who
tread and have trodden it, each of them with a story to tell, each
of them having

> scrambled up the screes of the slithering moment
> To seek a combe unquarried yet by change

Though *skarð* has lost its transparency to those who encounter it,
Nicholson used the place-name's etymology to reveal to us that a
name is not simply a label, impartial and abstract, but a term full
of history, intrigue and meaning. Through Nicholson's poem, we
can tap into the collective memory enshrined in this toponymic
monument, acknowledging the feet of previous generations who
have defined it and accessing something of the screes of the slith-
ering moments of the past.

The evolution of Scarth Gap Pass shows us the changes that a
name can undergo as its linguistic context ebbs, flows and trans-
forms, despite the name's essential meaning staying the same.
The first component of the name is now meaningless and yet it
is this component which preserves the place's linguistic memory,
enabling us to capture and express this process of linguistic
transformation.

To ignore a landscape's cultural aspect would be to weaken
our understanding of it, its processes, and how humans, wildlife,

and topography have evolved together. It would be an act of erasure, creating a void, a nothing-place for which we have no words to use. Though sheep and shepherds may not always be encountered on Scarth Gap Pass, it is not a wild place. To see its line cut into fell, rising above the lake, or to tramp the defile that resembles 'a pencil / Drawn diagonally across a slate' as Nicholson calls it in 'Scarf Gap, Buttermere' is to interact with its human significance, established with *skarð* and maintained in Scarth Gap Pass.

A landscape is not a blank canvas for people or for nature, but a tapestry of how they interact. In this instance, a place name reveals a distant cultural memory of migration, almost certainly not of people who came directly from Norway, but of Old Norse speakers who had a memory of that place—their ancestral homeland—not as a living memory in its common meaning, but in a memory that lived through the words they used and the naming practices they maintained. Here, now, in the twenty-first century, 'scarth' on its own no longer has any meaning; it needs its accompanying 'gap' and 'pass', and yet Nicholson has kept the idea of a cultural landscape alive, breathing story into place and language into rock.

Landscapes, seen in the bigger picture over a long period of time, are varied and multifaceted. They evolve with every new perspective and tick of the clock, amassing layers as they do so—layers of words and stories which do not present a linear picture but which are selective and discriminatory, elevating certain narratives while others fade. Some narratives are erased and lost forever while others mutate into forms unrecognisable; landscapes are constantly in flux. This flux makes them complex carriers of history and memory; and the membrane between past, present and future can be made to seem thin. This elision is what cultural geographers have drawn attention to as the palimpsest-like functioning of landscape. A palimpsest is the term used in the study of medieval parchment manuscripts to describe a process of use and re-use, of erasure and rewriting; a palimpsest is text that has been scraped off, entirely or partially, from the surface of a manuscript to be replaced with new words written on top, though often retaining traces of what was effaced, which enable us to know that there were previous layers. In a landscape, layer upon layer of human history is attached to place and yet written over, with fragments of past layers surviving beneath new ones, only partially scrubbed out.

The palimpsest-like functioning of a landscape can work both ways; language too is composed of layers, and to examine the etymology of a place is to shine a light through murky historical layers in the landscape. Place-names thus indicate past realities, linguistic, social and environmental; they are physical and imaginative meeting points. Nicholson's poem 'Scarf Gap, Buttermere' helps us to see this.

Crossings
JANE SMITH

Having grown up in an industrial city, I can't remember even seeing a toad until I was already an adult. Then again, I wasn't exactly looking for them. I didn't really like being outdoors, I didn't know anyone who regularly spent any significant time 'in nature', and I certainly wasn't equipped in any sense at all to get outside and engage with my wider environment.

In my early thirties, I took up hill walking, mainly because I'd started a new job in Manchester and the Lake District was suddenly within easy weekend reach. This opened up huge vistas, literally and mentally. I was coming across mountain streams for the first time, and chocolatey peat, and bracken, and lichens, and hares. I could feel a new kind of nourishment coming from the natural world now that I was seeing it, feeling it, hearing it and walking in it. Before too long, I was sitting in my office daydreaming about the walks I'd be doing at the weekend or relishing the things I'd seen during the previous weekend's walks – iced-over waterfalls, ancient trees, sunsets. And walking became a daily habit.

One evening, walking out of a local wood onto a country lane near my Cheshire home, I noticed lots of tiny dead frogs, which in fact turned out to be toadlets, on the road. They'd been run over. I contacted the national amphibian charity Froglife, who explained that the area must be toad-rich, and that the key time for toad fatalities on roads was in early Spring during their spawning migrations. They suggested I come back to the same site on an early Spring evening to check on the situation.

A few months later, in early Spring, I went back to the site one evening, and sure enough, dozens of toads were crossing the lane, while others seemed to be sitting in puddles or in the middle of the road. Some had been run over. I called Froglife the next morning and they told me I could set up a toad patrol where volunteers help the toads get across the road safely to their spawning ponds.

Behind this practical advice was an incredible natural phenomenon. Toads reach sexual maturity from around three or four years old, and at that point they make the arduous journey, sometimes of several kilometres, back to their natal ponds to mate. En route, they face multiple predators: most animals bigger than a toad will try to attack or eat them; toads breathe through their skin, so pollution, pesticides and herbicides are all a huge problem for them; many fall down open farm grids or road grids; and many are run over by vehicles, because their migratory route will usually include having to cross roads.

I recruited my ecologist friend Olivia, sent off for toad patrol packs from Froglife, and for the first couple of weeks it was just the two of us helping the toads over the road, either carrying them by hand or plopping them in buckets on busier nights. We were soon joined by our friend Claire; by the end of that first Spring season there were fifteen of us on the rota and we'd safely crossed 891 toads.

At the time I had no idea that the toads would bring me to question so many things I'd taken completely for granted about the world around us.

By the end of our first toad patrolling season, we realised that grids were a real problem. After spending many hours scooping toads out of grids with children's fishing nets, we knew we had to find a better way and we hit on the idea of temporary mesh over the grids to stop the toads falling in.

I would go over to our sites in the mornings pre-season to mesh the grids, always checking first to make sure no early migrants were already down there. One sunny day, I'd checked a grid and couldn't see any movement, so started to mesh it over. Standing back to admire my neat work, I was about to move on when I heard the unmistakable sound of amorous toads coming from the grid. Unpeeling the mesh but still unable to see the toads, I lowered my net, and bingo – a toad couple in flagrante, so attached to each other that I had to scoop them up as an entwined pair. Placing them down in a nearby field, they tumbled out of the net still embracing in the long grass, and that's how I left them.

It turned out, of course, that 'toad season' didn't finish once the toads had crossed, either. Knowing what I now knew about their hugely perilous journeys, having seen the wonder of the Spring migrations at first hand, the toads seemed to take a gentle hold of my consciousness and started to change, or more specifically to deepen, not only the way I saw the world, but also my place as a human, and human society's responsibilities, and our relationships, or lack of them, with the wider, wilder world. I had urgent new questions that needed answering.

Why did we build roads and runways and housing estates and high-speed railways so freely, with such scant consideration for all the other species who call those spaces home? Who gave us that right? And if it was a self-anointed sense of entitlement, where did it come from?

At the same time, my own species identity began to emerge. I'd hardly ever thought about what it meant to be a human being. I'd never really thought of myself as a-human-rather-than-a-something-else, but I did now. I could have been a cat, a bat, a rat or, indeed, a toad – but I was a human. Where did that leave me? And as a human, what were my obligations to other species?

I started to feel a heavy and uneasy sense of being part of human society – locally, nationally and globally. We were a species whose actions through industry and commerce and war and agriculture impacted on every other species. But where were we held accountable for them?

*

Sometimes we come across huge toads on our patrols, mainly elderly females. Toads can live twelve years or more in the wild, growing ever bigger as they age.

One night, I saw a very large toad making her way down the very middle of a lane. On closer investigation I saw she was elderly, and so big I couldn't even hold her safely in one hand, having to put my torch away and cup her in both my hands instead. She was as dry as paper, obviously in urgent need of water. When I put her down on the ground near the pond I gave her a spray of water and enjoyed her very visible appreciation of it before she took some last slow steps to the pond.

How many years had she been visiting this pond to mate? How many overly ardent males had she fought off? How many young had she produced, how many grids had she avoided and how many vehicles had she dodged? I often think about that dry old girl at the end of her journey, surviving for all those years in the wild and carrying herself with such dignity for what was almost certainly her last mating season.

Some very, very old toads have been found locally. A few years ago, archaeologists working at a site twenty miles from our patrol area found the 10,000-year-old fossilised remains of a natterjack toad. Natterjacks (*Bufo calamita*) favour open country over woodland, and after the spread of woodland across much of England many centuries ago, natterjacks became stranded on a coastal strip in the Wirral, where they're now highly protected and known affectionately as 'the Bootle organ' for their distinctive gribbet.

Common toads (*Bufo bufo*), on the other hand, thrive in or near woodland. And given that we've lost so much woodland to farming and construction, they've suffered greatly from habitat loss. Our toad patrol site is unusual in that it's part of a small hamlet which has only seen one new road built since the 1890s; the country lanes we patrol today were there over a hundred years ago. But even here, toad fatalities on the roads are very significant. Some toad crossings in other parts of England help toads cross busy main roads and even dual carriageways. Road-building has decimated so many toad populations, and in many places it has long rendered local toad populations extinct.

I myself have a car. I even drive to the toad patrol, as there's no public transport in the evenings. I park well away from the main toad sites but even still, I might be running toads over on the way there without even knowing it.

What must it have been like 10,000 years ago, when those natterjack toads were still living inland and we didn't have roads or trains or grids or housing estates or combine harvesters? We must have co-existed peacefully with other species – or those we weren't eating, at least. Did we make collective human decisions with other species' welfare in mind?

And if we ever did, why don't we do that now?

Two

RETROSPECTION

Voices from Before

The Blind Botanist

John Gough

I very well recollect surveying an earth-worm which was crawling in what appeared to me a collection of dirt perhaps in a Garden-bed; the reason for recalling so significant an object to memory with the greatest certainty may be this: my father, after the loss of my sight, was in the habit of teaching me to handle everything that fell in his way, which could be touched with safety & propriety; & I remember him giving me an earth-worm to feel, whilst he was angling, in the first year of my blindness; I concluded that the act of examining the reptile by the sense of feeling made me recognise the image formerly impressed upon the retina by a creature of the same denomination, accordingly I knew it to be an earth-worm. The want of similar comparisons seems to be the reason why many images still remain in my mind, to which it is impossible for me to assign their proper names with certainty. The foregoing facts & reflections contain a retrospective view of the brighter days, constituting the first stage of my infancy in which an attempt has been made to explain certain circumstances which are apparently connected with the premature loss of sight.

*

The first object that drew my attention to the properties of vegetables was a tall plant of Moldavian Balm (*Dracocephalum moldavica*) in flower.[1] It stood in the window of an apartment inhabited by an aged couple whom I frequently visited. In all probability, the powerful odour emitted by this herb was the cause which first attracted my notice, & I straight away began to examine carefully the stem, leaves & the whorl in which the lowers were arranged. After obtaining a pretty correct notion of the Moldavian Balm, I compared the different parts of it with the corresponding parts of another plant, which grew in a flower-pot standing near the former; & the result of the comparison led me to conclude that as much pleasure & information might be expected from the vegetable kingdom, as could be afforded by the study of animated Nature. At this time, I knew from information that plants of any particular species, grew up in succession from seeds which had been previously produced from others of the same denomination; & that they were fixed in the ground by roots, which supplied them with nutriment.

I also learned by my own observations, that water constituted a principal ingredient of this nutriment; because I had formerly remarked that a Poppy became flaccid & incapable of standing upright after being a short time upon a table, but which recovered its former vigour upon being placed with the extremity of its stem in a vessel of water. Without doubt many children enjoying the benefit of sight know as much as or more of botany than I knew at that age; but a person deprived of the use of his eyes in the earliest years of life has the advantage of tracing the progress of his own mind, which other men have not; for he acquires knowledge, as I may say accidentally.

This circumstance enables him to connect each enlargement of his understanding with some memorable date or event in his own private memoirs, or the history of some one of his friends or intimates. This I can do with certainty in the present instance; for I remember very well the foregoing to have been the state of my knowledge relating to the nature or variety of vegetables in the summer preceding Easter Sunday in 1765: for the person, in whose house I examined the Moldavian Balm, was buried that day; & on the same day I was obliged, by the groundless terrors of my parents, to take a quack medicine, which at the time was almost universally considered to be an infallible specific for Hydrophobia.[2] It is true, this most horrible of maladies never attacked me & the reason of my escape will be evident when the reader is informed that I had been scratched by a cat, which has supposed to go mad a few days after my hand had been wounded. Multiplied instances of this sort had at the time established the reputation of the remedy with the unthinking part of this nation; but where the danger was real, the efficacy of the Powder disappointed general expectations; for I recollected the failure of it in these instances in Kendal, or in the neighbourhood. The reputation, however, of the pretended specific maintained its ground a long time after the period here mentioned; but a gentleman, who had been severely lacerated by a dog which was known to be mad, & who had taken the Cohn Medicine as it was called, died of the Hydrophobia in London about the end of 1776, or the beginning of 1777. This unfortunate circumstance induced Dr Fothergill to warn the public through the medium of the newspapers, not to rely in similar cases on this nostrum, which he found to consist, when analysed, of little or nothing more than powdered chalk coloured with red powder.[3]

This information opened the eyes of the public, & very properly deprived the imposter of the profits arising from a wicked deception. But the preceding remarks on quackery & credulity threaten to lead e too far from my subject, which I will therefore resume. The circumstances which excited in me a taste for the study of vegetables have been already related; but my progress in Botany proved very slow for a long time. It is true I never desisted from the pursuit; for every plant that fell in my way became an object of careful scrutiny, & I treasured up in memory the forms of a multitude of vegetables, was to afterwards recognise many of them, when I came to read their descriptions. In the mean time I obtained by enquiring the names given by others, by my neighbours, such as were distinguished by their medical virtues, culinary uses, or which were cultivated for the beauty of their flowers, or the singularity of their structure. Ignorance, however, retarded my advancement in the science: for it was some years after I knew that animals were described by books, before I learned that there were also books in existence which described plants with equal accuracy & fidelity.

This error was entertained by me for some years; but a trivial occurrence shewed the opinion to be false in the year 1770, or when I was in my thirteenth year. My father took both my sister & myself into the fields on a fine summer's evening, when being reminded of my predilection for the products of the vegetable Kingdom by the circumstance of seeing me examine with the greatest care a plant of Henbane (*Hyoscyamus niger*) a few days before, he plucked several herbs, the names of which he knew, & presented them to me.[4]

This circumstance gave rise to a conversation respecting a celebrated Botanist called John Wilson who formerly resided in Kendal.[5] This man, my father observed, was in low circumstances, being a journey man shoemaker: but his desire for natural knowledge, particularly for Botany, was so strong, that he made himself the master of the Latin language, which enabled him to consult the writings of Ray & Thomson.[6] Wilson's wife was an industrious woman, who followed the business of a breadbaker, & her family was small, consisting of only two daughters. This was a fortunate circumstance for her husband, who not being incombered with domestic cares attached himself to an eminent land-surveyor of Newcastle, & became chain-bearer to his master, or more properly his intimate. This kind of life gave Wilson an opportunity of visiting various parts of England & thereby observing the rarer plants of the British catalogue in their native soil.

The labours & researches of this impecunious man were not entirely lost to the world: for being sensible, that Botany would not become a general pursuit & amusement until a systematic work on the subject should make its appearance in the English language, he published in 1744, the first volume of a Synopsis of

British Plants after the method of Ray, comprising the Genera & species of all the herbaceous vegetables, which were then known to be natives of the British Islands.

This information, which I received from my father, removed my error; & as there were many copies of the Synopsis in Kendal, I was in short time furnished with one. I began my systematic labours by studying the botanical dictionary, which I prefixed to the work, & the perusal of it afforded me both instruction & pleasure: for it gave me a first notion of the general structure of plants, as well as the different parts which compose them & it also taught me the technical landscape of the science then in use. After making myself master of this treatise I began to study the characters of the classes as they are described in the body of the Synopsis; & in a short time I acquired a pretty correct notion of the arrangement invented by Ray.

As soon as I thought myself master of the art of classification, my next business was to apply my newly acquired knowledge to practice. At first the undertaking appeared to be very discouraging; but constant assiduity, prompted by an ardent desire to learn, overcame in great measure all my difficulties. I began by referring my new indigenous plant to its proper class by a close examination of the fruit & flower; in the next place I discovered the division of that class in which it was to be found: lastly the generic & specific descriptions gave me the genus & species as well as the trivial names of the object of my research, with the synonyms ascribed to it by the elder English botanists, Gerard & Parkinson.[7] The necessity of referring frequently to Wilson's Synopsis excited in me a strong desire to become acquainted with the writings of the two ancient botanists last mentioned; & the wish was gratified in due time.

From *The Dark Path to Knowledge* (1852), Gough's autobiography. Blind from early infancy, Gough became a noted scientist and could identify plants by touch and smell.

Furness
THOMAS WEST

From the abbey, if on horse-back, return by NEWTON, STAINTON, and ADGARLY. See on the right a deep embayed coast, the islands of WALNEY, FOULNEY, and PEEL-CASTLE; a variety of extensive views on all sides. At ADGARLY the new works are carried on under the old workings; the richest iron ore is found here in immense quantities; one hundred and forty tons have been raised at one shaft in twenty four hours. To the right have a view of the ruins of GLEASTON-CASTLE, the seat of the FLEMINGS soon after the conquest; and by a succession of mariages [*sic*], it went to CANSFIELD, then to HARRINGTON, who enjoyed it fix descents, after that to BONVILLE, and lastly to GRAY, and was forfeited by HENRY GRAY Duke of SUFFOLK, A.D. 1559.

Leaving URSWICK behind ascend BIRKRIG, a rocky eminence, and from the beacon, have a variety of extensive and pleasant views, of land and sea, mountains and islands. ULVERSTON appears seated under a hanging wood, and behind that FURNESS-FELLS, in various shapes, form the grandest fore-ground that can be imagined. The back view is the reverse; when the tide is up, a fine arm of the sea stretching far within land, terminated by bold rocks and steep shores; across this expanse of sea a far country is seen, and LANCASTER town and castle is perceived in a fine point under a screen of high grounds, over which sable CLOUGHA rears his venerable head. INGLEBOROUGH, behind many other mountains, has a fine effect from this station.

If in a carriage, return from the abbey by DALTON. This village is sweetly situated on the crest of a rocky eminence, sloping to the morning sun. Upper-end is a square tower, where formerly the abbot held his secular court, and secured his prisoners; the keep is in the bottom of the tower, a dismal dungeon. This village, being conveniently situated in a fine sporting country, is honoured with an annual hunt, begun by the late Lord

RETROSPECTION

STRANGE, and is continued by his son, the truly noble Earl of DERBY. It commences the Monday after the 24th of October, and continues two whole weeks. For the better accommodation of the company, two excellent long rooms were built about four years ago, and called SPORTSMAN'S-HALL.

Return to ULVERSTON and from thence to the priory of CONISHEAD, the paradise of FURNESS, a MOUNT-EDGCUMBE in miniature; it well deserves a visit from the curious traveller. The house stands on the site of the priory of CONISHEAD, at the foot of a fine eminence, and the ground falls gently from it on all sides; the slopes are planted with shrubs and trees in such a manner as improve the elevation; and the waving woods that fly from it on each wing give an airy and noble appearance. The fourth front is in the modern taste, extended by an arcade; the north is in the gothic stile, with a piazza; the offices on this side form wings. The apartments are elegantly furnished; and the house is a good and convenient one: But what recommends itself most to the curious is a plan of pleasure ground, on a small scale, raised by improvement, to equal one of the greatest in ENGLAND. The variety of culminated grounds, and winding slopes, comprehended within this sweet spot, furnishes all the advantage of mountains and vales, woods and water. By the judicious management of these assemblages, the late owner did work wonders; and by well consulting the genius of the place called in to aid his plan, and harmonized the features of a country vast in extent, and by nature highly picturesque, whose distant parts answering, form a magnificent whole. Besides the ornamental grounds, the views from the house are pleasing and surprising, pastoral, rural, and marine. on one hand a fine estuary, spotted with rocks, isles, and peninsulas, a variety of shore, deeply indented in some places, in others composed of noble arched rocks, craggy, broken, and fringed with wood, over these hanging woods, intermixed with cultivated inclosures, covered with a background of stupendious mountains. The contrast of this view, at the other end of the gravel walk, between two culminating hills covered with tall wood, is seen, in fine perspective, a rich cultivated dale, divided by hedgerow trees, beyond these hanging grounds cut into inclosures; with scattered farms, above all, a long range of waving pasture ground and sheep walks, shining in variety of vegetation. This sweet pastoral picture is heightened much by the deep shade of the towering wooded hills, between which it is viewed. Turn to the left, the scenery is all reversed. Under a range of tall sycamores, an expanse of water bursts upon the eye, and beyond it, land just visible through the azure mist. Vessels traversing this bay are seen in a most picturesque manner, and from the lower windows, appear failing through the trees, and approaching the house, till they drop anchor just under the windows. The range of sycamores has a fine effect in this sea view, by breaking the line in the watery plane, and forming an elegant frame to a very excellent picture. By turning a little to the right the prospect changes; a the head of a sloping inclosure, and under the skirts of a steep wood, a sequestered cottage stands in the point of beauty.

There is a great variety of pleasing views from the different meandering walks and seats in the wood: At the moss-house, and the feat in the bottom of the wood, where ULVERSTON and the environs make a pretty picture. Under the shrubbery, on the eastern side of the house, and from the gate at the north end of the walk, in the afternoon and sun shining, behind a swell of green hills, the conical summits of distant mountains are seen, glistening like burnished gold in the sun beams, and pointing to the heavens in a noble stile. But as this sweet spot is injured by description, I shall only add that it is a great omission in the curious traveller, to be in FURNESS, and not to see this wonderful pretty place, to which nature has been so profuse in noble gifts, directed by the assistance she has had, under the conduct of an elegant fancy, a correct judgement, and refined taste.

From *A Guide to the Lakes (1778)*

Nature to the Invalid

HARRIET MARTINEAU

What is the best kind of view for a sick prisoner's windows to command? I have chosen the sea, and am satisfied with my choice. We should have the widest expanse of sky, for night scenery. We should have a wide expanse of land or water, for the sake of a sense of liberty, yet more than for variety; and also because then the inestimable help of a telescope may be called in. Think of the difference to us between seeing from our sofas the width of a street, evenif it be Sackville-street, Dublin, or Portland Place, in London, and thirty miles of sea view, with its long boundary of rocks, and the power of sweeping our glance over half a county, by means of a telescope! But the chief ground of preference of the sea is less its space than is motion, and the perpetual shifting of objects caused by it. There can be nothing in inland scenery which can give the sense of life and motion and connexion with the world like sea changes. The motion of a waterfall is too continuous,—too little varied,—as the breaking of the waves would be, if that were all the sea could afford. [...]

But then, there must not be too much sea. The strongest eyes and nerves could not support the glare and oppressive vastness of an unrelieved expanse of waters. ... Between my widnow and the sea is a green down, as green as any field in Ireland; and on the nearer half of this down, haymaking goes forward in its season. It slopes down to a hollow, where the Prior of old preserved his fish, there being sluices formerly at either end, the one opening upon the river, and the other upon the little haven below the Priory, whose ruins still crown the rock. From the Prior's fish-pond, the green down slopes upwards again to a ridge; and on the slope are cows grazing all summer, and half way into the winter. [...]

The winter beauty of the coast is a great consideration. The snow does not lie; at least rarely for more than a very few hours; and then it has no time to lose its lustre. When I look forth in the morning, the whole land may be sheeted with glittering snow, while the myrtle-green sea swells and tumbles, forming an almost incredible contrast to the summer aspect of both, and even to the afternoon aspect; for before sunset the snow is gone, except in the hollows; all is green again on shore, and the waves are lilac, crested with white. My winter pleasures of this kind were, at first, a pure surprise to me. I had spent every winter of my life in a town; and here, how different it is! The sun shines into my room from my hour of rising till within a few minutes of dusk, and this, almost by settled custom, till February, our worst month. The sheeny sea, swelling in orange light, is crossed by fishing-boats, which look black by contrast, and there is none of the deadness of winter in the landscape; no leafless trees, no locking up with ice; and the air comes in through my open upper sash brisk, but sun-warmed. Within-doors, all is gay and bright with flowering narcissus, tulips, crocus, and hyacinths. And at night, what a heaven! What an expanse of stars above, appearing more steadfast, the more the Northern Lights dart and quiver! And what a silvery sheet of moonlight below, crossed by vessels more black than those which looked blackest in the golden sea of the morning! It makes one's very frame shiver with a delicious surprise to look ... at a moonlit sea through the telescope.

From *Life in the Sickroom,* Tynemouth, 1844.

Cherryburn

Thomas Bewick

Cherryburn House, the place of my nativity, and which for many years my eyes beheld with cherished delight, is situated on the south side of the Tyne, in the county of Northumberland, a short distance from the river. The house, stables, &c., stand on the west side of a little dean [dene], at the foot of which runs a burn. The dean was embellished with a number of cherry and plum trees, which were terminated by a garden on the north. Near the house were two large ash trees growing from one root; and, at a little distance, stood another of the same kind. At the south end of the premises, was a spring well, overhung by a large hawthorn bush, behind which was a holly hedge; and further away was a little boggy dean, with underwood and trees of different kinds. Near the termination of this dean, towards the river, were a good many remarkably tall ash trees, and one of oak, supposed to be one of the tallest and straightest in the kingdom. On the tops of these was a rookery, the sable inhabitants of which, by their consultations and cawings, and the bustle they made when building their nests, were among the first of the feathered race to proclaim the approaching spring. The corn-fields and pastures to the eastward were surrounded with very large oak and ash trees. Indeed, at that time, the country between Wylam and Bywell was beautified with a great deal of wood, which presented the appearance of a continued forest; but these are long since stubbed up. Needy gentry care little about the beauty of a country, and part of it is now, comparatively, as bare as a mole-hill.

To the westward, adjoining the house, lay the common or fell, which extended some few miles in length, and was of various breadths. It was mostly fine, green sward or pasturage, broken or divided, indeed, with clumps of "blossom'd whins," foxglove, fern, and some junipers, and with heather in profusion, sufficient to scent the whole air. Near the burns, which guttered its sides, were to be seen the remains of old oaks, hollowed out by Time, with alders, willows, and birch, which were often to be met with in the same state; and these seemed to me to point out the length of time that these domains had belonged to no one. On this common,—the poor man's heritage for ages past, where he kept a few sheep, or a Kyloe cow, perhaps a flock of geese, and mostly a stock of bee-hives,—it was with infinite pleasure that I long beheld the beautiful wild scenery which was there exhibited, and it is with the opposite feelings of regret that I now find all swept away. Here and there on this common were to be seen the cottage, or rather hovel, of some labouring man, built at his own expense, and mostly with his own hands; and to this he always added a garth and a garden, upon which great pains and labour were bestowed to make both productive; and for this purpose not a bit of manure was suffered to be wasted away on the "lonnings" or public roads. These various concerns excited the attention and industry of the hardy occupants, which enabled them to prosper, and made them despise being ever numbered with the parish poor. These men, whose children were neither pampered nor spoiled, might truly be called—"A bold peasantry, their country's pride;" and to this day I think I see their broad shoulders and their hardy sun-burnt looks, which altogether bespoke the vigour of their constitutions.

*

At the beginning of this undertaking I made up my mind to copy nothing from the works of others, but to stick to nature as closely as I could; and for this purpose, being invited by Mr. Constable, the then owner of Wycliffe, I visited the extensive museum there, collected by the late Marmaduke Tunstal, Esq., to make drawings of the birds. I set off from Newcastle on the 16th July, 1791, and remained at the above beautiful place nearly two months, drawing from the stuffed specimens.

*

As soon as I arrived in Newcastle, I immediately began to engrave from the drawings of the birds I had made at Wycliffe; but I had not been long thus engaged till I found the very great difference between preserved specimens and those from Nature; no regard having been paid, at that time, to fix the former in their proper attitudes, nor to place the different series of the feathers so as to fall properly upon each other. It has always given me a great deal of trouble to get at the markings of the dishevelled plumage; and, when done with every pains, I never felt satisfied with them. I was on this account driven to wait for birds newly shot, or brought to me alive, and in the intervals employed my time in designing and engraving tail-pieces, or vignettes.

*

The sedentary artist ought, if possible, to have his dwelling in the country, where he can follow his business undisturbed, surrounded by pleasing rural scenery, and the fresh air. He ought not to sit at work too long at a time, but to unbend his mind with some variety of employment; for which purpose it is desirable that artists, with their little cots, shall also have each a garden attached, in which they may find both exercise and amusement, and only occasionally visit the city or the smoky town; and that chiefly for the purpose of meetings with their brother artists, in which they may make an interchange of their sentiments, and commune with each other as to whatever regards the arts. ...

Had I been a painter, I never would have copied the works of "old masters," or others, however highly they might be esteemed. I would have gone to nature for all my patterns; for she exhibits an endless variety not possible to be surpassed, and scarcely ever to be truly imitated. I would, indeed, have endeavoured to discover how those artists of old made or compounded their excellent colours, as well as the disposition of their lights and shades, by which they were enabled to accomplish so much and so well.

The work of the painter may be said to be as endless as the objects which nature continually presents to his view; and it is his judgment that must direct him in the choice of such as may be interesting. In this he will see what others have done before him, and the shoals and quicksands that have retarded their progress, as well as the rocks they have at last entirely split upon. On his taking a proper survey of all this, he will see the "labour in vain" that has been bestowed upon useless designs, which have found, and will continue to find, their way to a garret, while those of an opposite character will, from their excellence, be preserved with perhaps increasing value for ages to come. In performing all this, great industry will be required, and it ought ever to be kept in mind, that, as in morals, nothing is worth listening to but truth, so in arts nothing is worth looking at but such productions as have been faithfully copied from nature. Poetry, indeed, may launch out or take further liberties to charm the intellect of its votaries. It is only such youths as Providence has gifted with strong intellectual, innate powers that are perfectly fit to embark in the fine arts, and the power and propensity is often found early to bud out and show itself. This is seen in the young musician, who, without having even learned his A B C's, breaks out, with a random kind of unrestrained freedom, to whistle and sing. How often have I been amused at the first essays of the ploughboy, and how charmed to find him so soon attempt to equal his whistling and singing master, at the plough stilts, and who, with avidity unceasing, never stopped till he thought he excelled him. The future painter is shown by his strong propensity to sketch whatever objects in nature attract his attention, and excite him to imitate them. The poet, indeed, has more difficulties to contend with at first than the others, because he must know language, or be furnished with words wherewith to enable him to express himself even in his first essays in doggrel metre and sing-song rhymes. In all the varied ways by which men of talent are befitted to enlighten, to charm, and to embellish society, as they advance through life,—if they entertain the true feeling that every production they behold is created, not by chance, but by design,—they will find an increasing and endless pleasure in the exhaustless stores which nature has provided to attract the attention and promote the happiness of her votaries during the time of their sojourning here.

The painter need not roam very far from his home, in any part of our beautiful isles, to meet with plenty of charming scenes from which to copy nature—either on an extended or a limited scale—and in which he may give full scope to his genius and to his pencil, either in animate or inanimate subjects. His search will be crowned with success in the romantic ravine—the placid holme—the hollow dell—or amongst the pendant foliage of the richly ornamented dean; or by the sides of burns which roar or dash along, or run murmuring from pool to pool through their pebbly beds: all this bordered perhaps by a back-ground of ivy-covered, hollow oaks (thus clothed as if to hide their age),— of elms, willows, and birch, which seem kindly to offer shelter to an under-growth of hazel, whins, broom, juniper, and heather, with the wild rose, the woodbine, and the bramble, and beset with clumps of fern and foxglove; while the edges of the mossy braes are covered with a profusion of wild flowers, "born to blush unseen," which peep out amongst the creeping groundlings— the bleaberry, the wild strawberry, the harebell, and the violet; but I feel a want of words to enable the pen to give an adequate description of the beauty and simplicity of these neglected spots, which nature has planted as if to invite the admiration of such as have hearts and eyes to appreciate and enjoy these her exquisite treats, while she may perhaps smile at the formal, pruning efforts of the gardener, as well as doubt whether the pencil of the artist will ever accomplish a correct imitation. But, be all this as it may, she has spread out her beauties to feast the eyes, and to invite the admiration of all mankind, and to whet them up to an ardent love of all her works. How often have I, in my angling excursions, loitered upon such sunny braes, lost in extacy, and wishing

I could impart to others the pleasures I felt on such occasions: but they must see with their own eyes to feel as I felt, and to form an opinion how far the scenes depictured by poets fall short of the reality. The naturalist's poet—Thompson—has done much: so have others. Allan Ramsay's "Habbies Howe / Where a' the sweets of spring and summer grow," may have exhibited such as I have noticed, but the man endowed with a fit turn of mind, and inclined to search out such "beauty-spots," will not need the aid of poets to help him on in his enthusiastic ardour.

From *A Memoir of Thomas Bewick*, first published 1862

Bewick's Birds
CHARLOTTE BRONTË

I returned to my book – Bewick's *History of British Birds*: the letterpress thereof I cared little for, generally speaking; and yet there were certain introductory pages that, child as I was, I could not pass quite as a blank. They were those which treat of the haunts of sea-fowl; of 'the solitary rocks and promontories' by them only inhabited; of the coast of Norway, studded with isles from its southern extremity, the Lindeness, or Naze, to the North Cape –

> *'Where the Northern Ocean, in vast whirls,*
> *Boils round the naked, melancholy isles*
> *Of farthest Thule; and the Atlantic surge*
> *Pours in among the stormy Hebrides.'*

Nor could I pass unnoticed the suggestion of the bleak shores of Lapland, Siberia, Spitzbergen, Nova Zembla, Iceland, Greenland, with 'the vast sweep of the Arctic Zone, and those forlorn regions of dreary space' … Of these death-white realms I formed an idea of my own: shadowy, like all the half-comprehended notions that

float dim through children's brains, but strangely impressive ...
Each picture told a story; mysterious often to my undeveloped
understanding and imperfect feelings, yet ever profoundly interesting [...] With Bewick on my knee, I was then happy: happy at
least in my way.

From *Jane Eyre*

Pleasures of Spring
CHARLOTTE BRONTË

Spring drew on: she was indeed already come; the frosts of
winter had ceased; its snows were melted, its cutting winds ame-
liorated. My wretched feet, flayed and swollen to lameness by
the sharp air of January, began to heal and subside under the
gentler breathings of April; the nights and mornings no longer
by their Canadian temperature froze the very blood in our veins;
we could now endure the play-hour passed in the garden: sometimes on a sunny day it began even to be pleasant and genial, and
a greenness grew over those brown beds, which, freshening daily,
suggested the thought that Hope traversed them at night, and
left each morning brighter traces of her steps. Flowers peeped
out amongst the leaves; snow-drops, crocuses, purple auriculas,
and golden-eyed pansies. On Thursday afternoons (half-holi-
days) we now took walks, and found still sweeter flowers opening
by the wayside, under the hedges.[...]

I discovered, too, that a great pleasure, an enjoyment which
the horizon only bounded, lay all outside the high and spike-
guarded walls of our garden: this pleasure consisted in prospect
of noble summits girdling a great hill-hollow, rich in verdure
and shadow; in a bright beck, full of dark stones and sparkling
eddies. How different had this scene looked when I viewed
it laid out beneath the iron sky of winter, stiffened in frost,
shrouded with snow!—when mists as chill as death wandered to

the impulse of east winds along those purple peaks, and rolled down 'ing' and holm till they blended with the frozen fog of the beck! That beck itself was then a torrent, turbid and curbless: it tore asunder the wood, and sent a raving sound through the air, often thickened with wild rain or whirling sleet; and for the forest on its banks, that showed only ranks of skeletons.

April advanced to May: a bright serene May it was; days of blue sky, placid sunshine, and soft western or southern gales filled up its duration. And now vegetation matured with vigour; Lowood shook loose its tresses; it became all green, all flowery; its great elm, ash, and oak skeletons were restored to majestic life; woodland plants sprang up profusely in its recesses; unnumbered varieties of moss filled its hollows, and it made a strange ground-sunshine out of the wealth of its wild primrose plants: I have seen their pale gold gleam in overshadowed spots like scatterings of the sweetest lustre. All this I enjoyed often and fully, free, unwatched, and almost alone [...] That bright May shone unclouded over the bold hills and beautiful woodland out of doors. Its garden, too, glowed with flowers: hollyhocks had sprung up tall as trees, lilies had opened, tulips and roses were in bloom; the borders of the little beds were gay with pink thrift and crimson double daisies; the sweetbriars gave out, morning and evening, their scent of spice and apples.

But I, and the rest who continued well, enjoyed fully the beauties of the scene and season; they let us ramble in the wood, like gipsies, from morning till night ...

My favourite seat was a smooth and broad stone, rising white and dry from the very middle of the beck, and only to be got at by wading through the water; a feat I accomplished barefoot.

From *Jane Eyre*

Night into Morning

Charlotte Brontë

Evening

The evening was pitch-dark: star and moon were quenched in grey rain-clouds – grey they would have been by day, by night they looked sable. Malone was not a man given to close observation of Nature; her changes passed, for the most part, unnoticed by him: he could walk miles on the most varying April day, and never see the beautiful dallying of earth and heaven; never mark when a sunbeam kissed the hill-tops, making them smile clear in green light, or when a shower wept over them, hiding their crests with the low-hanging, dishevelled tresses of a cloud. He did not, therefore, care to contrast the sky as it now appeared – a muffled, streaming vault, all black, save where, towards the east, the furnaces of Stilbro' ironworks threw a tremulous lurid shimmer on the horizon – with the same sky on an unclouded frosty night. He did not trouble himself to ask where the constellations and the planets were gone, or to regret the 'black-blue' serenity of the air-ocean which those white islets stud; and which another ocean, of heavier and denser element, now rolled below and concealed. He just doggedly pursued his way, leaning a little forward as he walked, and wearing his hat on the back of his head, as his Irish manner was.

Morning

It was now the middle of the month of February; by six o'clock, therefore, dawn was just beginning to steal on night, to penetrate with a pale ray its brown obscurity, and give a demi-translucence to its opaque shadows. Pale enough that ray was on this particular morning; no colour tinged the east, no flush warmed it. To see what a heavy lid day slowly lifted, what a wan glance she flung along the hills, you would have thought the sun's fire quenched in last night's floods. The breath of this morning was chill as its aspect; a raw wind stirred the mass of night-cloud, and showed, as it slowly rose – leaving a colour-less, silver-gleaming ring all round the horizon – not blue sky, but a stratum of paler vapour beyond.

From *Shirley*

Haworth Village

ELIZABETH GASKELL

Right before the traveller on this road rises Haworth village; he can see it for two miles before he arrives, for it is situated on the side of a pretty steep hill, with a back-ground of dun and purple moors, rising and sweeping away yet higher than the church, which is built at the very summit of the long narrow street. All round the horizon there is this same line of sinuous wave-like hills; the scoops into which they fall only revealing other hills beyond, of similar colour and shape, crowned with wild, bleak moors—grand, from the ideas of solitude and loneliness which they suggest, or oppressive from the feeling which they give of being pent-up by some monotonous and illimitable barrier, according to the mood of mind in which the spectator may be.

For a short distance the road appears to turn away from Haworth, as it winds round the base of the shoulder of a hill; but then it crosses a bridge over the 'beck,' and the ascent through the village begins. The flag-stones with which it is paved are placed end-ways, in order to give a better hold to the horses' feet; and, even with this help, they seem to be in constant danger of slip-ping backwards. The old stone houses are high compared to the width of the street, which makes an abrupt turn before reaching the more level ground at the head of the village, so that the steep aspect of the place, in one part, is almost like that of a wall. But this surmounted, the church lies a little off the main road on the left; a hundred yards, or so, and the driver relaxes his care, and the horse breathes more easily, as they pass into the quite little by-street that leads to Haworth Parsonage. The churchyard is on one side of this lane, the school-house and the sexton's dwelling (where the curates formerly lodged) on the other.

The parsonage stands at right angles to the road, facing down upon the church; so that, in fact, parsonage, church, and belfried school-house form three sides of an irregular oblong, of which the fourth is open to the fields and moors that lie beyond. The area of this oblong is filled up by a crowded churchyard, and a small garden or court in front of the clergyman's house. As the entrance to this from the road is at the side, the path goes round the corner into the little plot of ground. Underneath the windows is a narrow flower-border, carefully tended in days of yore, although only the most hardy plants could be made to grow there. Within the stone wall, which keeps out the surrounding churchyard, are bushes of elder and lilac; the rest of the ground is occupied by a square grass-plot and a gravel walk. The house is of grey stone, two stories high, heavily roofed with flags, in order to resist the winds that might strip off a lighter covering. It appears to have been built about a hundred years ago, and to consist of four rooms on each story; the two windows on the right (as the visitor stands with his back to the church, ready to enter in at the front door) belonging to Mr. Brontë's study, the two on the left to the family sitting-room. Everything about the place tells of the most dainty order, the most exquisite cleanliness. The doorsteps are spotless; the small old-fashioned window-panes glitter like looking-glass. Inside and outside of that house cleanliness goes up into its essence, purity.

From *The Life of Charlotte Brontë* (1857)

Often rebuked, yet always back returning

EMILY BRONTË

Often rebuked, yet always back returning
To those first feelings that were born with me,
And leaving busy chase of wealth and learning
For idle dreams of things which cannot be:

Today, I will seek not the shadowy region;
 Its unsustaining vastness waxes drear;
And visions rising, legion after legion,
Bring the unreal world too strangely near.

I'll walk, but not in old heroic traces,
And not in paths of high morality,
And not among the half-distinguish'd faces,
The clouded forms of long-past history.

I'll walk when my own nature would be leading:
It vexes me to choose another guide:
Where the grey flocks in ferny glens are feeding,
Where the wild wind blows on the mountain side.

What have those lonely mountains worth revealing?
More glory and more grief that I can tell:
The earth that wakes one human heart to feeling
Can centre both the worlds of Heaven and Hell.

First published 1850

The Blue Bell

EMILY BRONTË

The blue bell is the sweetest flower
That waves in summer air:
Its blossoms have the mightiest power
To soothe my spirit's care.

There is a spell in purple heath
Too wildly, sadly dear
The violet has a fragrant breath,
But fragrance will not cheer,

The trees are bare, the sun is cold,
And seldom, seldom seen –
The heavens have lost their zone of gold
And earth her robe of green

And ice upon the glancing stream
Has cast its sombre shade
And distant hills and valleys seem
In frozen mist arrayed –

The blue bell cannot charm me now
The heath has lost its bloom
The violets in the glen below
They yield no sweet perfume

But, though I mourn the sweet Bluebell,
'Tis better far, away
I know how fast my tears would swell
To see it smile today

NORTH COUNTRY

And that wood flower that hides so shy
Beneath the mossy stone
Its balmy scent and dewy eye
'Tis not for them I moan

It is the slight and stately stem
The blossom's silvery blue
The buds hid like a sapphire gem
In sheaths of emerald hue

'Tis these that breathe upon my heart
A calm and softening spell
That if it makes the tear-drop start
Has power to soothe as well

For these I weep, so long divided
Through winter's dreary day
In longing weep – but most when guided
On withered banks to stray

If chilly then the light should fall
Adown the dreary sky
And gild the dank and darkened wall
With transient brilliancy

How do I yearn, how do I pine
For the time of flowers to come
And turn me from that fading shine
To mourn the fields of home –

--

How still, how happy! those are words
That once would scarce agree together
I loved the plashing of the surge –
The changing heaven the breezy weather,

RETROSPECTION

More than smooth seas and cloudless skies
And solemn, soothing, softened airs
That in the forest woke no sighs
And from the green spray shook no tears.

How still, how happy! now I feel
Where silence dwells is sweeter far
Than laughing mirth's most joyous swell
However pure its raptures are.

Come, sit down on this sunny stone:
'Tis wintry light o'er flowerless moors –
But sit – for we are all alone
And clear expand heaven's breathless shores.

I could think in the withered grass
Spring's budding wreaths we might discern
The violet's eye might shyly flash
And young leaves shoot among the fern.

It is but thought – full many a night
The snow shall clothe those hills afar
And storms shall add a drearier blight
And winds shall wage a wilder war,

Before the lark may herald in
Fresh foliage twined with blossoms fair
And summer days again begin
Their glory – haloed crown to wear.

Yet my heart loves December's smile
As much as July's golden beam;
Then let us sit and watch the while
The blue ice curdling on the stream.

1838

The Night Wind

EMILY BRONTË

In summer's mellow midnight
A cloudless moon shone through
Our open parlour window
And rose-trees wet with dew

I sat in silent musing –
The soft wind waved my hair
It told me heaven was glorious
And sleeping earth was fair

I needed not its breathing
To bring such thoughts to me
But still it whispered lowly
'How dark the woods will be! –

'The thick leaves in my murmur
Are rustling like a dream,
And all their myriad voices
Instinct with spirit seem.'

I said, 'Go, gentle singer,
Thy wooing voice is kind:
But do not think its music
Has power to reach my mind –

'Play with the scented flower,
The young tree's supple bough –
And leave my human feelings
In their own course to flow.'

The wanderer would not heed me;
Its kiss grew warmer still –
'O come!' it sighed so sweetly
'I'll win thee 'gainst thy will -

'Were we not friends from childhood?
Have I not loved thee long?
As long as thou, the solemn night,
Whose silence wakes my song?

'And when thy heart is resting
Beneath the church-aisle stone
I shall have time for mourning,
And thou for being alone.'

1840

Another Lovely Day

ANNE BRONTË

But now, — at evening, when I see the round, red sun sink quietly down behind those woody hills, leaving them sleeping in a warm, red, golden haze, I only think another lovely day is lost to him and me; — and at morning, when roused by the flutter and chirp of the sparrows, and the gleeful twitter of the swallows — all intent upon feeding their young, and full of life and joy in all their own little frames — I open the window to inhale the balmy, soul-reviving air, and look out upon the lovely landscape, laughing in dew and sunshine, — I too often shame that glorious scene with tears of thankless misery, because *he* cannot feel its freshening influence; — and when I wander in the ancient woods, and meet the little wildflowers smiling in my path, or sit in the shadow of our noble ash-trees by the waterside, with their branches gently swaying in the light summer breeze that murmurs through their feathery foliage — my ears full of that low music mingled with the dreamy hum of insects, my eyes abstractedly gazing on the glassy surface of the little lake before me, with the tress that crowd about its bank, some high above, but stretching their wide arms over its margin, all faithfully mirrored far, far down in its glassy depth — though sometimes the images are partially broken by the shirt of aquatic insects, and sometimes, for a moment, the whole is shivered into trembling fragments by a transient breeze that swept the surface too roughly, — still I have no pleasure; for the greater the happiness that nature sets before me, the more I lament that *he* is not here to taste it: the greater the bliss we might enjoy together, the more I feel our present wretchedness apart (yes, ours; he must be wretched, though he may not know it); and the more my senses are pleased, the more my heart is oppressed; for he keeps it with him confined amid the dust and smoke of London, — perhaps, shut up within the walls of his own abominable club.

From *The Tenant of Wildfell Hall*

Home
ANNE BRONTË

How brightly glistening in the sun
    The woodland ivy plays!
While yonder beeches from their barks
    Reflect his silver rays.

That sun surveys a lovely scene
    From softly smiling skies;
And wildly through unnumbered trees
    The wind of winter sighs:

RETROSPECTION

Now loud, it thunders o'er my head,
  And now in distance dies.
But give me back my barren hills
  Where colder breezes rise:

Where scarce the scattered, stunted trees
  Can yield an answering swell,
But where a wilderness of heath
  Returns the sound as well.

For yonder garden, fair and wide,
  With groves of evergreen,
Long winding walks, and orders trim,
  And velvet lawns between;

Restore to me that little spot,
  With grey walls compassed round,
Where knotted grass neglected lies,
  And weeds usurp the ground.

Though all around this mansion high
  Invites the foot to roam,
And though its halls are fair within —
  Oh, give me back my home!

First published 1846

The Cataract of Lodore
ROBERT SOUTHEY

"How does the water
 Come down at Lodore?"
My little boy asked me
Thus, once on a time;
And moreover he tasked me

To tell him in rhyme.
Anon, at the word,
There first came one daughter,
And then came another,
To second and third
The request of their brother,
And to hear how the water
Comes down at Lodore,
With its rush and its roar,
As many a time
They had seen it before.
So I told them in rhyme,
For of rhymes I had store;
And 'twas in my vocation
For their recreation
That so I should sing;
Because I was Laureate
To them and the King.

From its sources which well
In the tarn on the fell;
From its fountains
In the mountains,
Its rills and its gills;
Through moss and through brake,
It runs and it creeps
For a while, till it sleeps
In its own little lake.
And thence at departing,
Awakening and starting,
It runs through the reeds,
And away it proceeds,
Through meadow and glade,
In sun and in shade,

RETROSPECTION

And through the wood-shelter,
Among crags in its flurry,
Helter-skelter,
Hurry-skurry.
Here it comes sparkling,
And there it lies darkling;
Now smoking and frothing
Its tumult and wrath in,
Till, in this rapid race
On which it is bent,
It reaches the place
Of its steep descent.

The cataract strong
Then plunges along,
Striking and raging

As if a war raging
Its caverns and rocks among;
Rising and leaping,
Sinking and creeping,
Swelling and sweeping,
Showering and springing,
Flying and flinging,
Writhing and ringing,
Eddying and whisking,
Spouting and frisking,
Turning and twisting,
Around and around
With endless rebound:
Smiting and fighting,
A sight to delight in;
Confounding, astounding,
Dizzying and deafening the ear with its sound.

NORTH COUNTRY

Collecting, projecting,
Receding and speeding,
And shocking and rocking,
And darting and parting,
And threading and spreading,
And whizzing and hissing,
And dripping and skipping,
And hitting and splitting,
And shining and twining,
And rattling and battling,
And shaking and quaking,
And pouring and roaring,
And waving and raving,
And tossing and crossing,
And flowing and going,
And running and stunning,
And foaming and roaming,
And dinning and spinning,
And dropping and hopping,
And working and jerking,
And guggling and struggling,
And heaving and cleaving,
And moaning and groaning;

And glittering and frittering,
And gathering and feathering,
And whitening and brightening,
And quivering and shivering,
And hurrying and skurrying,
And thundering and floundering;

Dividing and gliding and sliding,
And falling and brawling and sprawling,
And driving and riving and striving,
And sprinkling and twinkling and wrinkling,

And sounding and bounding and rounding,
And bubbling and troubling and doubling,
And grumbling and rumbling and tumbling,
And clattering and battering and shattering;

Retreating and beating and meeting and sheeting,
Delaying and straying and playing and spraying,
Advancing and prancing and glancing and dancing,
Recoiling, turmoiling and toiling and boiling,
And gleaming and streaming and steaming and beaming,
And rushing and flushing and brushing and gushing,
And flapping and rapping and clapping and slapping,
And curling and whirling and purling and twirling,
And thumping and plumping and bumping and jumping,
And dashing and flashing and splashing and clashing;
And so never ending, but always descending,
Sounds and motions for ever and ever are blending
All at once and all o'er, with a mighty uproar, -
And this way the water comes down at Lodore.

1820

Esthwaite
Thomas De Quincey

Esthwaite, though a lovely scene in its summer garniture of
woods, has no features of permanent grandeur to rely upon. A
wet or gloomy day, even in summer, reduces it to little more
than a wildish pond, surrounded by miniature hills: and the
sole circumstances which restore the sense of a romantic region
and an Alpine character are the towering groups of Langdale
and Grasmere fells, which look over the little pastoral barriers
of Esthwaite, from distances of eight, ten, and fourteen miles.
Esthwaite, therefore, being no object for itself, and the sublime head of Coniston being accessible by a road which evades

Hawkshead, few tourists ever trouble the repose of this little village town. And in the days of which I am speaking (1778–1787) tourists were as yet few and infrequent to any parts of the country. ...

Wordsworth, therefore, enjoyed this labyrinth of valleys in a perfection that no one can have experienced since the opening of the present century. The whole was one paradise of virgin beauty; the rare works of man, all over the land, were hoar with the grey tints of an antique picturesque; nothing was new, nothing was raw and uncicatrized. Hawkshead, in particular, though tamely seated in itself and its immediate purlieus, has a most fortunate and central locality, as regards the best (at least the most interesting) scenes for a pedestrian rambler. The gorgeous scenery of Borrowdale, the austere sublimities of Wastdalehead, of Langdalehead, or Mardale—these are too oppressive, in their colossal proportions and their utter solitudes, for encouraging a perfectly human interest. Now, taking Hawkshead as a centre, with a radius of about eight miles, one might describe a little circular tract which embosoms a perfect network of little valleys—separate wards or cells, as it were, of one larger valley, walled in by the great leading mountains of the region. Grasmere, Easedale, Great and Little Langdale, Tilberthwaite, Yewdale, Elter Water, Loughrigg Tarn, Skelwith, and many other little quiet nooks, lie within a single division of this labyrinthine district. All these are within one summer afternoon's ramble. And amongst these, for the years of his boyhood, lay the daily excursions of Wordsworth.

***

One of the most interesting among the winter amusements of the Hawkshead boys was that of skating on the adjacent lake. Esthwaite Water is not one of the deep lakes, as its neighbours of Windermere, Coniston, and Grasmere are; consequently, a

RETROSPECTION

very slight duration of frost is sufficient to freeze it into a bear-ing strength. ... About the year 1810, by way of expressing an interest in "The Friend," which was just at that time appearing in weekly numbers, Wordsworth allowed Coleridge to print an extract from the poem on his own life, descriptive of the games celebrated upon the ice of Esthwaite by all who were able to skate: the mimic chases of hare and hounds, pursued long after the last orange gleam of light had died away from the western horizon—oftentimes far into the night; a circumstance which does not speak much for the discipline of the schools, or rather, perhaps, does speak much for the advantages of a situation so pure, and free from the usual perils of a town, as could allow of a discipline so lax. Wordsworth, in this fine descriptive passage— which I wish that I had at this moment the means of citing, in order to amplify my account of his earliest tyrocinium—speaks of himself as frequently wheeling aside from his joyous com-panions to cut across the image of a star; and thus, already in the midst of sportiveness, and by a movement of sportiveness, half unconsciously to himself expressing the growing necessity of retirement to his habits of thought.[107] At another period of the year, when the golden summer allowed the students a long season of early play before the studies of the[Pg 265] day began, he describes himself as roaming, hand-in-hand, with one companion, along the banks of Esthwaite Water, chanting, with one voice, the verses of Goldsmith and of Gray—verses which, at the time of recording the fact, he had come to look upon as either in parts false in the principles of their composition, or, at any rate, as far below the tone of high poetic passion; but which, at that time of life, when the profounder feelings were as yet only germinating, filled them with an enthusiasm "More bright than madness and the dreams of wine."

From *Recollections of the Lakes and the Lake Poets,* 1862

Resolution and Independence

William Wordsworth

There was a roaring in the wind all night;
The rain came heavily and fell in floods;
But now the sun is rising calm and bright;
The birds are singing in the distant woods;
Over his own sweet voice the Stock-dove broods;
The Jay makes answer as the Magpie chatters;
And all the air is filled with pleasant noise of waters.

All things that love the sun are out of doors;
The sky rejoices in the morning's birth;
The grass is bright with rain-drops;—on the moors
The hare is running races in her mirth;
And with her feet she from the plashy earth
Raises a mist, that, glittering in the sun,
Runs with her all the way, wherever she doth run.

I was a Traveller then upon the moor;
I saw the hare that raced about with joy;
I heard the woods and distant waters roar;
Or heard them not, as happy as a boy:
The pleasant season did my heart employ:
My old remembrances went from me wholly;
And all the ways of men, so vain and melancholy.

But, as it sometimes chanceth, from the might
Of joys in minds that can no further go,
As high as we have mounted in delight
In our dejection do we sink as low;
To me that morning did it happen so;
And fears and fancies thick upon me came;
Dim sadness—and blind thoughts, I knew not, nor could name.

RETROSPECTION

I heard the sky-lark warbling in the sky;
And I bethought me of the playful hare:
Even such a happy Child of earth am I;
Even as these blissful creatures do I fare;
Far from the world I walk, and from all care;
But there may come another day to me—
Solitude, pain of heart, distress, and poverty.

My whole life I have lived in pleasant thought,
As if life's business were a summer mood;
As if all needful things would come unsought
To genial faith, still rich in genial good;
But how can He expect that others should
Build for him, sow for him, and at his call
Love him, who for himself will take no heed at all?

I thought of Chatterton, the marvellous Boy,
The sleepless Soul that perished in his pride;
Of Him who walked in glory and in joy
Following his plough, along the mountain-side:
By our own spirits are we deified:
We Poets in our youth begin in gladness;
But thereof come in the end despondency and madness.

Now, whether it were by peculiar grace,
A leading from above, a something given,
Yet it befell that, in this lonely place,
When I with these untoward thoughts had striven,
Beside a pool bare to the eye of heaven
I saw a Man before me unawares:
The oldest man he seemed that ever wore grey hairs.

As a huge stone is sometimes seen to lie
Couched on the bald top of an eminence;

NORTH COUNTRY

Wonder to all who do the same espy,
By what means it could thither come, and whence;
So that it seems a thing endued with sense:
Like a sea-beast crawled forth, that on a shelf
Of rock or sand reposeth, there to sun itself;

Such seemed this Man, not all alive nor dead,
Nor all asleep—in his extreme old age:
His body was bent double, feet and head
Coming together in life's pilgrimage;
As if some dire constraint of pain, or rage
Of sickness felt by him in times long past,
A more than human weight upon his frame had cast.

Himself he propped, limbs, body, and pale face,
Upon a long grey staff of shaven wood:
And, still as I drew near with gentle pace,
Upon the margin of that moorish flood
Motionless as a cloud the old Man stood,
That heareth not the loud winds when they call,
And moveth all together, if it move at all.

At length, himself unsettling, he the pond
Stirred with his staff, and fixedly did look
Upon the muddy water, which he conned,
As if he had been reading in a book:
And now a stranger's privilege I took;
And, drawing to his side, to him did say,
"This morning gives us promise of a glorious day."

A gentle answer did the old Man make,
In courteous speech which forth he slowly drew:
And him with further words I thus bespake,
"What occupation do you there pursue?
This is a lonesome place for one like you."

RETROSPECTION

Ere he replied, a flash of mild surprise
Broke from the sable orbs of his yet-vivid eyes.

His words came feebly, from a feeble chest,
But each in solemn order followed each,
With something of a lofty utterance drest—
Choice word and measured phrase, above the reach
Of ordinary men; a stately speech;
Such as grave Livers do in Scotland use,
Religious men, who give to God and man their dues.

He told, that to these waters he had come
To gather leeches, being old and poor:
Employment hazardous and wearisome!
And he had many hardships to endure:
From pond to pond he roamed, from moor to moor;
Housing, with God's good help, by choice or chance;
And in this way he gained an honest maintenance.

The old Man still stood talking by my side;
But now his voice to me was like a stream
Scarce heard; nor word from word could I divide;
And the whole body of the Man did seem
Like one whom I had met with in a dream;
Or like a man from some far region sent,
To give me human strength, by apt admonishment.

My former thoughts returned: the fear that kills;
And hope that is unwilling to be fed;
Cold, pain, and labour, and all fleshly ills;
And mighty Poets in their misery dead.
—Perplexed, and longing to be comforted,
My question eagerly did I renew,
"How is it that you live, and what is it you do?"

He with a smile did then his words repeat;
And said that, gathering leeches, far and wide
He travelled; stirring thus about his feet
The waters of the pools where they abide.
"Once I could meet with them on every side;
But they have dwindled long by slow decay;
Yet still I persevere, and find them where I may."

While he was talking thus, the lonely place,
The old Man's shape, and speech—all troubled me:
In my mind's eye I seemed to see him pace
About the weary moors continually,
Wandering about alone and silently.
While I these thoughts within myself pursued,
He, having made a pause, the same discourse renewed.

And soon with this he other matter blended,
Cheerfully uttered, with demeanour kind,
But stately in the main; and, when he ended,
I could have laughed myself to scorn to find
In that decrepit Man so firm a mind.
"God," said I, "be my help and stay secure;
I'll think of the Leech-gatherer on the lonely moor!"

1802

In Borrowdale
SAMUEL TAYLOR COLERIDGE

A drizzling rain. Heavy masses of shapeless vapour upon the mountains (O the perpetual forms of Borrowdale!) yet it is no unbroken tale of dull sadness. Slanting pillars travel across the lake at long intervals, the vaporous mass whitens in large stains of light—on the lakeward ridge of that huge arm-chair of Lodore fell a gleam of softest light, that brought out the rich hues of the late autumn. The woody Castle Crag between me and Lodore is a rich flower-garden of colours—the brightest yellows with the deepest crimsons and the infinite shades of brown and green, the *infinite* diversity of which blends the whole, so that the brighter colours seem to be colours upon a ground, not coloured things. Little woolpacks of white bright vapour rest on different summits and declivities. The vale is narrowed by the mist and cloud, yet through the wall of mist you can see into a bower of sunny light, in Borrowdale; the birds are singing in the tender rain, as if it were the rain of April, and the decaying foliage were flowers and blossoms. The pillar of smoke from the chimney rises up in the mist and is just distinguishable from it, and the mountain forms in the gorge of Borrowdale consubstantiate with the mist and cloud, even as the pillar'd smoke—a shade deeper and a determinate form.

From Coleridge's notebooks, October 21st, 1803

Grasmere Journals
DOROTHY WORDSWORTH

Friday Morning, 16th [May 1800].—Warm and mild, after a fine night of rain.... The woods extremely beautiful with all autumnal variety and softness. I carried a basket for mosses, and gathered some wild plants. Oh! that we had a book of botany. All flowers now are gay and deliciously sweet. The primrose still prominent; the later flowers and the shiny foxgloves very tall, with their heads budding. I went forward round the lake at the foot of Loughrigg Fell. I was much amused with the busyness of a pair of stone-chats; their restless voices as they skimmed along the water, following each other, their shadows under them, and their returning back to the stones on the shore, chirping with the same unwearied voice. Could not cross the water, so I went round by the stepping-stones.... Rydale was very beautiful, with spear-shaped streaks of polished steel.... Grasmere very solemn in the last glimpse of twilight. It calls home the heart to quietness. I had been very melancholy. In my walk back I had many of my saddest thoughts, and I could not keep the tears within me. But when I came to Grasmere I felt that it did me good. I finished my letter to M. H....

Saturday.—Incessant rain from morning till night.... Worked hard, and read Midsummer Night's Dream, and ballads. Sauntered a little in the garden. The blackbird sate quietly in its nest, rocked by the wind, and beaten by the rain.

Sunday, 18th.—Went to church, slight showers, a cold air. The mountains from this window look much greener, and I think the valley is more green than ever. The corn begins to shew itself. The ashes are still bare. ... Walked to Ambleside in the evening round the lake, the prospect exceeding beautiful from Loughrigg Fell. It was so green that no eye could weary of reposing upon it. ... Did not reach home till ten o'clock.

Tuesday Morning.—A fine mild rain.... Everything green and overflowing with life, and the streams making a perpetual song, with the thrushes, and all little birds, not forgetting the stone-chats. The post was not come in. I walked as far as Windermere, and met him there.

*

RETROSPECTION

Sunday, June 1st.—Rain in the night. A sweet mild morning. Read ballads. Went to church. Singers from Wytheburn. Walked upon the hill above the house till dinner time. Went again to church. After tea, went to Ambleside, round the Lakes. A very fine warm evening. Upon the side of Loughrigg my heart dissolved in what I saw: when I was not startled, but called from my reverie by a noise as of a child paddling without shoes. I looked up, and saw a lamb close to me. It approached nearer and nearer, as if to examine me, and stood a long time. I did not move. At last, it ran past me, and went bleating along the pathway, seeming to be seeking its mother. I saw a hare on the high road....

Monday.—A cold dry windy morning. I worked in the garden, and planted flowers, etc. Sate under the trees after dinner till tea time.... I went to Ambleside after tea, crossed the stepping-stones at the foot of Grasmere, and pursued my way on the other side of Rydale and by Clappersgate. I sate a long time to watch the hurrying waves, and to hear the regularly irregular sound of the dashing waters. The waves round about the little Island seemed like a dance of spirits that rose out of the water, round its small circumference of shore.

*

Monday.[18th June]—Wm. and I went to Brathay by Little Langdale and Collath ... It was a warm mild morning with threatening rain. The vale of Little Langdale looked bare and unlovely. Collath was wild and interesting, from the peat carts and peat gatherers. The valley all perfumed with the gale and wild thyme. The woods about the waterfall bright with rich yellow broom. A succession of delicious views from ... to Brathay.

*

Saturday.—Walked up the hill to Rydale lake. Grasmere looked so beautiful that my heart was almost melted away. It was quite calm, only spotted with sparkles of light; the church visible. On our return all distant objects had faded away, all but the hills. The reflection of the light bright sky above Black Quarter was very solemn....

*

Monday.—Mr. Simpson called in the morning. W. and I went into Langdale to fish. The morning was very cold. I sate at the foot of the lake, till my head ached with cold. The view exquisitely beautiful, through a gate, and under a sycamore tree beside the first house going into Loughrigg. Elter-water looked barren, and the view from the church less beautiful than in winter. When W. went down to the water to fish, I lay under the wind, my head pillowed upon a mossy rock, and slept about 10 minutes, which relieved my headache. We ate our dinner together, and parted again.... W. went to fish for pike in Rydale. John came in when I had done tea and he and I carried a jug of tea to William. We met him in the old road from Rydale. He drank his tea upon the turf. The setting sun threw a red purple light upon the rocks, and stone walls of Rydale, which gave them a most interesting and beautiful appearance.

*

Tuesday, 26th. [August]— ... A very fine solemn evening. The wind blew very fierce from the island, and at Rydale. We went on the other side of Rydale, and sate a long time looking at the mountains, which were all black at Grasmere, and very bright in Rydale; Grasmere exceedingly dark, and Rydale of a light yellow green.

*

RETROSPECTION

Friday, 12th September.— ... The fern of the mountains now spreads yellow veins among the trees; the coppice wood turns brown. William observed some affecting little things in Borrowdale. A decayed house with the tall, silent rocks seen through the broken windows. A sort of rough column put upon the gable end of a house, with a ball stone, smooth from the river-island, upon it for ornament. Near it, a stone like it, upon an old mansion, carefully hewn.

Saturday, 13th September.—Morning. William writing his Preface—did not walk. Jones, and Mr. Palmer came to tea....

Sunday morning, 14th.— ... A lovely day. Read Boswell in the house in the morning, and after dinner under the bright yellow leaves of the orchard. The pear trees a bright yellow. The apple trees still green. A sweet lovely afternoon.... Here I have long neglected my Journal. John came home in the evening, after Jones left. Jones returned again on the Friday, the 19th September. Jones stayed with us till Friday, 26th September. Coleridge came in.

Wednesday, 1st October.—A fine morning, a showery night. The lake still in the morning; in the forenoon flashing light from the beams of the sun, as it was ruffled by the wind. We corrected the last sheet.

Thursday, 2nd October.—A very rainy morning. We walked after dinner to observe the torrents. I followed Wm. to Rydale. We afterwards went to Butterlip How. The Black Quarter looked marshy, and the general prospect was cold, but the force was very grand. The lichens are now coming out afresh. I carried home a collection in the afternoon. We had a pleasant conversation about the manners of the rich; avarice, inordinate desires, and the effeminacy, unnaturalness, and unworthy objects of education. The moonlight lay upon the hills like snow.

From *Journals of Dorothy Wordsworth, vol. 1,* 1800–1803

Peele/Piel Castle in a Storm

WILLIAM WORDSWORTH

I was thy Neighbour once, thou rugged Pile!
Four summer weeks I dwelt in sight of thee:
I saw thee every day; and all the while
Thy Form was sleeping on a glassy sea.

So pure the sky, so quiet was the air!
So like, so very like, was day to day!
Whene'er I looked, thy Image still was there;
It trembled, but it never passed away.

How perfect was the calm! It seemed no sleep;
No mood, which season takes away, or brings:
I could have fancied that the mighty Deep
Was even the gentlest of all gentle Things.

Ah! THEN, if mine had been the Painter's hand,
To express what then I saw; and add the gleam,
The light that never was, on sea or land,
The consecration, and the Poet's dream;

I would have planted thee, thou hoary Pile!
Amid a world how different from this!
Beside a sea that could not cease to smile;
On tranquil land, beneath a sky of bliss:

Thou shouldst have seemed a treasure-house, a mine
Of peaceful years; a chronicle of heaven: –
Of all the sunbeams that did ever shine
The very sweetest had to thee been given.

RETROSPECTION

A Picture had it been of lasting ease,
Elysian quiet, without toil or strife;
No motion but the moving tide, a breeze,
Or merely silent Nature's breathing life.

Such, in the fond delusion of my heart,
Such Picture would I at that time have made:
And seen the soul of truth in every part;
A faith, a trust, that could not be betrayed.

So once it would have been, – 'tis so no more;
I have submitted to a new controul:
A power is gone, which nothing can restore;
A deep distress hath humanized my Soul.

Not for a moment could I now behold
A smiling sea and be what I have been:
The feeling of my loss will ne'er be old;
This, which I know, I speak with mind serene.

Then Beaumont, Friend! Who would have been the Friend,
If he had lived, of Him whom I deplore,
This Work of thine I blame not, but commend;
This sea in anger, and the dismal shore.

Oh 'tis a passionate Work! – yet wise and well;
Well chosen is the spirit that is here;
That Hulk which labours in the deadly swell,
This rueful sky, this pageantry of fear!

And this huge Castle, standing here sublime,
I love to see the look with which it braves,
Cased in the unfeeling armour of old time,
The light'ning, the fierce wind, and trampling waves.

Farewell, farewell the Heart that lives alone,
Housed in a dream, at distance from the Kind!
Such happiness, wherever it be known,
Is to be pitied; for 'tis surely blind.

But welcome fortitude, and patient chear,
And frequent sights of what is to be borne!
Such sights, or worse, as are before me here. –
Not without hope we suffer and we mourn.

From *The Prelude*: Retrospect, Book VIII

Ribblesdale

GERARD MANLEY HOPKINS

Earth, sweet Earth, sweet landscape, with leavès throng
And louchèd low grass, heaven that dost appeal
To, with no tongue to plead, no heart to feel;
That canst but only be, but dost that long—

Thou canst but be, but that thou well dost; strong
Thy plea with him who dealt, nay does now deal,
Thy lovely dale down thus and thus bids reel
Thy river, and o'er gives all to rack or wrong.

And what is Earth's eye, tongue, or heart else, where
Else, but in dear and dogged man?—Ah, the heir
To his own selfbent so bound, so tied to his turn,
To thriftless reave both our rich round world bare
And none reck of world after, this bids wear
Earth brows of such care, care and dear concern.

1882

Journals in Stonyhurst

Gerard Manley Hopkins

Sept. 24 [1870]—First saw the Northern Lights. My eye was caught by beams of light and dark very like the crown of horny rays the sun makes behind a cloud. At first I thought of silvery cloud until I saw that these were more luminous and did not dim the clearness of the stars in the Bear. They rose slightly radiating thrown out from the earthline. Then I saw soft pulses of light one after another rise and pass upwards arched in shape but waveringly and with the arch broken. They seemed to float, not following the warp of the sphere as falling stars look to do but free though concentrical with it. This busy working of nature wholly independent of the earth and seeming to go on in a strain of time not reckoned by our reckoning of days and years but simpler and as if correcting the preoccupation of the world by being preoccupied with and appealing to and dated to the day of judgement was like a new witness to God and filled me with delightful fear.

Oct. 20—Laus Deo—the river today and yesterday. Yesterday it was a sallow and glassy gold at Hodder Roughs and by watching hard the banks began to sail upstream, the scaping unfolded, the river was all in tumult but not running, only the lateral motions were perceived, and the curls of froth where the waves overlap shaped and turned easily and idly.—I meant to have written more.—Today the river was wild, very full, glossy brown with mad, furrowed in permanent billows through which from head to head the water swung with a great down and up again. These heads were scalped with rags of jumping foam. But at the Roughs the sight was the burly water-backs which heave after heave kept tumbling up from the broken foam and their plump heap turning open in ropes of velvet.

What you look hard at seems to look hard at you, hence the true and the false instress of nature. One day early in March

[1871] when long streamers were rising from over Kemble End one large flake loop-shaped, not a streamer but belonging to the string, moving too slowly to be seen, seemed to cap and fill the zenith with a white shire of cloud. I looked long up at it till the tall height and the beauty of the scaping—regularly curled knots springing if I remember from fine stems, like foliation in wood or stone—had strongly grown on me. It changed beautiful changes, growing more into ribs and one stretch of running into branching like coral. Unless you refresh the mind from time to time you cannot always remember or believe how deep the inscape in things is.

March 14—Bright morning, pied skies, hail. In the afternoon the wind from the N., very cold; long bows of soft grey cloud straining the whole heaven but spanning the skyline with a slow entasis which left a strip of cold porcelain blue. The long ribs or girders were as rollers/across the wind, not in it, but across them there lay fine grass-ends, sided off down the perspective, as if locks of vapour blown free from the main ribs down the wind. Next day and next snow. Then in walking I saw the water-runs in the sand of unusual delicacy and the broken blots of snow in the dead bents of the hedge-banks I could find a square scaping in which helped the eye over another hitherto disordered field of things. (And if you look well at big pack-clouds overhead you will soon find a strong large quaining and squaring in them which makes each pack impressive and whole.) Pendle was beautiful: the face of snow on it and the tracks or gulleys which streaked and parted this well shaped out its roundness and boss and marked the slow tune of its long shoulder. One time it lay above a near hill of green field which, with the lands in it lined and plated by snow, was striped like a zebra: this Pendle repeated finer and dimmer.

End of March and beginning of April—This is the time to study inscape in the spraying of trees, for the swelling buds carry them to a pitch which the eye could not else gather—for out of much much more, out of little not much, out of nothing nothing: in these sprays at all events there is a new world of inscape. The male ashes are very boldly jotted with the heads of the bloom which tuft the outer ends of the branches. The staff of each of these branches is closely knotted with the places where buds are or have been, so that it is something like a finger which has been tied up with string and keeps the marks. They are in knops of a pair, one on each side, and the knops below, the bud of course is a short smoke-black pointed nail-head or beak pieced of four lids or nippers. Below it, like the hollow below the eye or the piece between the knuckle and the root of the nail, is a half-moon-shaped sill as if once chipped from the wood and this gives the twig its quaining in the outline. When the bud breaks at first it shews a heap of fruity purplish anthers looking something like the unripe elder-berries but these push open into richly-branched tree-pieces coloured buff and brown, shaking out loads of pollen, and drawing the tuft as a whole into peaked quains—mainly four, I think, two bigger and two smaller.

The bushes in the woods and hedgerows are spanned over and twisted upon by the woody chords of the honeysuckle: the cloves of leaf these bear are some purple, some grave green. But the young green of the briars is gay and neat and smooth as if cut in ivory.—One bay or hollow of Hodder Wood is curled all over with bright green garlic.

The sycamores are quite the earliest trees out: some have been fully out some days (April 15). The behaviour of the opening clusters is very beautiful and when fully opened not the single leaves but the whole tuft is strongly templed like the belly of a drum or bell.

The half-opened wood-sorrel leaves, the centre of spring of the leaflets rising foremost and the leaflets dropping back like ears leaving straight-chipped clefts between them, look like some green lettering and cut as sharp as dice.

The white violets are broader and smell; the blue, scentless and finer made, have a sharper whelking and a more winged recoil in the leaves.

Take a few primroses in a glass and the instress of—brilliancy, sort of starriness: I have not the right word—so simple a flower gives is remarkable. It is, I think, due to the strong swell given by the deeper yellow middle.

*

April 22—But such a lovely damasking in the sky as today I never felt before. The blue was charged with simple instress, the higher, zenith sky earnest and frowning, lower more light and sweet. High up again, breathing through woolly coats of cloud or on the quains and branches of the flying pieces it was the true exchange of crimson, nearer the earth/against the sun/it was turquoise, and in the opposite south-western bay below the sun it was like clear oil but just as full of colour, shaken over with slanted flashing 'travellers', all in flight, stepping one behind the other, their edges tossed with bright ravelling, as if white napkins were thrown up in the sun but not quite at the same moment so that they were all in a scale down the air falling one after the other to the ground.

April 27—Went to see Sauley [Sawley] Abbey (Cistercian): there is little to see.

Mesmerised a duck with chalk lines drawn from her beak sometimes level and sometimes forwards on a black table. They explain that the bird keeping the abiding offscape of the hand grasping her neck fancies she is still held down and cannot lift her head as long as she looks at the chalk line, which she associates with the power that holds her. This duck lifted her head at once when I put it down on the table without chalk. But this seems inadequate. It is most likely fascinating instress of the straight white stroke.

RETROSPECTION

May 9—A simple behaviour of the cloudscape I have not realised before. Before a N.E. wind great bars or rafters of cloud all
the morning and in a manner all the day marching across the sky
in regular rank and with equal spaces between. They seem prism-
shaped, flat-bottomed and banked up to a ride: their make is like
light tufty snow in coats.

This day and May 11 the bluebells in the little wood between
the College and the highroad and in one of the Hurst Green
cloughs. In the little wood/ opposite the light/ they stood in
blackish spreads or sheddings like the spots on a snake. The heads
are then like thongs and solemn in grain and grape-colour. But
in the clough/ through the light/ they came in falls of sky-col-
our washing the brows and slacks of the ground with vein-blue,
thickening at the double, vertical themselves and the young grass
and brake fern combed vertical, but the brake struck the upright
of all this with light winged transoms. It was a lovely sight.—The
bluebells in your hand baffle you with their inscape, made to every
sense: if you draw your fingers through them they are lodged
and struggle/ with a shock of wet heads; the long stalks rub and
click and flatten to a fan on one another like your fingers themselves would when you passed the palms hard across one another,
making a brittle rub and jostle like the noise of a hurdle strained
by leaning against; then there is the faint honey smell and in the
mouth the sweet gum when you bite them. But this is easy, it is
the eye they baffle. They give one a fancy of panpipes and of some
wind instrument with stops—a trombone perhaps. The overhung
necks—for growing they are little more than a staff with a simple
crook but in water, where they stiffen, they take stronger turns, in
the head like sheephooks or, when more waves throughout, like
the waves riding through a whip that is being smacked—what with
these overhung necks and what with the crisped ruffled bells dropping mostly on one side and the gloss these have at their footstalks
they have an air of the knights at chess. Then the knot or 'knoop'

of buds some shut, some just gaping, which makes the pencil of the whole spike, should be noticed: the inscape of the flower most finely carried out in the sliding of the axes, each striking a greater and greater slant, is finished in these clustered buds, which for the most part are not straightened but rise to the end like a tongue and this and their tapering and a little flattening they have make them look like the heads of snakes.

Journals, Gerard Manley Hopkins

Coniston Old Man
WG COLLINGWOOD

As we climb the zigzags to the highest quarries, over the slate which stands out in slabs from the sward, the crags of Brimfell and Buckbarrow opposite seem to rise with us. It is here, on a cloudy day when the tops are covered, that the finest impressions of mountain gloom may be found; under the cloud and the precipices a dark green tarn, savage rocks, and tumbling streams; and out, beyond, the tossing sea of mountain forms.

From the platform of the highest quarry, reached in ten minutes from the tarn, a rough and steep path to the left leads in five minutes more to the ridge, and the view of the lowland bursts upon us with the Westmorland and Yorkshire hills in the distance. Below, as Ruskin wrote when he first climbed here in 1867, "the two lakes of Coniston and Windermere, lying in the vastest space of sweet cultivated country I have ever looked over,—a great part of the view from the Rigi being merely over black pine-forest, even on the plains."

Fifteen minutes more take us up this steep arête to the top, 2626 feet above the sea.

There used to be three ancient cairns—the "Old Man" himself, his "Wife" and his "Son":—man, the Celtic *maen*, being the local name for a pile of stones, and the Old Man simply the name of the cairn, not of the whole mountain. These were destroyed to build the present landmark. The circle of stones we have passed marks the place of the Jubilee bonfire of 1887; the flare-lights of King Edward's coronation were shown from the top of the cairn, where in the days of fire signals was a regular beacon station.

The view on a clear day commands Ingleborough to the east, Snowdon to the south, the Isle of Man to the west, and to the north, Scafell and Bowfell, Glaramara and Skiddaw, Blencathra and Helvellyn: and beneath these all the country spread out like a raised model, with toy hills and lakes and villages. It is so easy to identify the different points with the help of the map that it is hardly necessary to name them in detail. Under the distant Pennines of Yorkshire lie Windermere, Esthwaite Water, and Coniston with Monk Coniston Tarns at its head. Southward,—over Walney Scar, Blind Tarn and Dow Crags close at hand,—are the shores of Morecambe Bay and the Duddon Estuary, with Black Combe rising dark against the sea. Westward, across the Duddon Valley, the steep rocky summits of Harter Fell and Hard Knott. The group close under our feet to the north includes Brimfell, Woolcrags, and the Carrs, with Grey Friar on the left and Weatherlam on the right, and in their hollows Lowwater and Leverswater. To the east of Helvellyn are Fairfield, Red Screes and Ill Bell, above the russet sides of Loughrigg and the distant detail of Ambleside.

At any time it is a fine panorama; but for grandeur of mountain line Weatherlam is the better standpoint. To walk along the ridge over springy turf is easy and exhilarating after the toil of the stony climb; and the excursion is often made. A mile to the depression of Levers Hause, another mile past Wool Crags and the Carrs, down Prison Band (the arête running eastward from the nearer side of the Carrs) to the dip at Swirl Hause; and a third mile over Blacksail, would bring you to Weatherlam Cairn. And a red sunset there, with a full moon to light you down the ridge to Hole Rake and the copper mines and home, is an experience to remember.

But for most of us enough is as good as a feast; and Weatherlam deserves a day to itself, and respectful approach by Tilberthwaite Gill. This walk leads from the village past Far End up Yewdale, turning to left at the sign post, and up between Raven Crag, opposite, and Yewdale Crag. At the next sign post turn up the path to the left, passing Pennyrigg Quarries, and then keep the path down into the Gill. The bridges, put up by Mr. Marshall, and kept in repair by the Lake District Association, lead through the ravine to the force at its head. Thence Weatherlam can be ascended either by Steel Edge, the ridge to the left, or breasting the steep slope from the hollow of the cove.

From the top of the Old Man we have choice of many descents. By Levers Hause we can scramble down—it looks perilous but is easy to a wary walker,—to Leverswater; and thence by a stony road to the copper mines and civilization.

From *The Book of Coniston*

The Lazy Tour of Two Idle Apprentices
Charles Dickens and Wilkie Collins

The Two Idle Apprentices drifted out resignedly into a fine, soft, close, drowsy, penetrating rain; got into the landlord's light dog-cart, and rattled off, through the village, for the foot of Carrock. The journey at the outset was not remarkable. The Cumberland road went up and down like other roads; the Cumberland curs burst out from backs of cottages and barked like other curs, and the Cumberland peasantry stared after the dog-cart amazedly, as long as it was in sight, like the rest of their race. The approach to the foot of the mountain resembled the approaches to the feet of most other mountains all over the world. The cultivation gradually ceased, the trees grew gradually rare, the road became gradually rougher, and the sides of the mountain looked gradually more and more lofty, and more and more difficult to get up. The dog-cart was left at a lonely farm-house. The landlord borrowed a large umbrella, and, assuming in an instant that the character of the most cheerful and adventurous of guides, led the way to the ascent. Mr. Goodchild looked eagerly at the top of the mountain, and, feeling apparently that he was now going to be very lazy indeed, shone all over wonderfully to the eye, under the influence of the contentment within and the moisture without. ...

The honest landlord went first, the beaming Goodchild followed, the mournful Idle brought up the rear. From time to time, the two foremost members of the expedition changed places in the order of march; but the rearguard never altered his position. Up the mountain or down the mountain, in the water or out of it, over the rocks, through the bogs, skirting the heather, Mr. Thomas Idle was always the last, and was always the man who had to be looked after and waited for. At first the ascent was delusively easy: the sides of the mountain sloped gradually, and the material of which they were composed was a soft spongy turf, very tender and pleasant to walk upon. After a hundred yards or so, however, the verdant scene and the easy slope disappeared, and the rocks began. Not noble, massive rocks, standing upright, keeping a certain regularity in their positions, and possessing, now and then, flat tops to sit upon, but little, irritating comfortless rocks, littered about anyhow by Nature; treacherous, disheartening rocks of all sorts of small shapes and small sizes, bruisers of tender toes and trippers-up of wavering feet. When these impediments were passed, heather and slough followed. Here the steepness of the ascent was slightly mitigated; and here the exploring part of three turned round to look at the view below them. The scene of the moorland and the fields was like a feeble water-colour drawing half sponged out. The mist was darkening, the rain was thickening, the trees were dotted about like spots of faint shadow, the division-lines which mapped out the fields were all getting blurred together, and the lonely farm-house where the dog-cart had been left, loomed spectral in the grey light like the last human dwelling at the end of the habitable world. Was this a sight worth climbing to see? Surely— surely not! Up again—for the top of Carrock is not reached yet. The landlord, just as good-tempered and obliging as he was at the bottom of the mountain. Mr. Goodchild brighter in the eyes and rosier in the face than ever; full of cheerful remarks and apt quotations; and walking with a springiness of step wonderful to behold. Mr. Idle, farther and father in the rear, with the water squeaking in the toes of his boots, with his two-guinea shoot- ing jacket clinging damply to his aching sides, with his over-coat so full of rain, and standing out so pyramidically stiff, in conse- quence, from his shoulders downwards, that he felt as if he was walking in a gigantic extinguisher—the despairing spirit within him representing but too aptly the candle that had just been put out. Up and up and up again, till a ridge is reached, and the outer edge of the mist on the summit of Carrock is darkly and drizzlingly near. Is this the top? No, nothing like the top. It is an aggravating peculiarity of all mountains, that, although they have only one top when they are seen (as they ought always to be seen) from below, they turn out to have a perfect eruption of false tops whenever the traveller is sufficiently ill-advised to go out of his way for the purpose of ascending them. Carrock is but a trumpery little mountain of fifteen hundred feet, and it presumes to have false tops, and even precipices, as if it was Mont Blanc. No matter; Goodchild enjoys it, and will go on; and Idle, who is afraid of being left behind by himself, must follow. On entering the edge of the mist, the landlord stops, and says he hopes that it will not get any thicker. It is twenty years since he last ascended Carrock, and it is barely possible, if the mist increases, that the party may be lost on the mountain. Goodchild hears this dreadful intimation, and is not in the least impressed by it. He marches for the top that is never to be found, as if he was the Wandering Jew, bound to go on for ever, in defiance of everything. The landlord faithfully accompanies him. The two, to the dim eye of Idle, far below, look in the exaggerative mist, like a pair of friendly giants, mounting the steps of some invisible castle together. Up and up, and then down a little, and then up, and then along a strip of level ground, and then up again. The wind, a wind unknown in the happy valley, blows keen and strong; the rain-mist gets impenetrable; a dreary little cairn of stone appears. The landlord adds one to the heap, first walking all round the cairn as if he were about to perform an incantation, then dropping the stone on to the top of the heap with the gesture of a magician adding an ingredient to a cauldron in full bubble. Goodchild sits down by the cairn as if it was his study-table at home; Idle, drenched and panting, stands up with his back to the wind, ascertains distinctly that this is the top at last, looks round with all the little curiosity that is left in him, and gets, in return, a magnificent view of—Nothing!

The effect of this sublime spectacle on the minds of the exploring party is a little injured by the nature of the direct conclusion to which the sight of it points—the said conclusion being that the mountain mist has actually gathered round them, as the landlord feared it would.

From *Household Words,* 1857

Pendle
WILLIAM BILLINGTON

Great Pendle Hill and Penyghent,
   And lofty Ingleborough,
Ye will not find three grander hills
   And trace old England thorough.

...

NORTH COUNTRY

We ranged the heights of lofty Pendle round
Where, gleaming through the dim-blue atmosphere,
We saw a cirque of hills, whose heads were crowned
With cloudy diadems, and some did peer
Above the clouds, and bask in sunbeams pure and clear.

With Blackstone Edge, and Cribden, and the Pike
Of Rivington before us,—full in view.
Huge Hambledon heaved his broad back, which like
Some Titan's form its giant shadow threw
On village, and on valley; but the blue
Of heaven, through the white clouds of the north,
Was glinting glory down; where well we knew
Old Skiddaw and Helvellyn, glooming forth,
With Scawfell Pike, appeared the boundary of the earth.

The Ribble, like a silver serpent, wound
Her gleaming course down to the estuary
By rock and scar, her devious way she found;
Through holme and dingle, clough and rugged quarry—
Among the meads mid cornfields seemed to tarry,
As loth to leave their fair and flowery nooks,
And lingering long, as though she meant to marry
Those offspring of the hills, the bounding brooks,
In such romantic wise as rhymed in poets' books.

We stood tiptoe on Pendle's highest point
And gazed around, until the scanty breast
Could scarce contain the heart, that fluttered, buoy'nt,
And bounding seemed to fly, as though 't would nest
In heaven; then, converging toward the west;
And, quite fatigued—bathed in a hot deluge
Of sunbeams—soon, the rest sat down to rest,—
I laid me down and gave my face refuge
Beneath my hat, and slept; and lo! broad, black and huge,

RETROSPECTION

I, dreaming, saw a pyramid arise
Spontaneous from the earth; its spire did make
A rent in the heaven's blue; and through the skies
The top gleamed like a tower through a lake;
Its weight did make the mighty Hill to shake,
And, trembling, rattle all her rocky bones;
Then, falling with the sound of an earthquake,
Or, like the rumbling of Jove's thunderstones,
Drew from the stars harsh echoes, loud as Titan's groans!

...

Strange tales were told of witches, long ago—
Old Mother Demdike, whose unholy power
Caused inky floods from Pendle's breast to flow,
And filched the blush from many a human a flower;
Whose midnight orgies, held in Malkin Tower,
Threw blight on harvests—blanched the bloom of spring—
Made summer clouds withhold the fruitful shower,
While withered at her will each living thing—
All ale turned sour, cows dry, and cuckoos ceased to sing!

Of Demdike's wrinked rival, Mother Chattox—
The abbot Paslew—the Dule-upo'-Dun—
The Pig bewitched—enchanted spades and mattocks—
The Dog Familiar and the Magic Gun;
Such webs were woven and such yarns were spun,
Of many a monk transformed into a tike,
And nymphs allured to fates they could not shun,—
Of fairies, banshees, boggarts and the like,
All wound up with a song, "The Devil and little Mike."

We took the road to Clitheroe once more,
And just arrived in time to take our tea,
And visit the old Castle, when 'twas o'er;
And well the same did with my soul agree,

For often had my spirit yearned to see
And minutely inspect its ruins, too,
To tread the prison yard with footsteps free,—
To scale the battlements, as now I do,
And view those splintered gaps where Cromwell's balls
   swept through.

For even now, in thought, I tread the height
Of those time-smitten battlements which crown
That Gothic pile—those relics ruin-bright—
Those huge moss-mantled walls, whose sullen frown
Hangs like a thunder-cloud above the town.
As when some Alpine rock, reared to the sky,
Upon the petty hills looks proudly down,
Tall forests dwarfed to furze beneath it lie,
So, from this height, the farmstead dwindles to a sty.

From 'The Times', Blackburn, 1876

Farewell Happy Fields

KATHLEEN RAINE

Over the high moss-grown stone wall of the manse garden,
behind the raspberry canes where on hot summer days I basked
and read the novels of Sir Walter Scott on the wooden bench of a
little holly-arbour, was the bull-field. There the bull lived his solitary life, marked out from the herd by the brass ring in his nose,
and the heavy wrinkled folds of his head and neck. We children
used often to play a dangerous game of 'last across' the bull-field,
climbing the five-barred gate from the farmyard when he was
quietly grazing at the far end of his field; or we would provoke
him with sticks, poked with safety over the wall, to make him
advance with lowered head, that ominous slowness gathering to
a rush that filled us with delight and terror. His high-pitched

bellow was well known to me, for from my bedroom window I could see into his field when the other children had gone home to their distant farms—in a special sense he was my neighbour.

Anyone who has live on, or by, a farm, knows in what respect a bull is held. There is no other creature on an English farm who has the power of death in his horns. For this reason, and also no doubt because of his sexual potency, equated with 'sin', he was the evil-one of our world. Yet by us children the bull's *mana*, his magical animal power, was recognized; he was a power among us; no human being in our world had such greatness as his. Theriomorphic gods are older than human, and children, like archaic man, recognize with immediacy the quality of animal-souls. He was, besides, not *a* bull, but *the* bull. Like the priest of the sacred wood, there is never more than one.

One day—I think in March, but this is no more than an impression of a clear cold sparse day of early spring—the news passed round among us that the bull had gored the farmer; not fatally, as it happened, for his eldest son, a boy of thirteen, and still on of the back row pupils in my Aunt's school-room, had arrived on the scene in time to save his father's life. But the butcher had been sent for, and the bull was to die.

So it was that I was one of the row of children who stood in the farmyard, where on an outcrop of rock the camomile was trodden by the clogs and hooves of all the village; the same farmyard where daily I filled our two buckets from the well. The farmyard was our Akropolis; and there we gathered to witness an event that held us not in partial, but in total, all-excluding participation. Never in amphitheatre nor temple of the gods nor circle of stone menhirs did the fate of consecrated victim more totally absorb the minds and souls of the spectators; what the theatre only represents, the bull-fight simulates, this was.

I recall the hush as the butcher drove his low dray into the farmyard; it stood there, empty, while the butcher walked over to the byre; empty; but we know what it was—a hearse for the dead. And the great one who was to be dead still lived, not knowing he was to die. The human world had passed judgement on the animal; the evil beast must yet again be slaughtered. Behind the immediate crime—the attack upon man—lay who knows what remote echo of archaic man's profound self-condemnation of his own animal nature, still not extinct in men so primitive as to be scarcely themselves securely rooted in the human principle to which on the Sabbath Day they aspired. Unreflectingly these hamlet-dwellers passed on the beast of age-old human verdict, laid down for the animal in the antiquity of pre-history; yet for them there was drama in his heath as though the struggle between man and animal remained still undecided, still the be waged. There was in this death the suspense of a struggle undecided: why else did we gather and stand so attentively on our lime-stone akropolis?

But to me the pity was greater than the terror: I was on his side. Everyone knew, as I did, that Farmer Bell was but a poor specimen of mankind; his stone dykes were falling unmended, his children were dirty and covered with ring-worm, his wife a slattern and he himself was good for nothing but breeding his kind; yet now all but I sided with him against the innocence of nature. Such was human solidarity; but I was on the side of nature against man; I felt the wrong man was committing against the wildness of the best, who, having no conscience had not sinned. Surely, surely he must not die! Justice would intervene, what justice I did not know, but I believed the world to be just.

There was the long waiting; the butcher, alone, crossing the yard, gun in hand; a muffled bellow; and as in a Greek tragedy the kind is slain behind the heavy doors of his palace, so we waited for the shot, and knew that the great one of our small world, the creature of power, had once again been slaughtered; the strong by the weak, the great by the small. Presently, as from those palace doors, the great body was dragged out of the byre and onto the dry, limp and powerless. I saw his pepper-and-salt purplish-brown hide with a sense of infinite compassion: I was him. My body suffered in itself the death of the beast, my skin mourning for his skin, my veins for his veins, my five senses for his; and when his anus slipped a mass of faeces, I was ashamed for the abasement of his death.

From *Happy Fields Forever*

To the River Duddon
NORMAN NICHOLSON

I wonder, Duddon, if you still remember
An oldish man with a nose like a pony's nose,
Broad bones, legs long and lean but strong enough
To carry him over Hard Knott at seventy years of age.
He came to you first as a boy with a fishing-rod
And a hunk of Ann Tyson's bread and cheese in his pocket,
Walking from Hawkshead across Walna Scar;
Then as a middle-aged Rydal landlord,
With a doting sister and a government sinecure,
Who left his verses gummed to your rocks like lichen,
The dry and yellow edges of a once-green spring.
He made a guide-book for you, from your source
There where you bubble through the moss on Wrynose
(Among the ribs of bald and bony fells
With screes scratched in the turf like grey scabs),
And twist and slither under humpbacked bridges—
Built like a child's house from odds and ends
Of stones that lie about the mountain side—
Past Cockley Beck Farm and on to Birk's Bridge,
Where the rocks stride about like legs in armour,
And the steel birches buckle and bounce in the wind

NORTH COUNTRY

With a crinkle of silver foil in the crisp of the leaves;
On then to Seathwaite, where like a steam-navvy
You shovel and slash your way through the gorge
By Wallabarrow Crag, broader now
From becks that flow out of black upland tarns
Or ooze through golden saxifrage and the roots of rowans;
Next Ulpha, where a stone dropped from the bridge
Swims like a tadpole down thirty feet of water
Between steep skirting-boards of rock; and thence
You dribble into lower Dunnerdale
Through wet woods and wood-soil and woodland flowers,
Tutson, the St John's-wort with a single yellow bead,
Marsh marigold, creeping jenny and daffodils;
Here from hazel islands in the late spring
The catkins fall and ride along the stream
Like little yellow weasels, and the soil is loosed
From bulbs of the white lily that smells of garlic,
And dippers rock up and down on rubber legs,
And long-tailed tits are flung through the air like darts;
By Foxfield now you taste the salt in your mouth,
And thrift mingles with the turf, and the heron stands
Watching the wagtails. Wordsworth wrote:
'Remote from every taint of sordid industry'.
But you and I know better, Duddon.
For I, who've lived for nearly thirty years
Upon your shore, have seen the slagbanks slant
Like screes into the sand, and watched the tide
Purple with ore back up the muddy gullies,
And wiped the sinter dust from the farmyard damsons.
A hundred years of floods and rain and wind
Have washed your rocks clear of his words again,
Many of them half-forgotten, brimming the Irish Sea,
But that which Wordsworth knew, even the old man

When poetry had failed like desire, was something
I have yet to learn, and you, Duddon,
Have learned and re-learned to forget and forget again.
Not the radical, the poet and heretic,
To whom the water-forces shouted and the fells
Were like a blackboard for the scrawls of God,
But the old man, inarticulate and humble,
Knew that eternity flows in a mountain beck—
The long cord of the water, the shepherd's numerals
That run upstream, through the singing decades of dialect.
He knew, beneath mutation of year and season,
Flood and drought, frost and fire and thunder,
The blossom on the rowan and the reddening of the berries,
There stands the base and root of the living rock,
Thirty thousand feet of solid Cumberland.

Wensleydale

Ella Pontefract

Wensleydale in Yorkshire is one of England's green valleys. You find the greenness from the beginning, as soon as the River Ure, after its first rush down Lunds Fell, takes the decisive bend which is to lead it through Yorkshire, instead of the gentler way of the Eden into Westmorland. It is a narrow line of cultivation at first, and the moor creeps down as if it would snatch it back to itself, but there are, nevertheless, meadows where grass is grown for hay, and pasture where cattle feed. Swiftly, as the valley dips and widens, the grassland increases, running in more level fields and climbing further up the fells, growing ever more luxuriant, to become at length some of the finest grazing land in the country. Near the foot of the dale a few ploughed fields appear, but these grow chiefly turnips and potatoes, so that they too are green for much of the year.

It is a grassy dale, and only for a few weeks in summer when the grass ripens does it change its face. Then the fields have their time of glory, to the making of which the whole year has gone. They are pink where the grass is still uncut, brown where hay is drying, yellow where it has just been led, and darkening where the grass begins to grow again.

The trees intensify the greenness, exaggerating its brightness by their dark outlines in the winter, showing it pale and weathered when they burst into their spring freshness, and joining with it in the summer as if to flaunt the many shades and changes which this colour can achieve. They too grow in the higher reaches, scattered, except where they climb the ravines or have been planted in clumps to break the winds, and always with a definite line above which they do not flourish. They follow the river on its downward journey, dotting themselves ever thicker in the meadows, until in the lower dale they attain a density which gives the valley the appearance of a park.

Through this green land the River Ure flows unobtrusively, cutting for the most part a silent, easy course, but in the one stretch where rocks bar its way, breaking into some of the finest waterfalls in England. But it is a dale river, fed by becks which drain from the fells, and its normal, almost noiseless, flow can change suddenly after storms to a torrent, flooding fields and roads and houses near its banks.

The fells which shut in Wensleydale, and without which it would not be a dale, emphasize its green fertility. They do not overshadow the valley, it is in most places too wide; nor, except for one ridge on the north, do they run up it in an unbroken line like a barrier, there are too many smaller dales cutting through them to allow for that. They do not rely for beauty on the turns and twists of the valley, for this is not a winding dale. It is the shape of them which is their attraction. They rise into isolated peaks, many of which end a ridge bounding a smaller dale. As a proverb says: 'There is a hill against a dale all Wensleydale over.' Their cliff-like faces often end in a series of terraces, formed by the wearing away of the softer layers of rock. Each has its own characteristics, and each dominates a stretch of the dale. You find yourself measuring your way up or down by them: Witton Fell, Penhill, Addleborough, Wether Fell, Cotter End. As one is left behind another appears, itself changing as the road passes it. But when they are named, it is a particular shape which comes to mind, as the dome-like summit of Penhill, or the crouching face of Cotter End. In their individuality and difference they are almost human, and you come to love them as you would love a person. They present an ever-changing background to the green valleys, from the almost monotonous green of those summer weeks when the line between it and them is nearly indistinguishable, to their autumn abandonment of rusts, ambers, and purples, and their winter moods when under their covering of bleached grass and rushes they seem to shrink into themselves, or white with snow sparkling in the sunshine they appear to expand and take to themselves the impenetrable look of mountains. But they are friendly hills, even the wildest of them. …

And there are the smaller dales, Coverdale, Bishopdale, Raydale, Cotterdale, and innumerable still smaller ones. They are like the branches of a big family of which Wensleydale is the head. Some are miniatures of her graciousness and repose; some have a fierce, untamed beauty, which far exceeds her wildest moods; some rest quiet and secure in their own loveliness; some are shut away like secret, forgotten valleys. They have an unexpected quality. Wandering about them you realize something of what Wensleydale itself was like in quieter, less restless days than these. Customs and sayings survive in them which are only memories here. Each has its separate life, but each is also centred in the town or village which, standing at or near its foot, links it up with the bigger dale.

This is Wensleydale as you find it to-day. There seems a per-manency about it, as if it had always been this green fertile valley under sheltering fells, with people settling there and villages growing up, because it was a good place to live in. But like most parts of England it has been made as it is by man.

*

The river rises as a trickle in the grass; now it cuts a feeble way through a stretch of peat; now struggles through rushes; now down a deep ravine. For a little way it runs underground, leav-ing its old bed dry with fallen rocks, and trees growing in the cracks, an eerie spot with its life, which was the river, gone. But it emerges and comes, always winding, past its first little bridge to Ure Crook, named after that critical turn down the valley. Here, within sight of its first trickles, farmhouses appear, and the life which follows its course begins.

The track from Hell Gill to Shaw Paddock is a wide grassy way, soft and springy to the feet... In spring the track is a sanctuary for birds. The hillside seems suddenly alive as a flock of golden plovers rises with a monotonous whistle, and settles again, hardly distinguishable from the moor. A pair of yellow wagtails skim along and perch on a tuft of grass, as if they know how well their yellowy green plumage is displayed against that sombre back-ground. Curlews give their liquid, burbling call, a call of pure happiness, the music of the fells. Seeing you, they swoop above, their long, curved beaks opening and shutting as they utter a harsh, agitated cry, angry at your intrusion. On the moor the curlews are in pairs, their calls of joy are warning are to each other; but at evening they come down to the lower land to feed in flocks of as many as eighteen. Green plovers —'tewits,' the dalespeople call them, and explain them as 'them wi' toppin's' — cry excitedly above, revelling in the joy of motion. Snipe rise exultantly into the air, and swoop downwards with their peculiar drumming sound. The birds come suddenly to the moor. One day it is empy and silent, and the next they fill it with their life.

From the door of our caravan we have watched a heron flying slowly up the valley, its great wings spread out and seeming to glitter as they caught the rays of the sun. It looked magnificent, a creature of power. Later it would fish in the river, catching numbers of trout, making itself disliked by the farmers who are fishermen, and who will shoot the 'hearinsew' if they can. It is a sign of bad weather when a heron comes as far up the valley as Lunds.

From *Wensleydale,* 1936

An icy rain fell
PRUDENCE MARY SCOTT

An icy rain fell in the afternoon; the white clematis
flowers stumbled and the half-ripe green figs struck the
ground like felted stones and the multitudinous and
disparate shapes on the herb leave parted and separated on
the pale stalks suddenly exposed.
It was the afternoon of cleaning and waiting and of
knowing nothing nor when, but we made gestures of preparation
as though we expected to live for a long time.
The staircase wound like a shell through our hopes,
a spiral bone that kept us tuned to arrivals and music
beyond walls, a strong voice singing the song of a newly-
discovered circular sea, three or four flights up, or down.
Even though the sun shone through the polished glass our
hands and feet grew cold, and we counted the occasional
pigeons fired from the barrels of the north west and
twisted our necks to accommodate roof tops and flightpaths,
and the mirror buildings bent those paths to alien dives
upon a twittering city. We wondered whether it was safe
to stay, and stitched our needles to our cuffs with

multi-coloured cottons for the unknown future; but later when the rain had passed and the clouds dropped their dust on cills and shoulders, the dark came suddenly when many were still aloft and without nightlight. Then from the gardens and parks of the city, and even from the balconies and window boxes and the flowerpots down deep areas where tortoises live and lament, there came upon the air a scent and warmth of full flowers and crushed herbs and skilleted spices, all the aromas one would ever need for however many weddings and births and burials. Everyone breathed deeply and slowed and halted, put down caskets and rods and bells and took off their shoes and stretched their hands and feet into the suddenly sparkling earth and sand, and drank of it deeply. Later they lay profoundly awake in the hindsight and foreknowing and asked nothing of touch and taste and desire, only let the newfurling green leaf appear from every brow by morning.

Blue and Green
John Ruskin

Look much at the morning and evening sky, and much at simple flowers – dog-roses, wood-hyacinths, violets, poppies, thistles, heather, and such like – as Nature arranges them in the woods and fields. If ever any scientific person tells you that two colours are "discordant", make a note of the two colours, and put them together whenever you can. I have actually heard people say that blue and green were discordant; the two colours which Nature seems to intend never to be separated, and never to be felt, either of them, in its full beauty without the other ! – a peacock's neck, or a blue sky through green leaves, or a blue wave with green lights through it, being precisely the loveliest things, next to clouds at sunrise, in this coloured world of ours.

From *The Elements of Drawing*

Three

RESISTANCE

*New Narratives for
Unprecedented Times*

Offcomer
KATIE HALE

I come from a land that was nobody's land
and anybody's. I come from a war
of accents and blood, from heather
taking root in the bones of clans,
while the wind whispers
the old names. I come from a land
where villages are crumbled and sunk, where stories
disturb the bottoms of lakes.
I come from a land of drownings.
I come from a land where water
is ammunition hurled from the sky. My childhood
was a scrap yard of animals,
of death and disinfectant, of 4x4s and smoke.
I come from a land where rivers
unburden themselves
into farms and villages, where they carpet the city
in a rainbow of diesel and mud.
I come from the fire and the flood.
I come from a land of scythed vowels, of consonants
let tumble like ghylls down the backs of throats. I come
from a land of poems trudged across the fells
like coffins. I come from a naked land, a land
veined in stone, baring itself to the wind. My land
is bracken and gorse and the slow
gorging of ticks. My land
is height and electric skies, is water
locked behind dams.
I cannot hold my land; it is a voice thrown
back across the valley. It speaks
with the deep-throated roar of fighter planes.

No, I am not *of* this land. My skin is a prairie,
my hair and eyes an Irish peat and sky,
my bones a midlands town.
But put your ear to my breast.
Between my stereo heartbeats, you will hear
water, the raucous gathering of clouds.

Those Who Can Afford Time
JASON ALLEN-PAISANT

Who wanders
   lonely as a cloud
with three golden retrievers?

Not me   no   not me
I could never understand this poetry

never understand what the poem was saying
and how this could be
poetry for me

when my English teacher drilled
the imagination of a white man's country

didn't know how but somehow I knew
this wandering was not
for me because

ours was not the same kind of time
   our wandering never so accidental
so entire so free

RESISTANCE

as if nothing was coming   as if no hawk was near
as if they owned the land and the mansion on it
as if tomorrow and forever was theirs

as if they had the right to take their time
  because
everything about them so refined   so secure
  so clean

So Wordsworth's poem never made sense
  I'd never stop to listen to the poems about trees
& mushrooms & odd cute things
& birds whose names I could never pronounce

My poetry was Tom the village deejay
more material   I said
  than the woods   than the lives of those who loafed

& bought their time
with money   I thought
those who had all the time in the world

Seagulls
JASON ALLEN-PAISANT

When I get to them they are a colony
picking and squawking
a white bar lying on the wide field

I am blessed to see them

175

Then   one thud raises them into the sky
suddenly all those wings flapping in unison
I thought   what a beauty of some
unknown mind deciding a precise moment
when that multitudinous flap of the wing
should happen

I heard a noise a call a song and thought
a soft moan of a pigeon or dove? And then I saw it
above   a machine flying among the birds

I swivel my head round and round
but there is no one

So the sound was no moan
of a pigeon or caw of a raven
but a motor purring where the birds fly

Some human extends its will over things
Some human has made a gadget
and doesn't remember the birds
no   doesn't remember the birds

The Most Mancunian of Trees
DAVID COOPER

> *If we are to restore any connection with nature at all, it is in
> the cities that we need to begin.* Bob Gilbert

There are trees in the centre of Manchester, but they are fakes.
Rush through the deadened space of Piccadilly Gardens on your
way to the station and you'll pass 'The Tree of Remembrance': a

memorial, made out of bronze and stainless steel, that Wolfgang Buttress and Fiona Heron designed to commemorate the sixtieth anniversary of VE Day. Dine out in Spinningfields – if your bank balance can take the strain – and you can eat Shanghai black cod beneath a four metre high dried cherry blossom that, miraculously, illuminates a restaurant interior for 365 days each year. It seems that Manchester, in the 2020s, is an unreal city, an arboreal simulacrum.

To say that the middle of Manchester is completely treeless, though, isn't strictly true. There are, of course, *some* real trees in the centre of the city. Just outside the Friends Meeting House, on Mount Street around the back of the Central Library, there's a giant London Plane. Redwoods and ash can be found between the beautifully brutalist buildings of the old UMIST campus. Further north, there's a thick line of trees, of various species, alongside the bijou Cathedral. There's a hornbeam on Market Street and a foxglove in St Peter's Square; there are willows overhanging the Bridgewater Canal and horse chestnuts in Castlefield. The centre of Manchester is a treescape, if you remember to look. It's just that, right now, you have to look pretty hard.

*

'St John's Gardens? Yeah, I know it really well,' Chris replied. 'It's just off Deansgate, not far from the Opera House. See you by the memorial at ten.'

*

In his 2017 collection of poems, *Mancunia*, Michael Symmons Roberts offers the reader a vision of the city that is rooted in the particularities of place: 'street-cleaners are out in force' in the 'post-drizzle glory' of the Northern Quarter ('On Your Birthday'); a first-person speaker seeks mercy from God whilst walking 'west on Cross Street' ('Mancunian Miserere').

Mancunia is also a book in which Manchester emerges as a city of geographical imaginaries and urban myths: a built environment of 'back-to-backs' where a modern-day Actaeon stalks 'the alleys' in the hope of glimpsing a sunbathing Diana ('Actaeon'); a post-industrial landscape in which a mermaid has evolved 'to live and hunt and thrive in this gotham of the north' ('Miss Molasses'). Manchester, then, emerges as a 'partly real, partly dream-country', to borrow the phrase that Thomas Hardy famously used to describe his own evocation of rural Wessex.

According to Rory Waterman, 'Great Northern Diver', the second poem in *Mancunia*, serves as 'a scene-setter' for the entire collection. Here, Symmons Roberts envisions – in a single, breathless sentence - Manchester viewed from above at night. To begin, the details in the cityscape are difficult to establish as, from this aerial perspective, the glow of street lights look 'like embers'. As the speaker describes moving towards the ground, though, it becomes possible to pick out specific features in the human-made environment: flyovers and stadiums; cul-de-sacs and factories; cars and shop windows. 'Great Northern Diver' then ends with the speaker addressing an unidentified interlocutor: 'the clay arrests you, holds you as a pulse for good/ so what keeps this city alive is you'. At the last, then, Symmons Roberts's poem seems to celebrate the grounded physicality of the city; Manchester is framed as a body which is kept beating by 'you'.

In the poem's penultimate stanza, as the speaker describes zooming towards the earth, there's a reference to the 'ragged tops' of 'black poplars'. I'm pretty sure that, when I first read *Mancunia*, I failed to pick up on this. In defence of my earlier self, it's only a fleeting mention as, in this poem of dizzying movement, the reader's gaze is immediately shifted from the trees to 'roof tiles' and 'kerbstones'. Looking back, though, I probably didn't pause at this point as I simply didn't get the place-specific significance of these particular treetops. I failed to realise that, in alluding to the black poplar, Symmons Robert was deliberately namecheck-ing what Andy Long – Woodlands Officer at the environmental charity, City of Trees – has labelled 'this most Mancunian of trees'.

*

It's a psychogeographic cliché, I know, but I sometimes wonder if I'm the only person in Manchester who still carries an A to Z in their bag. Bought at the Smiths in Piccadilly back in 2002 – price: £3.95 – my Mini Manchester is unsurprisingly battered these days: its back cover is coffee-stained; some of the pages have gone missing; and pages 3 to 72 reliably fall out each time it's opened. The tiny weatherworn book feels something of an anachronism on the increasingly rare occasions I take it out on Oxford Road or Cross Street or St Peter's Square. The cartographic contents of the book feel conspicuously out-of-date too given how, over the past twenty years, the city centre has been knocked down and rebuilt, erased and remade. That morning, though, the A to Z did its job as, walking down Quay Street, I looked for a left-hand turn which would take me towards an all-too-rare green square sandwiched between Lower Byrom Street, Byrom Street, and Quay Street. I was trying to find St John's Gardens.

Chris was already there, trying to keep warm by sipping from a flask of coffee on this fag-end-of-winter morning. From 1769, this patch of land was the site of a church built by Edward Byrom, one of the founders of the first bank of Manchester. Designed in the Gothic Revival style, and once deemed worthy of a sketch by Turner on one of his tours of the North, the congregation at St John's dwindled at the start of the twentieth century and, in the 1920s, the diocese merged the parish with St Matthew's on the nearby Liverpool Road. The church was eventually knocked down and, in 1932, the site was redeveloped as a formal garden.

As I headed towards Chris, I was aware that all around me, just beneath my feet, were the submerged tombstones of people once of this parish. The memorial at the centre of the Gardens indicated that one of those bodies below belonged to 'John Owens, the founder of the Victoria University'; it also revealed that William Marsden – 'who originated the Saturday half holiday' – was buried here. Yet another inscription gave a sense of the sheer scale of this once consecrated ground: 'around lie the remains of more than 22000 people'. Looking up towards the aircraft warning light at the top of Beetham Tower, I couldn't help but think of the recent framing of the city as *Manchattan*: a vertiginous urban landscape – 'cheered by the Financial Times and George Osborne', as the journalist Aditya Chakraborrty has put it - that's going higher and higher, pricier and pricier, with each passing year. Visiting St John's Gardens for the first time, though, was to remember that the vertical city also incorporates what continues to lie beneath.

'Right: where shall we begin?'

Chris's question was a reminder that we'd met up for a reason. We'd recently started to work together on a project exploring urban treescapes. We were here, in this patch of publicly owned green space, in search of Manchester poplars.

*

Over the course of the nineteenth century, Manchester became black. The buildings were blackened by smoke. Black snow fell from the sky in the winter months. As a result of industrial melanism, the local moth population became black too: an evolutionary adaptation that, astonishingly, enabled them to hide in plain sight.

Unsurprisingly, many of the city's trees were unable to withstand these punishing environmental conditions. However, black poplars proved to be an exception and were able to tolerate, in the words of the natural historian, David McClintock, 'the soot and filth of Manchester'.

*

'Let's go round together,' Chris suggested. 'Let's be systematic about this.'

I'm notoriously bad at identifying trees. I don't wear this inability as some sort of badge of honour: a self-righteous critique of the petty business of arboreal taxonomisation. For me, it's a significant *lack* as, on family walks, not knowing is the cause of frequent embarrassment. I *want* to be able to look and to name. For some reason, though, it takes a lot for the learning to sink in.

As we set off, I took out my phone to look at the checklist I'd cobbled together, on the way in that morning, from various websites and articles in obscure academic journals:

Populus nigra
Family: *Salicaceae*
'Manchester' is a cultivar of *P. nigra* subsp. *betulifolia* widely planted in northwest England.
Thick, fissured trunk
Knobbly 'bosses' and twigs
Buds spiral round the twig and are closely pressed to it
Spreading branches that often touch the ground, before sweeping upwards again in a mass of twigsLocation: sun to half-shade

We began by walking around the perimeter of the Gardens, sidestepping the pizza boxes and face masks. We also pretended not to notice the middle-aged man – linen suit, leather satchel over-the-shoulder – unselfconsciously pissing against the railings on his way, presumably, to a mid-morning meeting. For the most part, we were reasonably confident in our rejection of the trees that we passed. It was only as we headed back towards Byrom Street that we became a little unsure. There, on either side of the gateway to the church that once was, we found a line of trees that sort of ticked most of the boxes. Could these be them? Had I, in fact, walked past the black poplars on my way in? The trunks looked fissured and the branches seemed knobbly. And wouldn't it have made sense, given their remarkable resilience to industrial pollution, for these trees to have been planted on the edge of the Gardens? I started to send a photo to my sister-in-law – an ecologist turned horticulturalist – for confirmation when Chris interrupted...

'I've found them.'

I followed the line of Chris's finger to a pair of trees, leaning to the light, in the centre of the Gardens. He wasn't wrong. It was clear that there, just beyond the memorial where we'd started, was what we'd come to see.

*

There's nothing new about green jobs. Ninety years ago, unemployment levels were unprecedentedly high in Manchester as a result of the Great Depression. In an effort to get people back into work, the Manchester Parks and Cemeteries Committee – with the support of the national government – hired men to head out on bikes. Carrying small iron bars, and bunches of saplings cut from a single tree, these men were tasked with planting black poplars around Manchester. These trees began to grow in parks and on roadsides, alongside canals and in public squares.

To my mind, thinking about bikes and labour in the 1930s can carry unfortunate associations. Back in 1981, Norman Tebbit – Thatcher's rottweiler – responded to the Handsworth and Brixton riots with characteristic sensitivity by arguing that, fifty years earlier, his unemployed father had 'got on his bike and looked for work, and he kept looking till he found it'. The poplar planters offer an alternative cycling myth from that decade. I don't know where those Manchester men had to go to pick up the saplings. Nor I am sure where they were asked to take those cuttings. I like to think, though, that they gathered at the new public gardens off Byrom Street before pedalling off to Prestwich and Burnage, Eccles and Flowery Field. I like to think that there were hundreds of cyclists, dispersing from the centre of the city to its edges, with hope for the future hanging out of their pockets.

*

When I was little, there were two large silver birch at the bottom of our garden. Most of the time, I saw those trees as goalposts. I do remember, though, the deep satisfaction of going around and around the tree as I peeled off long, thin strips of bark. I also remember my Mum shouting from the back door, warning that I was 'taking off too much tree'. I always wondered what would happen if I just kept on peeling. Just how much trunk was needed to support the branches above? What would be the tipping point?

I thought of those silver birch as I rubbed my hands along the burred bark of one of the black poplars; in spite of the material differences, I was momentarily transported back to a time – the *only* time - when I had a diurnal relationship with a particular pair of trees. I'd returned to St John's Gardens on my own with the intention of closing my eyes and allowing my hands to get to know the texturality of the trees. But, in this edge-of-the-city-centre public space, I felt far too self-conscious to touch for too long. Instead, I took dozens of photos. I endeavoured to adopt an air of authoritative detachment which would convey, to any suspicious passers-by, that my interest in the poplar was purely professional.

There's an image still saved on my phone that provides a close-up of the bark. On the small screen, the photo of the black poplar resembles the plane surface of a geological map: a flattening of what is, in reality, a thickly contoured landscape of peaks and valleys, fissures and grykes. As I swipe, then, I can only imagine this gnarledness. What I can do, however, is to use my index and middle fingers to zoom down into one of the dark fissures in the trunk. The hole gets larger and larger until, eventually, the whole screen becomes black. I go deeper and deeper into this negative space on my morning commute. I sit deep inside the tree, thousands and thousands of caterpillars crawling across my skin as we wait, yet again, for a platform to become available at Oxford Road.

*

The twentieth century city belonged to the car. In the 1950s, there was congestion on Market Street and a line of cars parked outside the Royal Exchange in St Ann's Square. In the middle of the following decade, Harold Wilson officially opened the Mancunian Way: the 'highway in the sky' that was built on top of the West Manchester Fault. The city was reimagined, redesigned, and reconfigured to facilitate movement at speed. Given the cult of the private car, many roadside black poplars were removed to avoid their shedding branches proving to be troublesome for drivers wishing to get back home to Prestwich and Marple.

Then, in 2000, the young shoots and leaves of many of the remaining trees blackened and died as a result of a virulent airborne disease: *venturia populina* or poplar scab. At the turn of the new millennium, dozens of black poplars – trees that had been able to withstand the onslaught of industrialisation – suddenly disappeared from the local landscape.

*

To my surprise, the trees looked like they'd been draped with red decorations the next time I walked to St John's Gardens.

The black poplar is dioecious. In female trees, the catkins are yellow-green and, when they are fertilised, they develop into cotton-like seeds which fall towards the end of summer and are dispersed on the wind. In male trees, however, the flowers are pendulous red catkins. I turned to my phone, in an attempt to discover more, and learnt a new lexicon.

RESISTANCE

As I thought about heading back into town, I lifted a catkin that had fallen to the ground and tried to identify its bract and perianth. It was only when I got back home, and became buried deep within a rabbit-hole of folkloric websites, that I realised that, unwittingly, I'd picked up one of the Devil's fingers.

*

Over the past few years, the National Trust has been working on an ambitious project to create an urban skypark in Manchester. At the end of the nineteenth century, the 330-metre long Castlefield Viaduct was constructed to connect the railway line with the Great Northern Warehouse which now houses a major leisure complex at the junction of Deansgate and Peter Street. For almost eighty years, this viaduct carried improbably heavy traffic high over the Bridgewater Canal; but, since the closure of the line to the warehouse in 1969, the Grade II-listed structure has been redundant.

Working with a wide range of local organisations and communities, the staff at the National Trust have reimagined the viaduct as 'a garden in the sky': an experiment, influenced by the famous High Line on the west side of Manhattan, to create an accessible green space in a city that, according to Chakraborrty, has become defined by an Abu Dhabi-fuelled 'post-industrial regeneration' that is 'redbrick in tooth and claw'. Many of the species to be planted by the gardener and their team of volunteers will have local connections including cotton grass and native ferns to be found in the herbarium collections at Manchester Museum. It seems as if visitors to the skypark will also be able find shade beneath black poplars as they look out, through steel lattices, across the city.

*

Over the summer, the practice of everyday life invariably involved the black poplars. Some mornings, I'd catch an early train so that I could pop into St John's Gardens before work. Other days, I'd undertake a lengthy detour to Castlefield on the way back home. The Gardens, on one or two occasions, even served as a venue for en plein air meetings.

I like to think that, over those warmer months, I became a little less self-conscious around the black poplars. I pressed my left ear to the bark and tried to tune into the innumerable goings-on inside. I inhaled the balsamic scent of the trees in leaf. More than anything, I sat beneath and against them and read about black poplars.

In his brilliant book, *Ghost Trees: Nature and People in a London Parish* (2018), Bob Gilbert points out that black poplars can be found on the darkened left-hand side of Constable's 'The Hay Wain': a large-scale oil – painted in 1821 and originally entitled 'Landscape: Noon' - that was once voted 'England's favourite painting'. 'The Hay Wain', in the popular imagination, is beloved for its detailed depiction of a sleepily pastoral scene on the River Stour between Suffolk and Essex. As a result, when Peter Kennard, in 1980, produced a photomontage in which three nuclear cruise missiles were startlingly transplanted into this bucolic landscape, he was deliberately subverting an iconic symbol of national conservatism. There is, however, another – perhaps more nuanced - reading of 'The Hay Wain'. As Gilbert explains, the background of Constable's painting is split in two: the 'black poplars stand on the left, their billowing leaf branches seeming not just to catch a shade but to gather a darkness towards them'; but 'the eye is drawn' to the right of the canvas and towards 'a pleasant, level, sunlit plain where barely visible farm labourers are cutting the hay'. According to Gilbert, 'there is a tension in the picture that represents something of the tension of the times': a tumultuous period for many rural communities as the introduction of threshing machines led to mass unemployment and significant social unrest. In this interpretation, the black poplars 'radiate storminess, not just in their colour but also in their shape'.

RESISTANCE

I thought about Constable's painting hanging in the rarefied, temperature-controlled space of the National Gallery on Trafalgar Square as, at the start of what was going to be another alarmingly hot day, I sat in St John's Gardens beneath the black poplars. I thought about how, through the vital labour of organisations such as City of Trees and the National Trust, a sense of hope is being offered *through* Manchester's arboreal history. I put Gilbert's book in my bag and, as I headed back into town, I dreamt of Deansgate and St Peter's Square, Portland Street and Piccadilly, as forests of the future. As I walked, I imagined a city centre in which you won't have to look quite so hard to find the trees.

Great Northern Diver
MICHAEL SYMMONS ROBERTS

Mancunia at night looks like embers from above,
but hold the dive and it reassembles, cools,
coalesces into districts, flyovers, a motherboard,
now stadiums like unblinking eyes,
car lots set out as piano keys, parks with lake wounds,
counter-flow of arteries in red and white,
the bass clef curves of cul de sacs
in outlying estates, then factories with starting guns
of smoke that sting and make you squint,
now you can pick out individual cars, nags' heads
down in dark fields, glow of dressed shop windows,
drunks on their tightrope walk home,
black poplars' ragged tops, roof tiles, kerbstones,
air that drops from ice to cloud to everything a city
cooks at once until the road meets you
face-to-face, down and under, slower, denser
and the clay arrests you, holds you as a pulse for good,
so what keeps this city alive is you.

The Pier on Fire
SARAH HALL

In March of 1917, sometime between the hours of ten and eleven at night, a faulty fuse sparked on the western pier, inside its most majestic building. The little smoulder gathered strength and in the strong sea breeze it spun into a persistent glut of flame. Then the fire, suddenly very confident, spread to the ground-floor ceiling of the structure and lay upside down across its rafters. The great pavilion of the Taj Mahal went up in a blaze the likes of which the town had never seen before. The golden dome of the building shone in the darkness as reddish flames leaped upwards from the wooden strutting of the deck. Within twenty minutes the fire had created a bright Pharos of light to alert those not yet abed and to wake those who were. Cy pulled back the curtain of his window. He'd been reading when an undefined patch of light, out of keeping with the flare of the streetlamps on the promenade, caught his eye. His mother at her window saw wings of orange curving up the sides of the main dome, mimicking its shape, tormenting it with the authority to destroy it. Both ran to the front door, knocking awake their guests. An opportunistic buzz quickly went through Morecambe. It soon reached the back end of the town, those properties without a view of the fiery pavilion, through the slums of Moss Street and the train station, all were invited to the show.

The townsfolk and the first of the season's visitors made their way out of their houses and hotels and down to the beach, awed and hurriedly, as if late for the performance, though it looked in no danger of finishing before time. They came fully dressed or in nightgowns and slippers, rolling rags and winkie caps, caring nothing for appearance, drawn to the scene as if hypnotized, swaying quickly but thicky, like the frantic slowness towards the end of a strong dream. The tide was low, the entire mud beach stretching out for the spectators to take to like the apron of a stage. And take to it they did, thousands of people, standing close together on the sands, watching extraordinary light floating out above the bay. The wooden walkway to the pavilion had become a burning road above them, an almost biblical vision some said, and others passed that thought along.

Fire itself would have been incendiary beauty enough for one evening. But then, it snowed. First it snowed lightly, a flake or two on the heads of the bemused onlookers, like winter waving a handkerchief from a distant carriage of the train taking it away. Somebody close to Cy in the crowd cheered, presuming the snow would extinguish the blaze, as if one tear could put out the fire of a tormented heart! Then the wind turned, switched tracks, and brought with it an entire fast batch of plump snow, a blizzard in fact. Those in undergarments and long shirts shivered and reached for spouses and children for warmth, and some reached for convenient strangers. Those with rotting chests wheezed and couched but did not go inside. Reeda's consumptives benefited from her foresight and blessed her as she handed out a stack of woollen blankets. Cy found Morris Gibbs in the crowd, for his red hair seemed like a portion of fire itself in the light, and he pulled on his arm. They walked closer to the blaze, so close Cy could feel his face changing texture, crisping, broiling. Behind him Morris had hiked his jumper over his head for protection from the heat and was looking through the neck of it so the scope of his vision could have been no larger than that seen through a penny slot machine. The fire leaned slightly to the right, at an angle appropriate to the wind. The snow blew fast to the right, arced upwards, fell, was chaotic, then resumed its course. Cy looked up. Oh. The snow. The snow was on fire. How could that be? Though he understood that the two elements were seldom in cahoots, let alone conjoined. And yet it was so. Fire and ice. There above him. The brilliant snow moved like thousands of migrating, flaming birds across the sky, flocking, reforming, conflagrating. It was like meteors swarming and rushing on some swift and undisclosed passage, riding the rapids of the cosmos. Or like being spun with his eyes open in a circle on a clear night except that he was standing still and the sky was whirling of its own accord. It was like pieces of a mirror being smashed in the heavens, in a fury of narcissistic disappointment. He was ten years old and dizzy with amazement.

– Look at it. It's beautiful, Morris. It's beautiful.

– It is at that.

And the two boys stood watching the impossibility of the entire western portion of the sky alight with burning snowflakes. When the dome finally tumbled it did so without grace. It sucked into itself the way a drunk finally fives in to stupor and folds inwards to the floor. The noise of it crashing down one hundred feet to the shore below was equally ignominious, it was the uncontrolled groaning of something large and restricted becoming uncharacteristically mobile. Though the fall looked to be an implosion of sorts, an inverted tumble, at the end of its descent it altered shape to thrust outwards. The crowds on the beach gasped. A flush of warmth moved past them, as did a small tidal wave of sparks and fireworks.

By this point Cy's mother was looking for him. She had not liked the way in which the fire had leaped and streaked along the sand with the pavilion's collapse, chasing after the stray wood it was intent on devouring. The faces of those watching the show were orange and shadowy, even sicker guests looked momentarily healthy in the warm aura of the blaze. Those in the front row, closer to the volatile mass of cinder-spinning, roaring timber were only black silhouettes, and she could not see the one belonging to her boy. By the time she had reached the Bayview Hotel and checked that her guests did not need any calming spirits or rubs for their smoke-agitated chests, her son was already home, drinking milk in the kitchen with Morris Gibbs. His cheeks were blown read and his eyebrows were thinner than she remembered. And he had the look about him of a laudanum taker after a purchase. Lit up, let out and satisfied.

The next morning was Easter Sunday. Even for such a holy day the churches of the town were unusually packed for the morning services. Many had not felt at all comfortable with the previous night's events, and were comforted even less by the image of a burning pathway leading to a fiery temple which had been presented to them. It was interpreted by multiple citizens on a personal level as possibly being prophetic, an indication of what might be awaiting them upon their deathbeds. Caring little for damnation or days of reckoning, all the boys of the town went down to the wreckage of the pavilion to ferret around. It was now a huge pile of debris that the tide had been in and out over, extinguishing any residual smoulder. Some were climbing on the blackened heap, others rooting through the rubble looking for treasure, fake gold-leafing from the roof, tapestry from within the ballroom. After serving breakfast in the hotel Cy slipped out and went down to the beach. He walked about with his hands in his pockets, kicking bits of decking and bricks, tarnished tiles. The lads around him were excited by the proximity of destruction, by the fact that something formerly so grand and spectacular was now demolished. A strange exuberance and exhilaration roused them and they shoved each other around. Their behaviour reminded him of Reeda's comments about the present ugliness abroad that much of Europe was well and truly engaged in. She often said to him over the top of the morning paper that there was a certain pleasure for some people in violence. She said you could still hear it ringing in a few of the ones who came back from the war, and in those running the affair. Men especially suffered from this disposition, she informed him frankly and unapologetically. As if some were born hollow and there was a hole cut in their hearts that produced music when the breath of spite and madness was blown through them.

Cy looked up at the greyish March sky. Not a hint that it had once swum with flickering schooling light remained there. The fiery winter storm was gone. It seemed right that out of such beauty should come such awful devastation, he supposed, the things of the universe being equal and linked, like birth and death, his life for his father's. Fee Lung, the Chinese magician who played in the pavilion every Friday night, was standing by the desecrated spire of the dome, now half-buried in the sand, shaking his head. He looked over at Cy and smiled pristinely, solemnly.

– Yes, yes, all is gone.

Next to his polished feet, half hidden by spoiled wood, there appeared to be a stringed instrument of some kind, smallish, charred at the neck, perhaps a violin that had miraculously avoided being consumed by the flames. Cy pointed to it and Fee Lung stooped to retrieve the charmed item, bringing it out from under the wreckage like a rabbit from a black top hat. The Viennese Orchestra had been booked to play in the Taj Mahal that very evening.

Beauty and destruction, thought Cy, now there's a trick.

From the novel *Electric Michelangelo*

The Horses
TED HUGHES

I climbed through woods in the hour-before-dawn dark.
Evil air, a frost-making stillness,
Not a leaf, not a bird –
A world cast in frost. I came out above the wood

Where my breath left tortuous statues in the iron light.
But the valleys were draining the darkness

RESISTANCE

Till the moorline – blackening dregs of the brightening grey –
Halved the sky ahead. And I saw the horses:

Huge in the dense grey – ten together –
Megalith-still. They breathed, making no move,

with draped manes and tilted hind-hooves,
Making no sound.

I passed: not one snorted or jerked its head.
Grey silent fragments

Of a grey silent world.

I listened in emptiness on the moor-ridge.
The curlew's tear turned its edge on the silence.

Slowly detail leafed from the darkness. Then the sun
Orange, red, red erupted

Silently, and splitting to its core tore and flung cloud,
Shook the gulf open, showed blue,

And the big planets hanging -
I turned

Stumbling in the fever of a dream, down towards
The dark woods, from the kindling tops,

And came to the horses.
There, still they stood,
But now steaming and glistening under the flow of light,

Their draped stone manes, their tilted hind-hooves
Stirring under a thaw while all around them

The frost showed its fires. But still they made no sound.
Not one snorted or stamped,

Their hung heads patient as the horizons,
High over valleys in the red levelling rays –

In din of crowded streets, going among the years, the faces,
May I still meet my memory in so lonely a place

Between the streams and the red clouds, hearing the curlews,
Hearing the horizons endure.

Duplex: Horses
after Jericho Brown
RACHEL BURNS

Horse running wild through post code black spots
hooves ringing out through sink bin streets
echoing through the ginnel, the red brick streets
my last address I saw wild horses
my last address, horses, horses, horses
& small boys, dirt & neglect, burnt out cars
small boys climbing the wrecks of burnt out cars
small boys startled by the sound of police sirens
small boys throwing bricks; police sirens
the cracked pavements flooding with blue light
a car set on fire, sky flaming with orange light
until the heavens open, rain like a bullet shower
& the horses, horses, horses like an arrow shower
horses running wild through post code black spots.

'Spring Gentians'
MARK COCKER

As I head for Cow Green at dawn, with the sun at my back,
the whole landscape is cleanly engraved by low-angled soft light.
Below and immediately above Middleton-in-Teesdale is that

194

stock northern blend of cattle and sheep pasture segmented by drystone wall or stout wind-slanted thorn hedge. The River Tees flows by the town and at intervals bends close to the road as I climb west, all shallow blue shimmer and white-flecked stone. Then it is lost to view in the valley; the cattle fall away; so too the ash and the sycamores towering over the fields, while the lime-washed white cottages grow more distant from their neighbours. I pass the High Force Inn, where botanists have stayed since the 1840s, and just after the turning for Force Garth Quarry I ride out on to the upper reaches of the dale and the grandeur of it all seizes me.

Even as I absorb the panorama, a lapwing in full display blusters like a wind-slewed cloth just in front of the car, and even through the glass and engine drone I can pick out the ecstatic sweet ache of its song. A pair of pied wagtails flushes up from the road edge, and the cold dawn glow fringes all their feathers so that two birds look as if they had just been freshly minted from bright light.

But nothing equals the impact of the marsh marigolds. In the roadside fields, which weeks ago had been the pastel shades of snow-burnt grass, they are spread in such profusion that they embody the ideal of the colour yellow. I'm heading for Widdybank and Cow Green, but the flowers immediately unravel my programme. I fling the car door wide open. Within a minute the knees of my jeans are swollen with ground water (despite a plastic sheet I roll out to lie on), but there is also the joy of photography: forcing you to get on eye-level terms with flowers.

Our friend Polly Monroe (partner of Richard Mabey) calls the same species by their old Norfolk name – 'molly blobs' – which evokes the way that the stems and leaves of her local plants rise up with robust, water-filled, lily-like fleshiness. Here in Upper Teesdale, marsh marigolds are wind-sculpted creepers. I find a patch that has grown just high enough to meet my wide-angle lens, and behind their crisp detail is the blurred lustre of the yellow pool; beyond, a whitewashed gable end to a farm and, blurrier still, the Whin Sill plateaux of Cronkley and Widdybank Fells. The smothering of flowers reminds me of what has been lost with the destruction of 4 million acres of herb-rich meadow, of which this is such a singular, breathtaking example.

I have never seen its like before, and I a pitched into an elevated state of mind so that when I arrive, a few moments later, at a flower-lined trickle just by Langdon Beck it feels nothing to stop again. Weeks ago this very spot was a foam-flecked torrent, and the sound of angry water had been obliterated by the insane skitter of black plastic snagged in barbed wire.

Now I am straight across the brook and flat on my front before bird's-eye primroses. I saw the basal leaves last time – starlike rosettes of pale waxy green, prostrate to the ground – but here the plants are a spring song of exquisite colour. The petals are gently notched in their outer fringes so that a central yellow eye, formed by the cluster of pollen-bearing stamens, is encircled with five hearts of deepest pink. Almost without end they quiver in the breeze, and it is more than an hour before I align everything to my satisfaction: the blood pulse of my own hands, the detail of the flowers, a lull in the wind and then May sunshine coming and going between white cloud. As I lie to attend to this scarce resident of Upper Teesdale, I can listen to the sky songs of its most abundant bird neighbours – the lapwings and snipe, whose displays are fletched higher and higher by the morning's warmth and sunlight.

That hour with the primroses reflects how the whole day goes – a seven-mile distracted meander right around Widdybank Fell, which occupies me until seven in the evening, entirely alone, through scenes of overwhelming beauty punctuated with moments of absolute joy: the five-bar gates mottled white and grey and crusted along their upper beams by intricate gardens

of fruticose lichens; the weathered slabs of Whin Sill, so empa-
thetically curved to the human rear you would swear they were
hand-cut stone benches (yet the upper planes of the dolerite are
entirely smothered in a lichen cartography. My favourite, which I
photograph over and over and later select as screen saver for my
computer, is a Rothko-like blend of desert sand with islands of
black-flecked ginger or grey).

I have my lunch sitting on such a stone with the white rush
of Cauldron Snout boiling down beside me and my senses
immersed in its force-drenched music; and despite its power, a
dipper, nesting in the crag above where I sit, manages to pierce
the heart of all the water noise with song.

Around teatime a short-eared owl, wafting like some kind of
finned sea creature from the depths, performs a slow-savoured
display that makes it seem larger than it truly is. I notice as it
passes over the outcrops of sugar limestone, which are the
colour of an Aegean shore, how the whole of the owl's under-
wing acquires its own calcareous glow. Then it swims away with
the breeze and across the predominant rust-infused straw of
Widdybank's wider vegetation, and in direct sunshine the bird is
oat-white like setting steel.

This is all preparatory to the gentians. In a sense it has taken
more than 300 million years to create the conditions for this
flower. The decisive element is the Whin Sill itself, which began
as lava from deep within our planet's core around 295 million years ago. On its journey through the crust it met strata
of Carboniferous limestone, sand- and mudstones, which had
been laid down around 33 million years earlier when this part of
England lay near the equator.

The magma extruded through faults in the older sedimentary
rocks and, as it rose, so it cooked the adjacent limestone layers to
a coarse crystalline marble. When the latter weathers it acquires
the consistency of fine sand or, according to geologists, of white

sugar granules; hence the name: 'sugar limestone'. The surface outcrops of it are fond only on Cronkley and Widdybanks Fells, and it is these that in large measure give rise to the botanical significance of Upper Teesdale.

The special nature of the flora was noted by the late seventeenth century, when the pioneer botanist John Ray published records of shrubby cinquefoil, which grows in Upper Teesdale and in only one other English location, the Lake District. By the early nineteenth century botanists had found most of the famous Teesdale plants, including alpine bartsia, alpine distort, alpine cinquefoil, alpine meadowrue, alpine penny-cress, bearberry, bird's-eye primrose, bog orchid, hair sedge, hoary rock-rose, hoary whitlow grass, holly fern, another fern called kobresia, mountain avens, Scottish asphodel, sea plantain and three-flowered rush.

On paper the most special of all is a tiny tufted, glabrous perennial called Teesdale sandwort *Minuartia stricta*. Yet the five-millimetre flower is entirely insignificant. Were it not for the fact that the species grows on just two isolated patches here at Widdybank, and nowhere else closer to these islands than Norway, it would be hard to be aroused.

No so the gentians. And I find them eventually in good numbers. And I know, instantly, exactly what they are. Here's one. Quite soon, they surround me. I am routinely amused by the way in which a naturalist sets off with a long-brewed sense of longing for some rare organism – a bird or a flower – which one dreams to see; and then the ever-so-casual manner in which that anticipation confronts reality. There is no drum roll. No climax. Not even fumbling excitement. You simply pass quickly, efficiently almost, from one existential state to another.

With the gentians there may be no dramatic transformatory moment, but there is indubitably the life-lasting star-like beauty of them. It is not hard to see why they are the ultimate botanical symbol for Upper Teesdale. It is the colour. Of her own Californian gentians, the writer and pioneer feminist Mary Austin, a woman seldom lost for the extract word, could only pile up the one hue for added impact: 'blue-blue-eye-blue, perhaps'. One is not surprised to learn, she added, 'that they have tonic properties'.

It is a blue so much more striking than the sky, or the sea – as blue perhaps as the Earth when seen from outer space. The gentians are eyes of intense happiness in a brown and wind-troubled place. I drop to my knees to meet them.

Great Black-Backed Gull
PAUL FARLEY

The tide keeps bringing everything you need.
The tip is like a slowed down sea to gulls
who trawl behind the trucks or dip in strong
kinking glides above the ribbons and shreds
of dross, the spume and swell.
          Taken to see *Jaws*
at the ABC, the robot great white shark
made us jump, but later came the slower thought
of real great whites cruising the seas of the world
while I lay in bed. *What we are dealing with here*
is a perfect engine, an eating machine...

Now, a landfill lubber with binoculars,
I pick out great blacks from the smaller gulls
above the waste where, fathoms deep, the shark
still swims among the wreckage of who we were
forty summers ago. They're such powerful birds
and the tide keeps bringing everything they need.

Eagle Owl
Caroline Gilfillan

Bubo bubo hunches in her cage, bill
tight shut. Her eyes flame blood orange

but she can't see the dale to her left –
the fling of green dotted with plump trees,

or the narrow ribbon of a road stitched
to its hem, or the bare limestone ridge

shouldering the sky. Can't see the castle
to her right, battered by Cromwell's cannon

into a scoured shell. Her feet are dusted
in down. Her claws could snatch a fawn,

a cub, a snake, a vole in meadow grass –
but they won't. And she won't be waiting

for a male's staccato song to seduce her
to a shallow nest bowl scraped out of a cliff.

As I watch she launches her body – four kilos
clothed in feathers arranged into speckles,
splotches, vermiculation – upwards in a
a ten-foot flap from earth to skanky branch.

Her head pushes at the chicken wire roof.
In captivity she may live sixty years.

Windscale
NORMAN NICHOLSON

The toadstool towers infest the shore:
Stink-horns that propagate and spore
Wherever the wind blows.
Scafell looks down from the bracken band
And sees hell in a grain of sand,
And feels the canker itch between his toes.

This is a land where the dirt is clean
And poison pasture, quick and green,
And storm sky, bright and bare;
Where sewers flow with milk, and meat
is carved up for the fire to eat,
And children suffocate in God's fresh air.

Sellafield
CHARLIE GERE

On the day I visit, though clouds have built up, it is still a beautiful day, and the sun breaks out of the clouds to pick out the
mixture of sand and rock that make up the beach and to turn the
sea a luminous blue. From Seascale, I can already see the towers
of Sellafield. There is something strange about the juxtaposition
of the normality of the scene, with people walking dogs on the
beach. Yet, a few hundred metres up the coast there is a massive
accumulation of highly radioactive materials. There is a footpath
that runs right up the side of the complex, from which the trains
that carry nuclear waste can be seen. The tracks and the highly
protected gates which they go through to the plan remind me of
the perimeter in Tarkovsky's *Stalker*, through which the stalker

and his companions must enter the Zone. In an article in *The Guardian* in 2009, Building B30 at Sellafield was described by the deputy managing director of the site as 'the most hazardous industrial building complex in Europe'. He went on to describe Building B38 as 'the second most hazardous industrial building in Europe'. The article describes how in B30 'piles of old nuclear reactor parts and decaying fuel rods, much of them of unknown provenance and age, line the murky, radioactive waters of the cooling pond in the centre of B30. Down there, pieces of contaminated metal have dissolved into sludge that emits heavy and potentially lethal doses of radiation'.[1]

B38 is where the cladding and fuel were 'simply thrown' and 'left to disintegrate' during the Miners' Strike of 1972, when plants such as Sellafield were run at full stretch and it proved impossible to process all the waste. Meanwhile, Building B41 still stores the aluminium cladding for the uranium fuel rods that were burnt in 1957, while Building B29 is a 'huge covered cooling pond that once stretched between the heat stacks of Piles 1 and 2'. As the article puts it:

> *Nuclear waste was tipped in at the top of B41 once it was erected and then allowed to fall to the bottom. Later, when it was realised that pieces of aluminium and magnesium among this waste could catch fire and cause widespread contamination, inert argon gas had to be pumped in to smother potential blazes.*

Thus 'for the past 60 years, building B41 has remained in this state, its highly radioactive contents mingling and reacting with each other'.[2] It is for these reasons that Greenpeace describes Sellafield as a 'slow motion Chernobyl'.[3] A more recent report from 2015 in *The New Scientist* suggests that matters are no better now.

RESISTANCE

It must be said that nuclear power stations are much safer now. Recently, a colleague and I were given a 'writers' tour' around Heysham Nuclear Power Station, down the coast from Sellafield, just outside Morecambe. This visit offered a number of insights into nuclear power, one of which was that a nuclear power station is really little more than a massive kettle, and the sole purpose of the massive and potentially dangerous fission process at its heart is to millions of gallons of water to drive enormous turbines, which then turn a device that generates electricity based on the electromagnetic principles discovered by Michael Faraday in the 1830s. For all the mystique of nuclear power and the complexities of its operations, the basic idea is almost banally simple. It's exactly the same setup as a coal of water power station, with the proviso that, in this case, the power source is potentially incredibly dangerous. It is unsurprising therefore that the signage and, indeed, the whole interior environment of Heysham, evinced an obsessive concern with safety. From the moment a visitor approaches the site, he or she is confronted by endless signs informing anyone not aware of it that they are about the enter a controlled nuclear site, where specific laws and rules are in force. The United Kingdom has a specialist armed police service for guarding nuclear installations and nuclear materials in transit, the Civil Nuclear Constabulary, the motto of which is 'deter, defend, deny, recover'. Given understandable concerns about nuclear terrorism, the fact that the CNC is heavily armed is emphasised in any publicity. I felt perfectly safe in the station, despite being feet away from what is effectively a controlled nuclear explosion. The exterior of the station reminded me most strongly of the U.S.-Mexican border between San Diego and Tijuana which my daughter, sister and I had crossed a year or so earlier, with double sets of chain-linked fences, copious amounts of razor wire and heavily armed police. For my colleague, who had been a prison librarian, the interior of the station was exactly like a prison, particularly in relation to the various gates through which one might or might not be allowed to enter. We, of course, were massively restricted in terms of where we could go, and were only able to look at the reactors or the control room from special, glassed-in viewing platforms.

The only point at which this sense of safety was diminished was in relation to the trains taking the nuclear waste out of the station. As in Sellafield, the train line ran between chain-linked fences surmounted by razor wire. In the visitors' centre, we were shown a film of one of the metal containers in which the nuclear waste is stored for transportation being smashed into by a train, as a test. The train was almost entirely destroyed, while the container survived more or less intact, and now sits, slightly dented, outside one of the buildings at Heysham. The reassurance this was supposed to give was somewhat tempered by the knowledge that trains carrying nuclear waste in these containers were continually travelling from all over Britain to the one place where such waste can be stored until a proper, permanent solution to its storage can be devised, which is, of course, Sellafield. I once saw one of these trains pass as I sat in the Leighton Moss nature reserve near Silverdale at dusk. It was an eerie juxtaposition.

From *I Hate the Lake District*

Love Affair with Next Door's Birch
JANE BURN

when they came   two years ago
   to cut the neighbour's tree   I felt her pain
she was a tower   higher   than I ever knew a birch to be

a great mast   pinned   to a deck of grass   answering the rage
of westerly wind with   her own splintered songs
   it blew   it blew again   she stayed stood

they felled her partway   belted a chainsaw to her waist
cut her   down to size   I winced   at her halved length
   she had lost   her wavering heights   I got the gift

of amputated wood   stored her sideways   left her bones
   to be worried   in the mouth of each new month   yesterday
I took an axe   and split apart her limbs   saw her body

spalted   bloomed inside   with astonishing stains   today
I have used up many hours   to wear away the agony
   of the blade   soothed the rough skin   taken her remains

through all the sandpaper's grades   through the pleasure of
   working
her smooth   I have seen feathers and fjords   white rot angels
   intricate webs   zone line thaumaturgies   like she rotted

into her own beautiful world   like this is the map
   to her timber soul   like there is a message written here
like she is asking   *just hold me a moment and*   *look*

       This was the winning poem in the Future Places Prize 2022

Cresting the Hill
MARK CARSON

FOR *KIM MOORE*

There's a left-hand bend as we crest the hill
drop into second, 3000 revs
and another clichéd roadkill poem
bursts from the verge and one of the poets
dabs on the brakes, just in time,
and the other is thinking, *will she write it*
or shall I? Is there anything new
to be said about buzzards and flapping
or the sad little package gripped in its mouth,
I mean its beak. Well, is there?

Rain
BENJAMIN MYERS

In early November it begins to rain and it doesn't stop. Occasionally
it eases or abates, or sometimes shifts in tone or mood to evince
a false sense of optimism, before returning with renewed vigour.

There is more rain than there are adjectives to possibly
describe it.

Rain becomes the daily reality in a transaction between sky
and land over which we have no influence. Nature rears up to
pull us out of our internalised digital worlds and back into that
of the elemental.

Furious falls the rain like a snappy tantrum, a fit thrown by the
whims of time.

It is the force, the life source.

I watch it from my window, inching along the valley, a hodden-
grey scrim drawn close. At other times it falls in tall columns

like the old stone chimneys that rise, periscope-like, up above the trees, or it spits sideways, wet flecks flying like sparks from a farrier's furnace. I am out in it every day, exploring, exhausting the dog and observing the inflections, living in a permanent state of dampness.

It drills, it spears, it skewers. Niggles.

It touches, it caresses, it kisses.

Hisses.

The rain is hostile. Sometimes it is so ferocious it becomes comical – 'film-set rain', we call it – so insistent and pervasive as to be febrile. Sometimes it speaks, the sound of the rain becoming a shopping list: 'stamps wax pomegranate' it whispers in a dripping ear.

The showers sluice away the top layer of autumnal leaf loam of The Rock's floor, carving new ways through the routes of least resistance.

Winter groans on as flat as a school assembly Lord's Prayer and it feels as if it is raining in my mind, my subconscious soaked, and even in dreams I see deluges of cocoa-coloured water.

And the River Calder rises.

A local dog goes missing. It is a tan-brown terrier cross, female, about the same age as Cliff, spooked by the fireworks that whip-crack down the stone barrel of the valley without warning for weeks on end, a little earlier each year, the luminous paroxysms reflected in the eyes of trembling fox cubs born last spring, and sending the deer of The Rock into bounding frenzies over crag and wire in search of escape.

The squirrels scarper to the canopy, and another distant uni-dentifiable animal screams a fearful alarm.

But even as they run or burrow or scatter from their crag-edge eyries, the wild creatures still find themselves pursued by booms and whistles and blood-red flashes, the sound of these cheap Chinese pyrotechnics bouncing off The Rock below, the gritstones reflecting rather than absorbing, and echoing back a mindless mortar attack on the nerve centres of all animals.

The missing dog sparks a Facebook campaign, and I coax Cliff from his cellar dwelling to spend three days wandering Scout Rock Woods as I shout 'Pickle!' in an attempt to draw out a dog whose picture I have only seen online, yet feel somehow compelled to help find, as I routinely follow the progress of the scores of similarly sentimental animal lovers. I know no one else will think to search these woods. I doubt anyone else would dare.

For several days the search becomes an all-consuming, ever-shifting narrative whose conclusion I must know. After several days of terrible rain Pickle is found, shaken and half starved, but otherwise well. One sighting suggests we came within 100 yards of each other, my calls and whistles perhaps muted by the roar of the rain, or the missing dog merely looking on from a warm corner as I stumble and slip past it through the endless fucking mud.

And still the rain falls. It puddles and pools. Sits.

New streams emerge and stay for weeks.

The sky becomes a long and boring story without an ending. It just goes on and on, dispersing its wares, filling every nook and fissure, every trench and gulch, every divot, cleft and hollow.

It scours old rock and finds whorls there – grainy geological fingerprints free of the gelatinous algae that coats everything during the shorter days. It runs beneath our street, as ancient subterranean waterways are flooded back to life, and the old stone-lined springs and troughs where inhabitants drew their supply, and at which thirsty, steaming horses once lapped, are first refreshed and then overflow.

The woods below The Rock become a dank and desolate church of persistent dripping and leafless branches stripped bare, and the washed-away mud banks send me slipping arse-about-tit with increased regularity, thudding onto my shoulder one day, landing on my wrist the next.

Reanimated by the rain, the old town tip further reveals another trove of grubby treasures, as more junked pieces of the past poke through, including a very large moss-covered bone, one scorched-looking end the size of my fist. Species unknown.

Feeling like a meddling academic protagonist in a M. R. James ghost story, I carefully prise the jaundice-coloured bone from the soil and clan it with some dead leaves, then place it next to a glove for scale – it is twice the length of the glove and as wide as my wrist.

Another day during the same unbroken downpour I come across an old stone market inscribed 'PUBLIC FOOTPATH', with arrows pointing in either direction. The footpath has not been public for a long time, and season upon season of gorse and bramble and soil and leaves have grown over it, rotting down to the humus that is spread thick over the gritstone foundation. The rain has revealed this mid-twentieth-century marker to me, raising it up, another relic of The Rock's unending story told piecemeal through hints, teases and suggestions.

The rain grows oppressive and the valley shrinks to the narrowness of a birth canal. The sun is a foreign country, a nostalgic memory. The hills sigh. Everything folds in on itself like a sleeping dog.

And I find I am exhausted from too many writing projects, the worry of trying to exist on a four-figure annual income, never quite knowing what I will earn from week to week, and continually adjusting my lifestyle and diet accordingly. My muscles ache. My marrow feels damp.

The daily explorations of The Rock provide a distraction: 'I cannot stay in my chamber for a single day without acquiring some rust,' wrote America's hermetic crown price of woodland wandering, Henry David Thoreau in his 1862 essay 'Walking'. Knowing that I rarely feel worse at the end of a perambulation, I keep trudging the undergrowth. 'Roads are made for horses and men of business,' Thoreau also noted. 'I do not travel in them much because I am not in a hurry.'

Salvation from valley fever comes by way of a timely opportunity: a writing residency on Hadrian's Wall in Northumberland. Days later I'm driving through the worst storms in years before finding myself stuck in mud, in a raging wood where yards before me I see a tree being torn from the soil with an almighty splintering sound. I see snapped fences and a rising river. Back roads disappearing. Abandoning my car, I complete the final stage of my journey by foot in a total darkness and awake the next morning to acre upon acre of flooded fields shimmering in the metallic morning sun. From the back door I can make out in the far distance the line of the ancient Whin Sill banks, a natural tabular layer created by flows of lava 300 million years ago upon which Hadrian's Wall was built.

My stay continues in a similar fashion: short, drenched days exploring Hadrian's Wall, and long nights by the fire. I take a lot of field notes, drink a lot of Yespresso. I talk to no one but the wind and the ghosts of shivering, homesick Romans.

From *Under the Rock*

The Rose Experts
KATE DAVIS

This is a poor town and we who live here
are poor people. Still, we know all about
roses, rejoice in their existence.
Our TV screens are bright with adverts
for laundry liquid spilling slowly

from bottles gorgeous with roses;
our hoardings bloom sweetly with roses;
our museums keep rose paintings safe
in gloomy rooms; our curtains and clothes
are alive with roses, roses, roses!
We move through the detail
of our days grateful for roses in our lives.

There are parts of town where we poor
don't go; places set aside where important
business is done on our behalf by those
better suited than us. We see the high walls
and armed guards as we go about our work.
A few amongst us claim they've climbed
those walls, seen "real roses" growing
from the earth. They urge us to rise up,
seize the land, insist we could grow roses
ourselves. Of course, we ignore such
crazy talk; after all, don't we already know
all there is to know about roses.

Helks
MIKE BARLOW

The knock-kneed stile keels sideways
in the sodden ground, the path beyond
blocked by a fallen birch, many-legged
silhouette grazing on sunlight. You have to duck
and twist to get through and as you do
bright shafts drop from the horizon –
the brow of a field a hundred yards away.

This is a short-cut to the old road down
from the moor. It comes out where the beck

has undercut, flakes of cracked tarmac
peeled away above the landslide, plastic barriers
tumbled into the froth. Concrete slabs
block the way for traffic but a tractor
is all you need to nudge them aside enough
to let a quad bike through. This land still works
and those who mind it find a way, as always.

Just as the land itself always finds a way
to encroach on our encroachments, raw landslips
greening with new growth – hazel, whin, bramble,
blowdowns twisting fences, rushes crowding pasture
and from the fell road the whole kaleidoscope
shimmering after a downpour so it seems
it's not the land being farmed but the light.

Seeking Gods
PO YARWOOD

It always faces you, though it's never quite in the same place twice,
there's an inexplicable shift of position, walk slowly by and it turns
towards you realigning a greeting, and in return you nod.

The trunk is smooth belly-skin, secretly swelling,
the buttock-curve tender, the neck elongated,
arms are high, upper branches jubilant.

Its surface is pure androgyny, labial and phallic,
head, trunk, arms, groin beckon you to touch.
Lean in, place your forehead against the trunk,

heal me, you say, but this tree won't be hugged.
Put your arms around it and there's a recoil you don't expect,
a stiffening, a withdrawal, its own beautiful thing.

Weather Report, 3 March 2022
LAURENCE ROSE

*Low, East Rockall, one thousand and two, losing its identity by 0600
tomorrow; new low expected South-east England, one thousand and
fifteen by same time.*

*....Humber, Thames, Dover, Wight: south-east becoming cyclonic
later in Wight, three to five, occasional rain, moderate or good, occasionally poor. Portland, Plymouth, Biscay: cyclonic four or f...*

A week ago I stood at the waters' edge looking north across the
Humber. In the sunshine that had followed three storms, the
Humber's palette was three horizontal bands of Kodachromatic
intensity: corn-gold reeds, ultramarine water, electric sky.
Between the water and the sky was a thread of multicoloured
stippling formed by the edge of what was once the home-
land of the Parisi, then the Anglian kingdom of Deira, later
Northumbria, later still The East Riding of Yorkshire, then
Humberside, then and again The East Riding of Yorkshire: the
south of the North.

Today I remained at the same waters' edge, but 113 miles
upstream, two field-widths from home. Less than a mile farther upstream is the source. Well, *a* source: a modest headwater
unworthy of a remembered name. All the names it will acquire
between here and the North Sea will be granted by marriage,
when it conflows with four streams and four rivers in turn, each
bringing its own waters and its own name until the last, the Ouse,
concedes to the Humber, whose name belongs to the estuary
alone, formed when the waters of the Ouse of the North meet
the waters of the Trent of the middle counties.

There has been no sun and little colour here. Nor rain; at least
not from the heavens, but a constant deliquescence of saturated
air precipitated from winter twigs and holly leaves and conjured

an earthly rain that pattered into the stream. More so than the meagre trickle that rises from the hillside 1220 river-yards to the east, it was the air itself, and the tree-rain catalysed by millions of cold unformed leaves, that was the principal source of the Ouse headwaters this day.

Last month Storms Dudley, Eunice and Franklin brought down a rot-infused oak bough from one tree, and several smaller branches from an ash. I sawed a short section of the oak and another of a small, bark-naked ash branch and placed them side-by-side on a dry-stone wall. Both were as dead as wood-flesh ever can be, and as alive as long-dead wood always is: as alive as the soil or a city, as vivacious, as coloured and as fragrant. Each sported a strange excrescence, like convoluted bundles of rubberised cloth: black on the oak, golden-orange on the ash. Fungi for sure, but not any of the handful I can name. Except, that I had a vague recall that there is a fungus called witches' butter, and I guessed that the orange one may be that. It isn't, but the black one is - *Exidia glandulosa*. Creased and folded and as complex as a brain, it yielded to the touch and rebounded like gelatine. Two days later it had grown to twice the size, swollen like a contorted bellows. During the week between then and today, it has oscillated between these flaccid and tumescent states, like a slow-breathing lung.

The other is *Tremella mesenterica* – yellow brain fungus. Whereas the witches' butter is growing on the rough, convex surface of the oak's bark, the yellow brain seems to exude from the ripped end of the ash. They share the same contorted pattern of growth, with the yellow brain more lobed, like a pile of dried apricots. They also share the tendency to shrink and swell - even more so in *Tremella*, which expands at least five times in volume - and, side by side, they do so in imperceptible unison. They are natural hygrometers, responding to the humidity in the air around them; they have been at maximum distension today.

RESISTANCE

The gloom has not drained these fields of bird song entirely. At this northerly latitude, the daily increments of extended light, however veiled, are perceptible to birds, whose sensitivity to the smallest change in daylength enables them to sense the coming of spring well before time.

The special character of the spring in Britain is due to its lying at a more northerly position than its human inhabitants appreciate. I live in Yorkshire at 53°35'N. Follow today's weather along that line and, anywhere else, you'll find winter's hold unslackened. From the Humber you cross the North Sea to reach Germany west of Hamburg, where the temperature is a few degrees lower than here. Farther east, northern Poland is a little colder still; everywhere east of there, in Belarus and Russia the land has been ice-locked for weeks. Even at the edge of the Pacific, at Kamchatka, it has been minus 8°C today. The line crosses the northern Pacific to reach Unalaska Island, Alaska. Here, ocean influences raise the winter averages, to a few degrees below what we experience in West Yorkshire. Continuing along the line, this relative balm is extremely short-lived. After crossing Graham Island and the low-lying western edge of the Canadian province of British Columbia the continental influence holds sway once more: Edmonton, Alberta is minus nine. The ice grip tightens across Saskatchewan, Ontario and Quebec to Churchill Falls in Labrador where todays' high is -14°C. You need to arrive at the Atlantic Ocean at North River to return to freezing point.

Only once back across the Atlantic, completing our circumnavigation with landfall at the Renvyle peninsula, County Galway, separated from home by a final 364 miles comprising a slice of Ireland, the Irish Sea and Lancashire, do we experience conditions as clement as those we left behind. For it is the ocean itself, some of whose waters bring with them what remains of the tropical warmth of their origin in the Gulf of Mexico, that creates the British winter and sets up the slow onset of spring.

Birdsong is the defining soundtrack to spring, but here in Britain one doesn't have to wait until the birds return from Africa to hear it. There are many birds who never leave to fly south, because here they find the winter is liveable enough. Those that do depart are replaced by refugees from the east and north, land birds to exploit an abundance of berries and beech-mast, and water birds from the tundra who expect to find lakes and estuaries free of ice. If the beech crop fails one year, the bramblings continue until they reach southern France or Spain. Redwings and fieldfares roam widely in poor berry years. They are not bound to a particular location as they would be in the nesting season. They can strip a valley or a county or a country of its fruit and then move to the next. For such birds, spring is less a season, more a place. No matter that a local robin may already be gathering moss for her nest by now; for these northern and eastern immigrants, it is winter here as long as it is winter there.

It is all finely-tuned. Freedom to roam in search of food is a two-edged sword: there must be enough at end of the search to replenish drained reserves of energy, then enough more to cover the greater mileage home through lands already depleted. For some birds, there is no such freedom anyway. Waders and waterfowl come to the estuary that joins my stream to the North Sea, the Humber, in their hundreds of thousands because it is often the closest ice-free wetland to the land they left behind at the start of the autumn. But some of those birds have suddenly declined in number. So much so, that the dunlins that nest on the tundra, and the goldeneye who spend the summer on the forest lakes of the taiga have been marked 'Red' in the classification of UK Birds of Conservation Concern. It is a strange new phenomenon: short-stopping. Whether or not they are declining overall, the numbers reaching the UK have plummeted because as the planet heats, more wetlands and estuaries remain ice-free to the east and north of here, in the Baltic. Some birds no longer need to travel to Britain to find a typically British winter.

Despite our being almost equidistant from the east and west coasts (slightly west of half-way), the sound of pink-footed geese is as likely as not to colour the early spring chorus here, for the minute or two that it takes for them, and their calls, to pass overhead in arrowhead skeins a few dozen to a few hundred strong. Each goose calls infrequently during that time; the smallest flocks make a sound I liken to a squeaky pub sign swinging in the breeze. The same sound multiplied among the largest groups is like a distant kennels inhabited by dozens of members of the same small, yappy breed of dog. We are directly beneath the flight-path between the Lincolnshire coast and the Ribble Estuary. Exactly when they choose to use it, and in which direction, is a complicated matter.

In 1638 Gísli Oddsson, the Bishop of Skálholt in southern Iceland, observed that 'throughout the winter they do not dwell amongst us and are not even observed. In springtime they occupy the island in an almost countless number. It is commonly said that every year in autumn, they make for the neighbouring countries of England, Ireland and Scotland.' Hundreds of thousands arrive in Aberdeenshire and north-east Scotland in September. Some push on farther south, overland to north-west England. A proportion of these cross over eastward later in the autumn, to join the great flocks that had travelled into Lincolnshire and Norfolk direct from Scotland. Then, in late winter, there is a noticeable northward shift as birds begin making their way back to Scotland in stages, in response to grass growth. They will remain for the rest of the winter, until ready for the long, non-stop over-sea flight to Iceland, when Iceland is ready for them.

So in an average year, skeins would cross our sky heading south east in October and November, and north west in January and February. But these days an average year is as rare as an average family. The geese seem to respond freely to conditions as they find them. A cold snap in the east early in the autumn may see the traditional pattern reverse, to reverse again when conditions allow. Short-stopping is not for them; between their breeding and wintering areas, there is only ocean.

I have lived in Yorkshire for twenty-three springs and write this on the eve of my twenty-fourth. In our first spring I was told, categorically, that swallows arrive here on the twenty-sixth of April. My neighbour had gone outside to look for them on that date, and as I stood alongside him, sure enough, there was a male, singing as he darted across our line of sight and jinking left towards the barns. So fixed was this idea that the birds were faithful to their calendar that he had not looked for them until now. Had he done, he would have seen the one that arrived twelve days earlier, and its mate the next day, and the pair of them every day thereafter. They have been arriving earlier each year since, with the odd break in the pattern when a cold spell might hold them over the continent for a while. I await them over the coming weeks, wondering if they will be here before the end of March, or at least earlier than the current record of 3rd April. Or at all.

It is an expectant month, March. It is impossible not to worry. In two decades the voice of the cuckoo has been extinguished here, and swallows seem to be on the same trajectory. At first sight, they appear to have adapted their behaviour in a rapid response to the changing climate, to take advantage of the summer flush of insects that also starts earlier each year. If there were such a thing as an average year, then the body clocks of birds and insects might, on average, remain synchronised. The occasional drought, deluge or summer frost might insert the odd poor year between years of recovery. But it is not like that any more. The light-and-temperature triggers that determine when leaves un-bud are not the same as those that un-egg the caterpillar or call upon mayflies to un-river. The old stability had 11,000 years of the post-Ice Age in which to settle. Instability will be the new stability.

Kneeling African: Dunham Massey
Maxwell Ayamba

On a field trip a few years back I visited the statue of the kneeling Black man at Dunham Massey Hall, near Altrincham, which depicts an African man holding a sundial. Formerly the home of the Earl of Warrington, Dunham Massey is now in the hands of the National Trust. The sundial recently caused controversy because it used to sit in the most prominent position imaginable at Dunham Massey, right outside the front door. The figure is considered a survivor of what was then a popular motif in eighteenth-century art. A notice next to it read: "This sundial is in the style of one commissioned by King William III. It represents Africa, one of four continents known at the time. The figure depicts a Moor, not a slave, and he has knelt here since before 1750."

The 'Blackamoor' was removed and put into storage just four days after the removal of Edward Colston's statue in Bristol in June 2020; the National Trust had to seek retrospective planning permission for this action.

An article in *The Mirror* quoted a spokeswoman from the National Trust, who said: 'The statue has caused upset and distress because of the way it depicts a Black person and because of its prominence at the front of the house. We don't want to censor or deny the way colonial histories are woven into the fabric of our buildings." However, the Trust did not then proceed to explain why this historical knowledge has in the past been denied and refuted, contributing to the structural and institutional forms of racism upon which Black people face daily in British society.

More recently, the Trust said that they are reviewing each example of kneeling black figures on a case-by-case basis. "As a conservation organisation, we believe the physical legacies of our collective histories, including buildings and objects, can serve society by giving evidence and helping us learn and understand the past. Removal can take away the opportunity to understand what's gone before, now and for future generations. It's vital that where statues are in place, they genuinely help us learn about and understand the past. We're working with partners to ensure these are fully explored and interpreted."

There are further examples of 'Blackamoor' figures on display at other stately homes and National Trust properties across the UK. The Blackamoor figure at Wentworth, South Yorkshire, for example, is now accompanied by this updated notice: "Sir Thomas Wentworth helped to negotiate the Treaty of Utrecht in 1713. This international treaty confirmed Britain as the most important commercial power in Europe. It included a lucrative monopoly over the Atlantic slave trade. Wentworth represented this in his house and gardens, including the statue of a kneeling African man supporting a sundial that now stands in the conservatory. Like many of his contemporaries, Wentworth made a great deal of money from the sale and labour of enslaved Africans. This human misery helped pay for the house and gardens he built."

Many Black people are still unaware of this history. Seeing the sundial of the kneeling Black man on my visit to Dunham Massey made me reflect on the kind of inhumane treatment that my Black ancestors might have experienced. I question whether by contextualising the statue, the National Trust had done enough to raise public awareness of this past history.

Subsequently, though, the signage on the plinth of the removed figure was changed to the following: "A sundial supported by the figure of a kneeling African man once stood in this location. In 2020 we temporarily removed the sundial to protect it from harm after complaints about the man's subjugated pose. We are taking time to review how to sensitively redisplay and interpret this historic object. We are working closely with different people and organisations including Trafford Council and Historic England on the next chapter of the statue's history."

RESISTANCE

The narrative about the historical presence of Black people and how they are depicted in Britain has not changed enough. The example of the sundial being displayed, hidden, and possibly displayed again indicates the contentious place of Black people in the history of the British countryside. On the other hand, the kneeling Black man figure now shines a light on the histories of empire and colonialism. That alone is a revelation of the place of Black people in the countryside, and our relationship to the legacy of British colonialism and slavery.

Salvage job, he said, this hedge of yours
JANE ROUTH

When I get back with the tea,
    old rails and thorns are heaped in the field,
        three liggers already laid low on the cop.

He's tender with it, the axe
    working behind the bark with his right,
        his left hand coaxing a stem till it creaks,

the lightest of taps, another inch of caress,
    a small groan and the stiff old thornbush
    compliant as when it was a whip.

He looks at the knot of roots and thick stems
    and says strange thing is, he can hear
        his Old Man telling him which to take out,

how to dig round a bole
    and swivel the stock
        on the hold of a single good root

NORTH COUNTRY

– he wouldn't have thought
    he'd been listening, his mind as a lad
        always on Fridays and the Floral Hall.

When I get back with more stakes,
    he says *It's come back to me now,*
        you'll like this, it's a geb

so I write in my pocket book *geb (hard G)*
    and sit drawing the crook-shape
        he cut from an angle of trunk and drove into the cop

to clamp springy lengths inwards and down –
    there being no word I can think of
        to explain what it does.

Soon be cowing-up time, I say,
    giving him back the word on my previous page
        – a word, it says not just (underlined) about milking

but straw for the calves,
    a handful of grain for the hens,
        gathering in tools at the end of a day –

Looks fine to me,
    but the Old Man's having a field day today,
        out of his grave again and elbowing between us

to stab at the hedge with the stem of his pipe
    telling us – like they say he always did
        when it came to judging competitions –

No good going by how it looks, fresh laid;
    what it's like come July
        is what counts.

Grange-Over-Sands: 2027
MAGGIE REED

In the second week the Bay search and rescue team
locates the clock tower. As the waters settled
to the new high tide, the promenade
became an underwater playground
for flukes, crabs and shrimp.
The abandoned lido has never been so full;
sea water two meters above the parapets,
graffiti collaged with seaweed.

The divers go in on the third week.
Those who'd stayed on long swept away;
no bodies but bottles floating in lines
from the Commodore Hotel. Beer pipes rinsed,
packets of crisps still in their boxes salvaged.
A huddle of walking boots launched from Lancaster Shoes,
washed up in the church porch alongside a sodden sock.
Butterfingers' freezer is still on the blink.

The post office counter, swept clean of forms,
an echo of *next please,* but there is no queue.
The tides subsided, rooftops shone bright,
stripped of their mosses, choked chimneys
belch trapped air. The roundabout by the Crown
was the first road to appear, the following Thursday
you reached the station in your wellington boots.
The ornamental pond was more or less intact

On the morning of the fifth we see the edge of town,
black iron railings rimming the tide,
saw that the river had changed its path,
flowed close to the Prom over the salt marsh,

so boats could return bringing rescuers, workers;
no need for the Queen's Guide to the Sands.[1]

The pool is now full, perfect for swimming.
It took a tsunami, but we got our lido back.

White on Black: The Ongoing Problematic Narrative of ★★★★★'s Grave
KAREN LLOYD

On the southern edge of Morecambe Bay in North-west England, Sunderland Point is one of those places within striking distance of society – housing estates, caravan parks and a nuclear power station – that still feels far from the centre of things. I'd first written about the grave of the African who was buried here in 2013 in my book *The Gathering Tide*. I'd set off to find it one January morning. The tide was far out, rendering the sands a purplish red under heavy grey clouds. Walking towards the point where the River Lune meets the waters of the tidal estuary, redshanks had lifted from the saltmarsh uttering unnerving, tremulous calls. In those days the grave was indicated by a weather-beaten signpost, accessed by a low stile and situated in a small enclosure bounded by barbed wire and drystone walls. In the corner of the site was a hawthorn, gorse bushes, a robin singing.

Dating to the year 1736, the grave is an unostentatious affair; a grey flagstone set flat into the grass with a poem inscribed in a brass plate and at its head, a simple wooden cross. I'd written how the grave has a life of its own, noting the kinds of twenty-first-century grave goods that people leave in an ever-renewing cycle of objects. Then, there'd been a doggy key ring, a bangle, a wooden antelope, a tiny angel, a rusted metal Christmas tree and scattered around the grave various decorated beach pebbles painted with the words 'We love you Sambo,' along with other messages of love. Through these diverse objects there arises a movement towards atonement – not only for the death of this Black individual – but for nearby Lancaster city's wider involvement in the slave trade.

After the burial the grave remained unmarked for some sixty years, until a local priest commemorated it in verse and paid for the poem's installation to be appended to the slab.

> *Here lies poor Samboo*
> *a faithful Negro*
> *Who*
> *(Attending his master from the West Indies)*
> *Died on his Arrival at Sunderland*
> *Full sixty Years the angry Winter's Wave*
> *Has thundering dashed this bleak and barren Shore*
> *Since Sambo's head laid in this lonely Grave*
> *Lie still and ne'er will hear their turmoil more.*
> *Full many a Sand-bird chirps up on the Sod,*
> *And many Moonlight Elfin round him trips*
> *Full many of Summer's Sunbeam warms the Clod*
> *And many a teeming Cloud upon him drips.*
> *But still he sleeps – till the awakening Sounds,*
> *Of the Archangels Trump new Life impart,*
> *Then the GREAT JUDGE his Approbation founds,*
> *Not on Man's COLOR but his WORTH OF HEART*

Mawkish doggerel it may be, but here at least an individual appears to be grappling with the injustices of trafficking in the later part of the eighteenth century, a time when the anti-slavery movement was growing. It marks the first attempt to disrupt the grave's troubling history.

From the seventeenth century, Lancaster's entrepreneurs developed a particular model of slave ship, one whose shallow draught enabled slave traders to journey far into Africa's interior, navigating rivers such as the Gambia into modern-day Liberia and the Ivory Coast. The kinds of gewgaws traded for human lives included bracelets, beads, brass bells, mirrors, clothing, hats and pans. Lancaster became the fourth most prolific slaving city in the UK,[1] trafficking around 30,000 individuals. Half a mile from the grave the village of Sunderland was built as an 'outport' for the loading and offloading of cargo in the decades before wharfs were constructed upriver in the city itself.

Around 1736 a ship arrived at Sunderland. As the cargo was offloaded (likely to have included mahogany, sugar, dyes, rice, spices, coffee, rum and cotton from the Caribbean and the Americas), the story goes that a Black male was put, or, as was reported in the *Lonsdale Magazine* a century later, 'ran' ashore.[2]

The article asserts that this person was housed at the inn on full wages, but then, *after some time, supposing himself deserted by his master and being unable to speak English, he had fallen 'into a complete state of stupefaction.' Such was this strength of feeling that the man took himself into the loft of the village brewhouse where, stretching out on the bare boards, he refused all sustenance. He continued in this state only a few days, when death terminated the sufferings of poor Samboo.*

The account follows the removal of the body to a dell in a rabbit warren across the fields and close to the edge of the bay where the body was interred without coffin or bier. Thus begins the appropriation of a story whose ramifications endure to this day.

Perhaps we can excuse, or at least begin to understand, this kind of representation of events. But who knows; the *Lonsdale Magazine* account could very possibly be just a made-up story. Whatever the case, its effect is to imply that the individual had been responsible for their own death, or even, that they had chosen to die.

RESISTANCE

Re-reading my earlier representation of events, I was troubled by the certainty with which I'd written that this person had been a servant, a cabin boy or a personal assistant. Here I was, stamping my own authority on the grave. Now my own sense of culpability has inspired the need to metaphorically revisit the grave and its surroundings, and to consider what they communicate to me in 2022.

I try to imagine him as a person, this mother's son, this boy, this beloved, this husband, this father. This body of so much economic value. Where had he been born? What kind of community had he come from? Had he cried much as a baby? Had he and his whole family endured the ordeal of being trafficked together? Or ripped apart. What height? What build? Had he the ability to stand upright in the face of abuse? What kinds of horrors had he been witness or subjected to? Indeed, what age was he? The term 'boy' of course, was just another weapon in the slavery's arsenal of de-individuation.

Then again, there was also the nagging doubt, aided by a woman I once met in the village of Sunderland who questioned whether indeed a body had been buried. And short of a full-blown archaeological dig, we can never know for sure. So, yes, the story could be apocryphal, something concocted by sailors and villagers to keep themselves amused on long winter nights. There's a big part of me who wants to subscribe to this version, this lack of a body; story-making as a method way of trying to understand something taking place far away and out of sight. If a man or a youth had existed, he may well have been powerless to disrupt the narrative of his own destiny. And we should not forget that it is the same powerlessness which pertains amongst trafficked people today; even those who pay to be trafficked, like the twenty-four Chinese whose families borrowed significant sums to send them to the UK, and who had drowned on the bay in the cockling disaster in 2004.

I revisited the grave in the summer of 2014. A piece of slate had been secured to it, obscuring most of the small cross itself. The slate had been inscribed with the words to 'Amazing Grace' in meticulous white lettering. Below this the writer continued, 'I come to this peaceful and beautiful place to give thanks and enjoy this charming and delightful special burial ground.'

Now, the writer no doubt made and fastened the sign to the cross with the best of intentions, yet it was deeply troubling. The slate dominated the view of the grave, an emplacement that resonated with the systematic imposition of chapels and oratories on Pagan sites, or the sites of alternate religions, under the rise of Christianity. Then there's the issue of the imposition of a Christian prayer when nothing can be known of the religious inclinations or practices of the deceased. Most troubling of all was the use of that word, 'charming.' The dictionary tells me that *charming* pertains to 'something very pleasant or attractive, such as a charming country cottage.' I don't understand in what kinds of ways such a word can be applied to the grave of an individual who may or may not have existed, but if he had, may have been trafficked, beaten, raped (the 'cabin boy'; the personal assistant) and who had almost definitely been put ashore because of suffering some horrible contagious disease.

By now I'm on the horns of a dilemma. Do I remove the slate and place it to the side along with the rest of the offerings, which would be respectful (perhaps) to the writer but also show greater respect to the deceased? There was no one in sight, so why not? In the event, I did not. To this day I don't know why. At the time of writing, some seven years later, the slate, the prayer, along with that troubling word, remain firmly in place.

In Lancaster Maritime Museum a poem expresses the dilemma of the Quakers who, amongst the city's merchant class, perpetuated the invidious trade in human lives.

RESISTANCE

I own I am saddened by the purchase of slaves
And fear those who buy them and sell them as knaves
What I hear of their hardship, their torture and groans
Is almost enough to draw pity from stones.
I pity them greatly but I must be mum,
For how could we do without sugar and rum?

There are many ways we can talk about how best to honour and represent the grave. We can tell ourselves that this unknown individual's death was inevitable because he could not speak our language/was abandoned/died of a broken heart/died of stupefaction/of refusing sustenance/of being stretched out on wooden floorboards. Anything; anything at all, as long as we don't also tell ourselves that he died because of the project of Colonialism.

A few years ago I took friends of mine from the south for a walk at Sunderland Point. We'd taken the binoculars to see what birds might be about, but after rounding the point from the river and finding nothing much doing, I suggested we walk the short distance to the grave. Chatting away, eventually I realised we'd walked past the place where the grave should have been. I was puzzled, and not a little embarrassed by my inability (me, the local!) to locate it. Where was the signpost? The stile? Something was being constructed, though I couldn't tell what, and so eventually we turned and walked back the way we'd come.

Shortly afterwards a local television item alerted me to a commission by a local tourism development agency at Sunderland Point. My sensitivity radar went into hyperdrive. There'd been no mention of Sambo's grave in the news item. Was it possible the installation had been built adjacent to the grave?

I went to investigate. A new sea-defence wall had been constructed. No doubt this was necessary to protect the grave from storm damage under climate chaos, but the wall felt like an ugly, if practical, intrusion. And there was something else. A new gate at the side led into a new enclosure just north of the grave. A broad wheelchair-accessible path had been constructed, which was strange, as there's no wheelchair access along the headland or to and from the village. Between the path and the new wall, dozens of saplings had been planted inside those plastic tree protectors, but these incipient trees had given up the ghost and if not already dead, then dying, the plastic tubes spilling nettles and desiccated twigs. Dominating the new space was the sculpture *Horizon Line Chamber*, by artist Chris Drury, commissioned by the development company Morecambe Bay Partnership.

The chamber is a replica of an oratory, such as the Gallarus Oratory I'd visited several times on Ireland's Dingle Peninsula. Inside the chamber the eye takes time to adjust to the dark, and when it has, a faint inverted projection is cast onto the far wall in which the sea (or the sand) is the sky and the sky is the sea. And it's an interesting piece – one that might invite us to see things differently, at least whenever the lens is not smeared with salt – or from a different perspective. But, once again, the way the piece has been placed infers that this in itself is the main event, the destination, the point of the journey.

Beyond the chamber a small gate leads into the original grave site. There's a new interpretation board, but regrettably the term 'Sambo's Grave' remains, with no attempt to make sense of the relevance of the sculpture to the site or the grave to the sculpture. Indeed, no attempt at all to rationalise our deeply troubled past against our new assemblages.

As I turned to leave, in the corner I found a stash of bags of rubbish dumped behind the wall. As I attempted to make sense of it all, what I felt most of all was anger.

Once again, we white people had failed to understand or acknowledge the uncomfortable truth of the grave. We had simply appropriated it as a means of directing tourists to the site (and thence into the local economy) without any attempt or reference to meaning. Indeed, a piece in the *Lancashire Post* about the granting of permission for the installation to remain permanently makes no mention of its relevance to the grave, stating simply that 'The installation is part of wider work to regenerate the area and to celebrate arts in the local area.' Quite how such an isolated place should be regenerated is not made apparent. And that it was thought appropriate to simply ignore the grave means that the development is an appropriation, or worse – an embarrassment. Now, far from being remote, strange but strangely compelling, the grave is just an appendage to our white narratives; the installation an object superimposed on our refusal to engage with uncomfortable truths.

During my processing of the developments at the grave I needed to include something at least from a Black perspective. I spoke with academic and writer Maxwell Ayamba, whose work addresses access for Black and other minority groups to the British countryside. I'd recently read Maxwell's piece about the kneeling Black slave sundial at The National Trust's Dunham Massey in Cheshire, and about how the Trust had failed to engage with that highly visible underlying narrative of oppression. Here on the shores of Morecambe Bay, the 'boy Sambo' continues to kneel under the weight of our refusal to deal with the issues the site raises, but we continually cast aside.

Maxwell and I wondered how such inarticulacy had come about. Specifically, I asked him what could be done to with the use of the term 'Sambo.'

'Instead of being avoided,' he said, 'these kinds of uncomfortable truths have to be recognised – dealt with. In this case, the uncomfortable truth is that the term 'Sambo' is offensive; it's a non-name, right? It was part of the system of the Colonial project, used with the intention of dehumanising the individual. To continue the use of the term is a desecration, or more – an abomination.'

Maxwell continued, 'We can't rewrite the past, but we can initiate recovery, and do this by challenging and changing these problematic narratives. Stopping the use of the term 'Sambo' is an urgent part of that reparation.'

I recall how, when dictating this essay into my computer from earlier hand-written notes, the software had been programmed to exclude the term 'Sambo,' substituting it with a series of asterisk. However many times I typed the word, the computer refused. This is what we need to do; to refuse a term that confronts us with all that has been staring us in the face, but that we have repeatedly chosen to turn away from. Much, I suppose, in the same way I'd fallen into the trap of using the term 'Sambo' and 'boy' and chosen to leave the slate with the prayer and the word 'charming' attached to the cross – which is in itself another imposition. But lasting reparation can only be made through conversation and agreement, rather than through division.

'It's about social justice,' Maxwell explained, 'about the lives people are leading now and about lived experience. If we don't do it, the divisions between us will be perpetuated. Imagine a Black person visiting the grave today, being confronted by the term 'Sambo,' and seeing that the problems with that are not being articulated. Imagine; how would that person feel? Being able to empathise with others is a necessary part of the process.'

In other words, without direct and meaningful conversation and without action, we are stuck in a horrible stasis. 'Inarticulacy is that stasis,' Maxwell said.

'So tell me,' I said, 'What do we call him?'

'We call him 'The Unknown African.'

The African-American writer James Baldwin states that 'the past is all that makes the present coherent, and further, that the past will remain horrible for exactly as long as we refuse to assess it honestly.' The use of 'Sambo' must no longer be normalised – either here on the shores of Morecambe Bay, or anywhere. As long as this Black body (or even this imagined Black body) remains 'Sambo'; as long as we are unable and unwilling to scrutinise our white selves in relation to the story and its unceasing Colonial aftermath, century after century, decade after decade in the stasis of an unengaged present; if we continue to unsee the problem of the body interred beneath the weight of the word 'charming,' then we have also failed utterly to come to terms with our part in the legacy of Black history and the lives of Black people today. Most essentially, we have chosen to unsee the expression of our own history, how it pervades, how it poisons, in the light of all this, absolutely. Baldwin again: 'As is the inevitable result of things unsaid, we find ourselves until today oppressed with a dangerous and reverberating silence.'

Queen Elizabeth ll is dead. King Charles III is the tenth monarch to reign over the UK since the unknown African died at Sunderland at the beginning of the Georgian period. Throughout those three hundred years, white narratives prevailed.

Marilynne Robinson states, 'The willingness to indulge in ideological thinking – that is … thinking that by definition is not one's own, which is blind to experience under the contradictions that arise when broader fields of knowledge are consulted – is a capitulation no one should ever make. It is a betrayal of our magnificent minds and of all the splendid resources our culture has prepared for their use.'

There is another way of thinking about the grave at the edge of the bay, one that I'd previously missed altogether, though its evidence is all around us in books, paintings, television programmes and more. As Maxwell reminded me, we should not assume that the unknown African at Sunderland was, in fact, enslaved. Africans and Black people have been part of our culture as individuals *within*, rather than *apart from*, society, for centuries. They *had* self-determination. They *had* acceptance – even of a sort. Think of those who lived and worked alongside Romans on Hadrian's Wall; in the Tudor court; in the paintings of the Dutch masters where they are seen to have been equals to their white compatriots; the Black citizens who, together with many other minority groups, enlisted to fight for our country in the causes of peace and freedom and self-determination in two World Wars. When we think like this – when finally, we get it – that to be African and Black is not always to have been enslaved – then it establishes a more open, more engaged view of Black lives and the principles of social justice and equality.

By admitting my previous assumptions, by us all admitting our previous assumptions and our mistakes, by making these urgent and necessary reparations at the grave on Morecambe Bay, we will have shown ourselves capable of at least reaching for those principles. Until then, we white people are shackled to the memory of this Black individual, buried under the weight of our collective amnesia.

In 2003 Lancaster's Litfest commissioned a sequence of poems titled Lancaster Keys, by the London-born, Barbadian-descended poet Dorothea Smartt, subsequently distributing 24,950 copies – one for each person shipped into slavery by Lancaster traders between the years 1750 and 1800 – to secondary school pupils across the city. The poems spoke to a city grown rich from the trade in misery, but that continues to suffer from what historian Alan Rice of the Institute for Black Atlantic Research calls the 'traditional amnesia' of its slaving past.[3] Smartt's poems then, provide a radical counter-memory.

Here I lie. A hollow
Sambo. Filled with your tears

and regrets. The tick in the eye
of Lancaster pride; the stutter,

the pause, the dry cough, shifting
eyes, that cannot meet a Black man's

gaze[4]

In her poems, Smartt renames the person Bilal, which is a con-
templative and imaginative act of the restoration of identity. At
the outset of the collection Smartt provides 'a few words on samboo's grave;' definitions, actually, including 'Sambo: a pet name
given to anyone of the negro race' from the Dictionary of Phrase
and Fable of 1898 and 'Sambo; a colloquial or humorous appel-
lation for a negro' from Websters Dictionary, 1913. Twenty
years have lapsed since Litfest's commission of Smartt's poems,
yet the pejorative use of the term 'Sambo' persists. Some histo-
rians call for the term to remain because it represents a moment
in time; one that we need to be reminded of, and that in the
common parlance of the past the significance – the word's aura,
if you like - was very different to what it is now.

Smartt's sequence includes a poem titled '99 names for
samboo,' which is a list of words, some of which speak to his
having a family and relationships. Others are the kinds of offensive words now relegated to history, and some speak to the
physical and economic properties of slave bodies. Smartt also
renames him Bilal, which, following that comprehensive list, is
an act of restoration of an individual identity.

The toppling of Edward Colston's statue in Bristol instigated the
swift removal of other slavery-related objects from public display
around the country. In the grounds of Lancaster Priory Church,
a grave monument to the Rawlinson family – city traders who had

acquired significant wealth through slavery – was graffitied in red with the words 'Slave Trader.' I went to take a look. The monument sits behind iron railings, but there the words remain, sprayed in red paint. I was glad that they have survived; a chink in the city's armoury against coming to terms with its slaving past.

Recently, I took another walk to the grave. The door to the chamber was off its hinges, lying on the floor of the interior. With daylight admitted, the lens and its peculiar way of showing the world was redundant. Perhaps worse, the new trees that had survived were now growing contorted from the plastic tubes that were still here a number of years on. Poor unknown African. Whilst the world stumbles incrementally towards equality, you remain 'Sambo'; you remain 'boy'. What would I say to you now? What can I do other than to apologise? To say I am sorry?

A189 Hymn
JAKE MORRIS-CAMPBELL

Suppose we're driving out to Newbiggin-by-the-Sea
spying on the couple solemn on that plinth.
Meadow pipits hover over redemptive waves
snarling an old pit town's song: where all the broken bottles
cemented into walls behind the Iona Club collage
carlin peas and gospels from Woodhorn's diamond days.
Or there's a northwesterly cleansing the Cheviots
and the Wansbeck shimmers like tinfoil in spring air
that fooled us into thinking we had it so good.
Bindweed gleams in the central reservation
and all along the verge from Cambois to Seaton Sluice
we send down the windows drawing lungfulls
of the afternoon's coconut staves.
How sweet-smelling the gorse, how little to be saved.

Errata Slip for a Northern Town
JAKE MORRIS-CAMPBELL

> *'The choices open to women and men today—even amongst the underprivileged—may be more numerous than in the past, but what has been lost irretrievably is the choice of saying: this is the centre of the world.'*
>
> John Berger, *and our faces, my heart, brief as photos*

For:	**Read:**
'The Metro in a hurry to pass the sunken gasometer.'	'The end of the line is also its beginning.'
'Crumbling asbestos of failed industrial units.'	'Glow of fireweed against rusted railing.'
'Identikit new houses no-one round here can afford.'	'It's the people that make the place.'
'Midday drinkers outside Annie McCarthy's.'	'Hazy summer evenings at the Shields Riviera.'
'Seagulls screaming down Keppel Street.'	'Melody of seabirds strumming the shore.'
'The congestion and overpriced car parks.'	'The end of the oil age is soon upon us.'
'Tombstone suicides at Marsden Bay.'	'She lived a long life soothed by the sea.'
A dead-end high street with no decent shops.'	'A thriving local economy of independent retailers.'

'An absolute lack
of intellectual curiosity.'

'The streets are named
after long-dead poets.'

'A barren peninsula
of backward-looking bigots.'

'A stunning seaside town
open to the world.'

'Those who had to leave
and those who burn to.'

'You could spend your life here;
you could be happy.

The White Lands:
The Otterburn Training Area
WILLIAM ATKINS

Between Longtae Burn and Trouty Sike it is possible to trace a section of the Roman branch-road that extended east from the fort at High Rochester, just north of Otterburn, to the camp at Low Learchild on the Devil's Causeway. High Rochester – Bremenium – was a key camp on Dere Street, the chief instrument of the empire's incursion into the unpacified north. Extending three hundred miles from York to the legionary fortress on the river Tay, Dere Street passed the smaller camp of Chew Green, which lay in what is now the northwestern corner of the training area.

Now the stones of Dere Street lie beneath the tarmacked military road from which modern-day officers watch their men manoeuvring on the moorland plains below. It was a matter of pride for the commandant that his soldiers marched along the line of the very road, Dere Street, that Roman legionaries had trodden on two thousand years before.

*

I came to a right-hand junction that led north toward the impact zone. From this aggregate track a series of eighteen 'hardstandings' extended north. From these hardstandings, observation crews in Challengers were to look over the ridge, into the enemy valley below, and, using lasers, acquire and relay target coordinates to the guns situated on the spurs three kilometres to their rear, before jockeying back from the ridge to safety. Like much of what was visible of the military presence here today, these 'tactical observation posts' were new, having been constructed during the massive works that occurred in the early twenty-first century.

The same things that suited the moors to military training had always presented a challenge to transportation. Even tracked vehicles became mired. Main Battle Tanks could not be deployed here, as they were on the harder chalk of Salisbury Plain, and so-called 'free tactical manoeuvring' was impossible. You only had to look down on the cratered impact zone to see how soft the ground was, like the bubble-putted surface of a sponge. Or push your walking pole into any patch of wet ground. There were stories here, as there were of the ranges of Fylingdales and Dartmoor, of howitzers complete with horses and crew being sunk forever in bogs. And it was this softness that had made essential (as far as the MOD was concerned) many of the developments that were proposed in the 1990s to allow training on the ranges with those new 'artillery systems', the AS90 and the MLRS. The ranges lay within Northumberland National Park.
...

The National Parks Act of 1949 had conceded that 'It may be necessary ... to permit some part of the national park area to be used for purposes of national defence.'

From *The Moor*

Tempest Avenue
IAN MCMILLAN

It is 5 am, and I am standing
in the half light bedroom
holding our son. He is finally asleep

and I lay him gently in the cot,
trying not to rattle the toy bear
attached to the bars. Next door

Mr Lowe is having a dream about
the glassworks at Stairfoot. Look:
all the workers have turned to glass,

what a strange dream. Across
the road, Mr Ford is cycling
out of his drive to the pit. He

cycles during the week, takes the car
at weekends, Down the street
my mam is standing at the kitchen

window, looking at our house, thinking
'Our Ian will be asleep. I hope
Mr Ford's squeaky cycle doesn't wake him up.'

And I am being careful, so careful
with these words, laying them
gently into this poem, turning to the door.

The Blue Lonnen
KATRINA PORTEOUS

The crunch of mussel shells under the boot heel;
The bramble-patch where the cottages were rooted;

The stone ring of the mussel bed, the stair
To the drying-green, the ballast heap, the beach of
    creeve-stones;

The tarry stain where the bark-pot reeked; the wicket
In the wall; on the bridge to the limpets, the blade-worn
    groove;
The iron pin that marks the sea-road to the haven;
The nail driven into the door jamb – they are illegible

Without the rudder and the anchor,
Without the twine, the needle and the knitter:

For these are the paths they beat to the shore – The Nick.
    The Blue Lonnen –
And each is a road with a boat at the end of it.

Gaps
HARRIET FRASER

On the hill that summer's day, grey cloud hung low like a lid.
Under foot: wet grass, bracken and tormentil standing in for sun.
We passed Low Bridge Beck and Shepherd Gill,
walked beneath broad bog patches and Dawson Pike,
tracing the wall, the line between intake and fell.

We looked back along Duddon Valley, beyond Turner Hall
over a land of ruffled shadows, woodlands, rock and sky,
onto distant ridges, England's highest crumbs of earth,
across tracks followed by shepherds, for generations,
        while above, two ravens, silhouettes, soared.

Michael's hand raised rocks as big as lambs, and heavier.
As stones were lifted, passed and teased into spaces
and boulders hauled from the chill flow of a beck,
gentle banter and laughter, like moss on rock, formed
        around the edges of this elemental graft

These walls, land's bones borrowed and stitched by man,
may stand solid for a century. But on a farm this size
there are always gaps, forced by unforgiving rains and snow.
Today two hundred stones are fetched, fitted, back in place.
        Two gaps, three men, one rhythm.

Later, in the kitchen, cups of tea, cake, and Anthony's drawn face
as he tells us that Michael is leaving. All those years
treading this land, learning its ways, kenning the sheep.
His choice forced, no choice, no farm to take on here.
Now the valley has a gap   a man gone, a rare breed.

There's that many, says Anthony,
raising four fingers of a weather-worn hand,
that many young ones in Cumbria who could take over a farm.
        How will you find another like that?

Tinker's Tea
JO CLEMENT

The Settle line brought me to these hills.
Maned with winter, he makes tea the old way
and I thank stars for the lack of a service desk,
pylons or ticket checks. Behind the private road,

I put a leaf back in my book, to watch blue shadows
hawk the snow. He tells me my hair has grown,
asks how my studies go, pours the best hot air
from spout to mouth. Her recipe breathes spice.

The right berries steeped with cloveroot, woodruff
and hogweed: it's no secret I came for the leaves
in this pot. But the real gift was seeing
him for the first time in a coat.

A Trip to the Countryside
ANITA SETHI

The huge grey road wound its way up through the hills, further and further up. Out of the M6, the heavy greyness, the
cluttered-up world gradually spaced itself out, lifted itself up.
Up and up and up we drove, into the high regions of the earth,
where the space dived straight into my belly, leaving me winded.
The world grew softer, wider, dragged me out of myself and
into something larger, layering into the mountains. Suddenly,
everything was slightly warmer. Everything was slightly lighter.
The world seemed to open itself up, lift itself, lighten up, shrug
a weight off its shoulders.

We were on a journey to Cumbria with Mum. Mum had got a
weekend stay in a bungalow in a place called Barbon, subsidised
through the nursing association at her workplace.

I wonder if I would even have had this early experience of the countryside had it not been for that nurses' subsidy. My earliest memories of nature were visiting the local park in my hometown of Manchester, which had felt like a safe space before I heard about the guns. After hearing that guns belonging to gangs were rumoured to be buried beneath the trees, I could not walk through the park in quite the same way. My childhood home was just two miles from the city centre in the M16 postcode, which criss-crosses Old Trafford, Moss Side and Whalley Range, and at the time my hometown had acquired the nickname 'Gunchester'. It was a world away from Cumbria.

There were some trips to parks further afield than our local park, to Lyme Park and Dunham Massey. I found a colour photo with my mother, siblings and two cousins, all gazing at a deer, which must have been taken in Lyme Park. This is the closest I came to nature, beyond a school trip to Chester Zoo. For the most part, though, growing up in a single-parent family with a mother who worked multiple jobs, there was not much time or money for many trips away. I rarely ventured out of my home city in early childhood.

But one day we did leave the city behind and venture beyond it; we ventured higher up in the world than I'd ever been before. I don't have a photo of it, but now it's coming out of the dark and into full colour. Before leaving, Mum stuffed all valuables into black bin liners and hid them in the cubbyhole, scared – we all were – of burglars.

We drove away from the city and up through the hills, up and up and up, the roads growing thin and steep and winding, and I looked out of the car window and gasped as the grey fell away into an astonishment of green and blue and gold. It was as if a surface had been stripped off the world to reveal its colours beneath.

It was a shock to step out into this new world and breathe in, for the air was so much clearer, the light so lucid, the sky vast and blue, reflected in water. I breathed more deeply than I ever had done before and for the first time I could remember, it was a joy to breathe, and the oxygen was flowing through the lungs, around the body, lifting the heart, clearing the head. I walked through the grass, which tickled my bare brown legs.

I played outside, picking flowers, and watching an elderly couple who pruned vegetables in the garden next door. They were not saying much but appeared to be watching and listening to us.

'You don't see many brown folks out here in the countryside,' mumbled the man as he paused from pruning to gaze towards me, squinting, his face contorted in a frown, then going back to his gardening.

It would be true to say that there were not many brown people to be seen in the countryside.

One morning I went for a walk with Mum, watching how the great expanse of green gave way to water and watching the wide-open spaces. Mum held my hand as we walked and walked through this new world, stopping to inspect flowers and plants that grew and watch as birds and butterflies fluttered past. We walked through a place filled with so many species I had never known existed. We stopped near a huge tree and I stretched out my limbs so I was standing firm and proud like the tree. For the first time I remember, it felt right to be. I felt strong, as if, like that tree, I would be able to withstand any fierce gale that may come battering. The heart was opening; somewhere a tulip that had been trapped in darkness was unfurling itself in the daylight. The heart was growing, becoming as vast and deep as the lakes, as wide as the woods.

As I walked, the grass brushed my skin and the sweet scents of the flowers filled my lungs and a bright purple butterfly fluttered by so quickly that my heart leapt, and I forgot about myself entirely as the world flooded in and bad feelings drained away into the hills, which absorbed them, and Mum's rage seeped away into the water, which swallowed it up and washed it away. The hard shell that had built up around me began to melt away amidst all this beauty. Love came flooding in. The world came flooding in, pouring into the emptiness.

*

After the bank holiday, we loaded everything back into the Peugeot and drove back down, the softness fading away, the car splattered in grey rain.

It felt strange thinking about our house in Old Trafford without being in it, thinking about it while being so far away from everything that had gone on inside it. From up there, near what seemed like the top of the world, I had gained a new perspective.

Down down down we drove, away from that place where the light is clear, where the fresh air is abundant, down down down until soon it seemed we were driving into the very heart of a thick blanket of grey clouds. I looked out of the window and the world had vanished beneath the cotton-wool grey as if it had been snuffed out, and even the car headlights made only a thin orange gleam through the fogginess. We drove towards our city until soon it had grown dark and the streetlights appeared.

I can't remember going to the Lakes after that; Mum mustn't have got another subsidised place. I can't remember going to the countryside much, either. I think of how we move through the world; social mobility, race and class – how certain places have been for too long inaccessible to too many people, and how important it is to break down such barriers of place. It's vital that children of all backgrounds have ready access to nature and the countryside.

Adapted from an essay in *Common People,* ed. Kit de Waal, 2019

Four

RESTORATION

Deep Time

Rain

SIMON ARMITAGE

Be glad
of these freshwater tears,
each pearled droplet
some salty old sea-bullet
air-lifted out of the waves,
then laundered and sieved,
recast as a soft bead
and returned.

And no matter how much
it strafes or sheets,
it is no mean feat
to catch one raindrop
clean in the mouth,
to take one drop
on the tongue, tasting
cloud-pollen,
grain of the heavens,
raw sky.

Let it teem, up here
where the front of the mind
distils
the brunt of the world

Puddle

SIMON ARMITAGE

Rain-junk.
Sky-litter.
Some May mornings
Atlantic storm-horses
clatter this way,
shedding their iron shoes
in potholes and ruts,
shoes that melt
into steel-grey puddles
then settle and set
into cloudless mirrors
by noon.

The shy deer
of the daytime moon
comes to sip from the rim.
But the sun
likes the look of itself,
stares all afternoon,
its hard eye
lifting the sheen
from the glass,
turning the glaze
to rust.
Then we don't see things
for dust.

Lordenshaw, Northumberland

SUSIE WHITE

From Rothbury our path runs steeply uphill, the view opening out with every calf-pulling step. The sun is shining, a church bell chimes the quarter and a farmer on a quad bike is feeding sheep and lambs. We walk past Sharpe's Folly, a round tower built by the 18th-century rector as an observatory and to relieve unemployment. Then it's out on to the moorland, where latticed heath moths flicker past and skylarks sing.

The first sign of something unusual is a jagged upright rock like a molar, with deep grooves running down from its apex. It is speckled with lichens in grey, silver and pewter, and echoed by further tooth-like forms. Across this flat spur of land known as Lordenshaw, more than 100 carved stones are scattered among the heather, one of the largest assemblages of prehistoric rock art in the country.

The Simonside hills rise above us, but to east and north this is a prominent position overlooking the fertile valley, the distant Cheviots and a gleam of the North Sea. Maybe that is why it was important to the neolithic and bronze age people who etched their symbols into the sandstone. Using a harder rock as a tool and striking it with a mallet, they decorated the surfaces of huge boulders with cup and ring markings, grooves, channels and concentric rings. In places, they enhanced and deepened the natural crevices in the rock.

The largest is Main Rock, pecked with cup-like hollows, some embraced by single, double or triple rings. We look for meaning in the decorations. Perhaps they marked out territories or routes, or were sacred spaces. Prehistoric rock art expert Stan Beckensall speaks of their "indefinable power and beauty".

Added to this are further layers of history. Lordenshaw was chosen 1,000 years later by iron age people as the site for a hillfort, their hut circles enclosed in multivallate ramparts. Later still, the tumbled walls of a 13th-century deer park.

As I search for more carvings, there's a crackle of dead bracken as a hare springs away from beneath my feet. And adding further to the magic of the day, a cuckoo calls from a far-off wood.

First published in *The Guardian*, Country Diary

Foxglove Country
ZAFFAR KUNIAL

Sometimes I like to hide in the word
foxgloves – in the middle of *foxgloves*.
The *xgl* is hard to say, out of the England
of its harbouring word.
Alone it becomes a small tangle,
a witch's thimble, hard-to-toll bell,
elvish door to a door. *Xgl*
a place with a locked beginning
then a snag, a *gl*
like the little Englands of my grief,
a knotted dark that locks light
in *glisten, glow, glint, gleam*
and Oberon's banks of eglantine
which closes in on the opening
of *Gulliver* whose shrunken *gul*
says 'rose' in my fatherland.
Meanwhile, in the motherland, the *xg*
is almost the thumb of a lost mitten,
an impossible interior, deeper than forests
and further in. And deeper inland
is the gulp, the gulf, the gap, the grip
that goes before *love*.

The Northern Hay Meadow
LEE SCHOFIELD

> *How does the Meadow-flower its bloom unfold?*
> *Because the lovely little flower is free*
> *Down to its root, and, in that freedom, bold.*

William Wordsworth

William Wordsworth had a fine way with words, but these lines suggest he hadn't spent a huge amount of time thinking about haymaking, for it would be hard to argue that a meadow-flower has much in the way of freedom. Derived from a Germanic word meaning *to mow*, a hay meadow's persistence, and the lives of the flowers that grow in it, rely entirely on human stewardship. Whether that makes a hay meadow less or more special depends on your point of view.

Perhaps William can be forgiven though, as *meadow* is a slightly slippery term. It's sometimes used (lazily, if you ask me) to describe a generally open, grassy area. In high mountain environments, alpine meadows never see a mower, staying open and flower-rich due to their being above the treeline. A hay meadow though, can be more accurately defined, being a place to produce winter fodder for livestock. Hay meadows are usually found in valley bottoms, often close to a river. As a habitat they lie at a crucial interface between the needs of humans and the needs of nature.

In a temperate climate, where the seasons govern our lives, storing the summer's bounty in order to feed livestock through the winter is an agricultural technique that is pretty much essential to the rearing of livestock. This is the central purpose of a hay meadow. Harvesting and drying plants at the peak of their lushness retains their goodness. The sugars manufactured by photosynthesis don't get pulled back into the roots as they otherwise would, and so the nutritional value of the growing season is deferred, providing the sustenance for livestock through the months of nature's dormancy.

Hay meadows have origins extending deep into the murk of history. They weren't invented – they are the result of thousands of years of incremental innovation. Neolithic people hacking rough fields out of ancient wildwoods began the process. As the centuries rolled by, small-scale wild harvests of tall vegetation evolved alongside our technological ingenuity. By 1066, hay meadows were almost ubiquitous – the Domesday Book recorded them in 80% of settlements. Although sickles, scythes, pitchforks, and horses have been replaced by tractors, mowers and balers, the core principle of hay making remains central to livestock farming.

For a crop of hay to be grown, grazing animals must be excluded. In many hilly regions of the world, including the Lake District, where I live and work, this 'shut-up' is part of what drove the development of transhumance. Although myriad variations exist, transhumance in its most basic form involves livestock being moved up into hill pastures by shepherds for the summer months, giving the valley bottom a rest for hay and other crops to burgeon unmolested. Distinctive field patterns, the construction of seasonal hill dwellings, and locally characteristic cultural practices have grown up around this system, and hay meadows lie at the heart of all of it.

Freed from grazing for the growing season, plants in a hay meadow get to live their best lives. Not only do they grow tall and nutritious, but they take the chance to flower in astonishing profusion. A hay meadow in summer can be one of the most-flower rich habitats in the temperate world; a decent one can have more than 150 plant species. With the resulting explosion in nectar and pollen, the invertebrates also bloom. A summer meadow is alive with butterflies and moths, hoverflies and bees, grasshoppers and spiders taking advantage of the flowery largesse. Then come the birds – swallows and house martins skimming low over grass tips to scoop up the insects, the linnets and goldfinches snaffling seeds.

The soils of traditional hay meadows are characterized by having low nutrients and, perhaps counter-intuitively, this is part of what keeps them so rich. With an annual cycle of cutting and then grazing, nutrients are slowly stripped from the land into the bodies of the animals and the hay. Lower nutrients tend to favour flowers over grasses, and species like yellow rattle and eyebright, which parasitize grasses, give the flowers a further advantage. There is something of a positive feedback loop here; as the grasses are suppressed the sward becomes more open, creating more space and open ground for even more flowers to establish. The annual cutting, traditionally carried out after seeds have been set, helps to scatter the seeds across the meadow while at the same time giving them access to bare ground in which to germinate.

Once upon a time, it was the amount of hay that could be produced which determined how many livestock could be fed through the winter, setting the upper threshold of how many animals a farm could carry. Anyone seeking to push these limits took a massive risk – a hard winter with too many livestock could leave a farm with a whole load of deadstock. So, trying to increase the hay crop makes sense, but this is much easier said than done. Cutting hay before mechanisation involved enormous toil. To ensure it doesn't rot between harvest and use, hay must be properly dried. After the scythe laid it down, the crop had to be turned, ideally more than once, before being heaped or moved to a barn for storing. The effort required meant haymaking was a community affair, and everyone lent their hands, even the children. It's no coincidence that hay time fell during long the school summer holidays.

Creating more meadow land as a means to increase yield was if anything even more labour-intensive, involving picking stones, levelling and draining, and enclosing it to keep grazing animals out. Even if this toil could be achieved, there might not be the labour available to cut the extra hay during the often-short, late summer weather window, or the barn space to store it. In order to boost soil fertility, livestock would traditionally aftermath graze the meadows following the hay cut, their dung directly fertilising the ground to boost next year's crop. Dung from elsewhere would also be spread along with periodic dressings of lime, produced with vast effort in local kilns. The work involved in all of this, and the lack of other options, meant that the quantity of hay that could be produced was naturally limited, and so farming had no choice but to operate within a carrying-capacity determined by the sun, soil and rain. Not so anymore.

The so-called Green Revolution that took place following the Second World War ushered in an arsenal of new innovations focused on increasing agricultural yields. Fertilisers, pesticides, tractors of fearsome power, plastic bale wrap, synthetic feedstuffs and a host of other technologies all appeared at the same time as financial incentives designed to boost production. Having played out so recently, this grimmest of chapters in the story of the hay-meadow can be told with clarity. The recollections of Wilson Robinson, a Cumbrian farmer born in 1916, captured by Cumbria Wildlife Trust as part of an oral history project, describe how everything changed.

In 1947, Wilson was approached by the chemical company ICI. They asked if he would be interested in trialling the use of fertilisers in order to demonstrate their impact on his land and his business to others. The ethos ICI wanted Wilson to showcase was a simple one: "more fertiliser, more grass, more cows, more profit". Adhering to this ethos transformed his farm, ecologically and economically. Multiple cuts of silage – cut while green and stored without drying – replaced the traditional annual summer hay cut. Thanks to the fertiliser, his yields exploded, meaning his farm could carry more livestock and keep them all well fed. It took three years for his pale green, traditional meadows to turn into lurid silage fields. The flowers paid the price, and Wilson describes how the vigorous growth of the grass smothered the "geraniums and other herbs". His partridges and lapwings vanished at the same time, thanks to the earlier cutting that he was now doing. Observing the change over the hedge, his neighbours wanted a slice of the action, and soon enough, they were all buying in the "bagged stuff" for themselves and so their flower-filled meadows disappeared too.

Just as ICI predicted, more silage meant more animals could be carried. For big dairy farms, this meant bigger sheds had to be built to house the cattle. This meant more slurry was produced, which then needed to be spread onto the fields, and so the intensity of the whole system ratcheted further and further up. It took a little longer, but the bagged stuff eventually reached the hill farms too. Although the fertiliser was only applied on the enclosed land, increased yields enabled livestock numbers to swell, which then took a heavy toll on the habitats up in the summer hill pastures.

Wilson was proud of the changes he'd made on his farm, and the way it inspired others to go the same way, but it wasn't all plain sailing. He was criticised by people horrified that the meadows that had persisted for generations were being erased, and so rapidly. But progress was progress – fertiliser use proliferated, and wildlife dwindled.

In part, Wilson blamed Cumbria's soggy climate for the rapid transition from hay cutting to silage making. Cutting hay is a gamble, needing a period of least three days of fine weather to allow the hay to be cut, dried and removed. As anyone living in Northwest England can attest, that's not something that can be counted on. Silage isn't as weather dependent, removed straight after cutting and compacted, still moist, into a clamp, or baled and wrapped in plastic. Wilson reckoned that if we lived in a drier climate where the summer was more reliable, silage wouldn't have caught on anything like as quickly as it did.

Wilson's story played out on virtually every farm in the land. It explains why 97% of hay meadows have been wiped from the countryside, the vast majority converted into sterile, silage factories. It explains too why we no longer have corncrakes.

Because meadows were so much more widespread than they are today, a hundred years ago, corncrakes were common as muck, so common in fact that they occasionally even nested in people's gardens. Up until the 1960s their distinctive nocturnal call would have been a familiar feature of farmland up and down the country. Accounts from the time give no hint that their numbers were soon to take a dramatic nosedive. Corncrakes are secretive, more often heard than seen. Their repetitive raspy call, which they make most during the night, sounds like a pencil being dragged across the teeth of a comb and earned them their onomatopoeic Latin name, *Crex crex*. They are most vocal soon after they arrive from their African wintering grounds in April, making their call a sleep-shattering 20,000 times per night.

Corncrakes rely on a degree of general untidiness. When they first arrive on their breeding grounds, they need to find tall vegetation in which to hide straight away, but hay meadows haven't usually grown to a height to give them the cover they need by then. While they await the growth of the crop, corncrakes make use of beds of nettles or irises, which grow in the scruffy, wet and weedy parts of the landscape that have in so many places been swept away, drained and turned into something agriculturally more productive. Once the hay grew, the corncrakes would move in, usually laying two clutches of precious eggs beneath a swaying canopy of flowers. As traditional hay meadows leaked out of our landscapes, these sanctuaries of colour, nectar and insect life that used to be undisturbed oases for corncrakes to rear their chicks became sterile green deserts, through which tractors ripped two or three times a year. The corncrakes didn't stand a chance.

Hay meadows provided for people and for nature for thousands of years. In the last 70, despite them retaining an unrivalled place in our folk memory, they lie in tatters. But redemption is possible.

*

A suite of hay meadows lie in the palm of Swindale, a secluded glacial valley at the eastern edge of the Lake District National Park. This jewel of a place is one of two hill farms on the catchment of the Haweswater reservoir looked after by the RSPB, who I have the privilege to work for as site manager. My colleagues and I have spent years tending to Swindale's meadows, picking up the baton from the generations of farmers who came before us, in the hope of handing them on to whoever follows in a richer condition than we found them. When you work a piece of land, be it for food production, for nature conservation, or for both, a relationship forms. As I've poured time and energy into Swindale's meadows, some of their richness has flowed back into me.

These meadows aren't just special in a personal sense. To Natural England, the statutory nature conservation agency, they are known as Swindale Meadows Site of Special Scientific Interest (SSSI). Originally designated in 1985, they are recognised as being of a particularly special upland type, known as Northern Hay Meadows. Assemblages of plants are referred to by ecologists as communities. Using a rather arcane and complex method of surveying called the National Vegetation Classification (NVC) system, plant communities can be described and named. A northern hay meadow community is prosaically referred to as MG3 *Anthoxanthum odoratum-Geranium sylvaticum* grassland. While this might sound a bit niche and technical, describing plant communities in this way is tremendously helpful. Plants come together in a community as a result of a complex range of factors. Soil type, depth, pH and moisture are important, as is locality, the land's aspect and altitude and how it's been managed over time. An NVC code summarises all of this, and crucially, helps us to understand how rare a plant community is.

There are fewer than 900 hectares of northern hay meadow left in the UK, virtually all of which is in Northern England. They have been at the sharp end of meadow loss. Our meadows in Swindale are about 3% of the national total, so looking after them is a serious responsibility.

A Northern Hay Meadow is characterized by big chunky flowers such as wood crane's-bill, globeflower and melancholy thistle. These species were still present in Swindale's meadows when RSPB took over the farming tenancy of the valley, but they were few and far between. The valley was down to a single globeflower plant, bravely clinging to one of the banks of the beck as it flowed through the meadow. The previous tenant of Swindale apparently wasn't very interested in wildflowers and so, despite legal obligations to manage the meadows in a way that was intended to protect them, he spread too much manure and fertilizer on them, and grazed them too heavily. I don't mean to knock him. The fact that he didn't hand the meadows on to us in as pristine a state as we might have liked was not through any malicious intent. He was just farming in the way that was the norm at the time, focusing his energies on food production rather than nature conservation. That the meadows are still there at all is a feather in his cap. He could have easily ploughed them up, destroying them completely.

One slender upside to the catastrophic loss of hay meadows is that there is now a huge bank of knowledge about how best to restore them. Working with Natural England, we've been putting that knowledge into practice in Swindale over the course of the past decade.

Our soils were a bit rich, but that was easily addressed by ending the application of fertilizer and manure. We still had most of the important big, blowsy species present in the meadow, but they weren't as numerous as they should have been. To encourage them to spread, changing the timing of grazing was key. In order to attain their larger size, bulky wildflowers start growing earlier in the year than some of their smaller companions. The previous tenant in Swindale frequently used the meadows for lambing, meaning the meadows were grazed right through to April or May, disproportionately impacting earlier growing species. We have fewer sheep now, and by lambing elsewhere on the farm, we can shut up the meadows much earlier in the year, and so the bulkier plants are spreading.

Moving to an earlier shut-up date for our meadows is more in line with local farming traditions, too. At different periods through history, the traditional shut-up date has varied, but I've found several references to it being in February or March. Before fertiliser sunk its insidious tendrils into the soil, the obvious way to ensure a good crop was to allow the hay as much time as possible to grow, so an early shut-up makes total sense. The fact that the wildflowers also benefited from this is a happy accident. The timing of cutting is also important. We never cut our hay before late July to ensure that the seeds can ripen and drop back into the meadow as the hay is turned to dry.

Further up Swindale, towards where Hobgrumble Gill waterfalls come tumbling into the valley, we have other undesignated meadows. Because these lacked the protection afforded them by a SSSI badge, their wildflowers had been even less well looked after. To get these back up to scratch, we harvested seed from the best bits of the SSSI meadow, and then after gently harrowing to open the soil, we scattered the seed into it. We added a selection of locally grown plug plants to add further diversity. Then all we had to do was sit back and wait for nature to take its course.

RESTORATION

Today, Swindale's meadows are pure botanical joy. Colourful, diverse and buzzing with life, walking through them in late June is one of the most uplifting experiences there can be. Great clumps of melancholy thistle tower over the herbal understorey, a haze of eyebright peering up from below. Patches of bright pink bistort are spreading, and heath spotted orchids have appeared. In late summer the staccato of dried yellow rattle seed heads accompanies every step. There are hundreds of globe-flowers now, spreading alongside saw-wort, ragged robin and meadowsweet in the wetter areas. Tinkling flocks of linnets and goldfinches feast on the abundant seeds, jostling with chimney sweeper moths, meadow brown butterflies, bees and hoverflies for airspace.

With a remeandered beck winding its way through this flowery wonderland, we've got a lot to be proud of in Swindale. What's perhaps most satisfying is that we've done this work while continuing to farm. The crop we take from the hay meadows still feeds our sheep and cattle through the winter. True, we get less bulk of hay per hectare than a silage field, but with reduced numbers of animals we've found a balance. Keeping the meadows alive relies on keeping them in use, retaining their cultural, as well as their ecological richness.

Although a meadow's primary function has always been fodder production, it is seeing them only through this lens that has put them in jeopardy. Trading tractors for corncrakes seems like too high a price. To an ecologist, a meadow is an ecosystem, all be it one that relies on humans to sustain it. To a historian, a meadow is a fragile, but living link to the past, part of an ever-evolving system that enabled our ancestors to survive and flourish. To an artist a meadow is a source of inspiration, a living palette that flows with the seasons. A meadow is all of these things, and more. It is farming elevated to the status of art, a living repository of nature and culture. We must handle our meadows with care.

High Borrowdale Farm

KERRY DARBISHIRE

Great burnet, daisies, yellow rattle,
pignut, star bright, bedstraw
and a hundred other flowers
I can't name,
have found their way home.

Horse hair and lime-wash
barely patch the walls. Windows,
curtains and bread oven are gone,
nettles burn through a grate standing proud
of the hearth.

The open flue maps the last draw
of peat smoke from the kitchen
and bedroom – open wide
to sycamores filtering
today's hot sun.

A lintel crumbles to dust where salt
and spices were stored oak-dark
and dry. One thistle coming into flower,
sits at the table in its July best.
The pantry floor dips, slate slabs stare

at the sky. I count five
stone steps up to the half-way turn
and see the giant fallen ash. Here
a family caught the last glimpse of stars
before bed. Here

candles cast shadows from the sill –
danced themselves to sleep
as prayers rolled out to hay meadows
where now a pair of buzzards cry
shadowing the summer-long lane.

Heron Time
JOANNA C. DOBSON

Before we got our allotment, I'd never noticed a heron in flight. Then one day when I looked up, red-faced and sweaty from digging out bramble, bindweed and couch grass, I saw it. High up in the blue, a heron floating above the plot, wingspan vast as an eagle's, legs trailing behind like an undercarriage.

The allotment lies on the northern slope of the Porter Valley in Sheffield and I guessed the bird was on its way to the Porter Brook, which runs along the bottom. I've often seen them there. Once I hid behind a beech tree to spy on a heron fishing. It held itself perfectly still, reptilian neck frozen to an S, raggedy sweep of slate-grey body bunched behind like a bustle, everything balanced on two scaly, hinged legs that disappeared into the peat-brown water. It seemed to have hardly any head: the neck flowed into an enormous, dagger-like bill as if that were the whole point of the bird. Only the circular yellow eyes gave the impression of a face.

As I watched, the heron gradually stretched out its neck, peered towards the stream, slowly, slowly lowered its head and then, suddenly, stabbed. There was a great splash, then back it came, shaking off droplets and swallowing. I didn't see the fish itself, but a small lump jerked inside the pouch beneath the heron's bill, then rippled down its neck. The heron shook itself again, stilled and resumed the watch.

The herons that visit this valley probably roost in some ancient woodland about two kilometres south of the allotment, where there's been a heronry for as long as anyone can remember. When I get home, I spread out the map of Sheffield and Barnsley on my study floor to get an idea of how my first flying heron might have reached our plot. The map shows rows of little blocky houses between the heronry and the allotment site, along with a few small patches of green. The A625, which links the Peak District to the city centre, snakes through them, a bold red line that the humans from this part of Sheffield would use to orientate themselves.

I imagine the heron flying north above the houses and barely registering the road. I guess that it steers by the light that glints off streams and pools. Before long it would get a view of Porter Brook, and, if it tracked the water towards the east, it would soon be over the Hangingwater Allotments. From its flight path above the sycamore tree where the song thrush sings all summer, it would be able to take in the whole site. It might see the sun glancing off greenhouses, mostly wonky structures of cracked glass and rotting planks. Its eyes could travel over upturned wheelbarrows, plastic compost bins, woodchipped paths and bamboo ridge supports for runner beans. It might clock a scattering of humans, some digging, weeding or planting, the odd one resting in a deckchair outside a tool shed.

Unlike the pigeons, which devour any brassicas that aren't covered with nets, the heron probably wouldn't be that interested in the allotments. It might, instead, come to rest beside the old millpond that lies just beyond the wall bordering the site. This millpond, known locally as a 'dam', belongs to Shepherd Wheel, a seventeenth-century knife-grinding workshop. One of a string of small, water-powered forges that used to thread the length of the valley, it stopped production in the 1930s but was recently restored. At weekends you can visit and watch the slow turning of the water wheel that drove the grindstones where steel blades were sharpened for the cutlery industry that made Sheffield famous.

RESTORATION

A few days after I saw the heron, I stopped at Shepherd Wheel on my way to plant out broad beans. It was early morning in mid-April and the air was chilly, but somewhere a chiff chaff was announcing the start of spring. Mostly the millpond was still and clear, but one patch shivered in the breeze, the choppy water flickering between silver and grey. Beside my bench I spotted the tiny, bright green flowers of dog's mercury, a remnant of ancient woodland that must have been cleared in the 1500s to make way for the first of the workshops.

Apart from the chiff chaff, a robin was singing from the tops of the lime trees that edge the allotment site. Its glassy song had kept me company all winter and now it sounded louder, more full-throated, as if it too was heralding the shift towards longer, lighter days. Further over towards our plot, a blackbird was carolling and a pair of wood pigeons called to each other. Otherwise everything was quiet, apart from the intermittent hum of traffic from the road on the north side of the allotments.

I wondered what the soundscape of this place would have been in the days when Shepherd Wheel was in full production. Men worked long days, crouched over the grindstones for eight to ten hours, turning roughly forged metal into fine, sharp blades. The valley would have resounded with the scrape of metal on sandstone, the shouts of the boys charged with ferrying finished blades into town in wheelbarrows, and the hacking coughs of the older grinders, their lungs irreparably damaged from years inhaling the metallic particles that showered from the wheels as they worked.

Suddenly I realised I was being watched. Another heron – or even, perhaps, the same one – was sitting on the wall across the dam, and looking straight towards me. I looked back at it and thought of the humans who've shared this space with them, from medieval woodcutters, through the last of the knife grinders, to all of us busy allotment holders. It seemed that the gaze of this reptilian bird was holding us all.

Grange-over-Sands

JENN ASHWORTH

Our fine house lies on the outskirts of a little town, the grey
houses and hotels and hydros huddled on the gentle lower slopes
of the fells, tucked between them and the northern edge of
Morecambe Bay. Grange-over-Sands looks out across the River
Kent right where it leaves the land and disgorges itself into the
sea. A perfect place to settle down. Rest for fell walkers, res-
pite for the sick and a perfect place to bring up children. It's
what we've always said. We have a duck pond and some nice
gardens and all kinds of things for guests. The lovely cast-iron
railings saved because the civil munitions people didn't get this
far north when they moved across the country stripping towns
of iron during the war. It's not late yet, but at this time of year
it gets dark early. The narrow, jumbled streets are deserted. The
fells are dark. It's the off season, and the promenade is empty.
There's the lido, boarded up. No way to get in, but the water's
still in the concrete bowl of the place, an old supermarket trolley
in the deep end, and the little yachting pool bright green and
thickened with algae.

Reminds us of the times we used to come here. The summers,
getting in early before the tourists arrived and took the whole
place over, leaving no room for anyone else. We could walk there
– ten minutes from the house it was, and easy enough to pop
back in case something wanted doing. Looking after the boys
– a full-time job. Not much time for recreation. And look: the
day brightens and the sun comes out and there's Jack. We watch
him lie back on his towel. Eyes closed. Nothing but the bloody
orange glow of the too-bright sun through his eyelids.

When winter comes, everything changes. Didn't she see? The
water in the bay loses its bright metallic sheen; the tidal pools
and tributaries at the estuary no longer act as mirrors to the

rough sky but become muddy brown lakes, hopping with sand shrimp and siphoned by crowds of godwit, stopping off on their annual migration south. Even before the summer is over there is a certain coolness to the place. The wind does other things too. The bay is dangerous and unpredictable: it always has been. It changes daily and without notice: that's part of the microclimate of the area and the reason for the siren charm and danger of the edgelands. The gullies and channels shift, the sands run like mercury: no one can trace the same path across them twice. But these daily fluctuations are part of a larger turn – in our time there was a beach here but now the salt marsh is encroaching on the foreshore and we gaze, without recognition, on a landscape transformed.

The Kent, which flows alongside the promenade, is on the move. The wind has taken it further and further away from the town. It will continue to retreat inch by imperceptible inch, taking whole decades to make its slow migration south and away from the town. The beach got choked up with silt, then disappeared entirely under a harsh scruff of spartina grass. Those of us returning after years away will lean over the old railings to measure the view against our memories, squint at maps, and consider ourselves lost. We'll wonder where the water went, where the ice-cream kiosks disappeared to and where the amusements have gone.

There's nothing to be done about it. It is the nature of all deep-water channels to be cyclical; to go where the wind takes them. Those who stay say the salt marsh covered the sands so slowly that the locals in sight of it every day didn't notice the shift at first. Now farmers graze lambs there. Because the creatures eat samphire and seaweed they're something of a speciality; the restaurants charge a lot for them. Salt marsh lamb: raised on the tidal range of the town, their short lives lived on the very spot where the pleasure boats used to plough up and down with their horns tooting and their passengers waving to queues on the shore. It's all gone now and even if people did still want to come, the mill towns don't keep the wake weeks any longer; the Glasgow fair that used to see the city empty and decant itself down here, discharging from the train stations and filling up boarding houses and hotels in Blackpool, Morecambe and Grange, is only a memory, reminisced about in half-empty pubs in need of modernisation and refurbishment. The odd confused tourist still arrives at the train station and immediately heads for the coast in search of the sands, loaded up with picnic baskets and windbreaks. Bored cafe owners stare out of drizzle-speckled windows and smirk. What the visitor finds is a beach transformed into grey, mud-streaked grass, the odd sheep skull, and silence. On bright days the sea is a shining thread on the horizon pressed between the salt marsh and the low-slung swollen clouds. Miles out.

But one day the wind will turn again and when it does the Kent will remember itself and advance on the marsh to drown the cordgrass. After the spring tides new channels will emerge overnight and turn the sea-washed turf into a treacherous maze of unmapped islands, slippery knolls and sucking mudflats. Those that mourned the disappearing beach will, if they last long enough, live to grieve the eroding salt marsh. Farmers will move their grazing lambs inland, the sea will return the sand to the town and the curlews and oystercatchers will come home. Walkers trying to take their bearings from the old coordinates between Holme Island and Great Crag will become disorientated: the tide will boil through the channel, proceeding at the pace of a galloping horse and the outcrops will seem to move, to change appearance, to shift their relation to the mainland entirely.

From the novel *Fell*

Anthropophony
KAREN LLOYD

I'm tuning in to territories
like we'd tune in to stations on the radiogram.
The shortwave chiff-chaff
with the dial stuck, the maudlin willow warbler,
the blackcap trying and failing to be a nightingale.
And this is work.

In the airwaves of Africa
the switch turns on
and it's 3,000 miles from Senegal.
Swallows, martins and swifts
are charged particles inside storms
that bloom like static over the Med.
Somewhere west of Hilversum
the migrants enter our reception
and this is work and fortitude.

And it's all noise; the time-lapse of
trees engineering chlorophyll.
The way the light gets in   the way life gets in.
The Lune's analogue hauls itself towards the hills
with curlews and oystercatchers
broadcasting from shingle and field.
And this is work and fortitude and fortune.

And right on cue, hoverflies
and all the other insect gizmos
begin transmissions.
For one night only, the mayfly dancehall of desire
is in full swing above the river's glitterball.
And this is work and this is food.

I'm trying hard to unscramble the signals
but our human frequencies make so much din.
Take away the machines
and this is all that's left.
Pull up a chair.
Lean close   listen to the view.

Anthropophony is the term used to describe all human-made
sounds from language to music and machines. The poem was
commissioned by the BBC Contains Strong Language Festival
in 2021 and responds to Ruskin's View in Kirkby Lonsdale. It
was first published on Ink, Sweat and Tears National Poetry Day
Environment Feature, 2022.

The Lost Garden

LINDA FRANCE

The conservatory's on its last legs. Several panes of glass on the
roof are slipping out of their rickety wooden frames, in danger of
crashing onto the untidy stretch of grass, nettle and fern below.
Moss grows up the inside walls like a luxuriant emerald beard. A
fine silt of leaves, seeds and soil has gathered in drifts on the stone
floor. As if Nature is trying to regain control of what is rightfully
hers, the atmosphere is dank, primeval, a touch Gothic. A gen-
erous froth of cobwebs exudes a morbid mustiness far beyond
anything you'd expect with Autumn creeping in now, withering
leaves and shrinking days.

On the flaking sill a few plants in ancient terracotta pots are
hanging on for dear life – pelargoniums, leggy, dry-stalked and
flowerless; a stubborn fremontodendron, given by a friend and
brought inside after being ravaged by hungry rabbits one particularly harsh winter; a Japanese mock-orange (*Pittospermum*

tobira) from the Eden Project I bought at a charity auction, keen on the idea of importing a little bit of paradise to my wind-blasted patch of ground, just shy of Hadrian's Wall, overlooking the bare expanse of Stagshaw Fair and then the Tyne valley to the south.

I've ventured into this uninviting tumbledown space to retrieve the only four renga lilies (*Arthropodium cirratum*) to have survived the depredations of some invisible but ruthless leaf-cutting beetle that has made its home here, alongside green-fly, numerous spiders, flies, wasps and the occasional mouse or small lost bird. The seeds arrived in the post, unannounced, all the way from New Zealand, their natural home – another gift from another friend aware of my love of plants and the stories behind them. The attraction of the renga lilies was their name – *renga renga* in Māori; but in Japanese, the term for a classical poetic form I've been practising since the turn of the millennium. This fellow rengaista had the seeds sent to me for my birthday in May and, against the odds, all fourteen germinated. But the unexpectedly valiant seedlings proved no match for the appetite of those incognito insects in the survival-of-the-fittest world of my so- called 'conservatory' – which is really too grand a name for what it's turned into in the twenty-five years I've lived in this place. Even 'lean-to' sounds too kind. Only four plants proved to be a match for the various challenges the alchemy of my inhospitable northern garden and laissez-faire style of gardening pose. On the verge of leaving for a week to visit the world's oldest botanic garden, I've come to gather up these precious survivors to take them to what I know will be a place of greater safety and more reliable nourishment.

I pack them carefully in a cardboard box, load them in the boot of my car and drive twenty-five miles east across open agricultural land, merging into the familiar straggle of suburbs and city. It is a regular commute for me, from rural to urban, from where I live now to the place where I was born, where my father was born, my rootstock. In the middle of Newcastle, just off a slip road from the busy dual carriageway, the road curves back on itself, houses on one side, a thin screen of trees on the other, till I pull up opposite a black metal gate. After making a quick phone call, the wide grille glides slowly to the left so I can drive in and park outside the modest building and old glasshouses. This is Moorbank Botanic Garden, where I spent the previous year as poet in residence and, at the end of it, couldn't stay away. It's one of those places that draws you in, makes you feel at home, part of what the American poet Mary Oliver calls 'the family of things'.

For nearly ninety years this garden at the hub of the city has nurtured new plant species and been a haven for wildlife. Walking down the long corridor between the offices, storerooms, teaching space and the Tropical House, I can't help feeling embarrassed by these poor specimens I've dared to bring into this world of lush healthy foliage and exotic blossoms. A bright red bottle-brush feathers the wall above a rank of strappy agapanthus. Sleek orange and blue birds of paradise flutter past. The air is sweet and ripe and warm. Just across the threshold this is already about as far from a chilly field in Northumberland, closely cropped by sheep and cattle, tented by brooding clouds, as you could get. I feel my shoulders relax. All is well.

I quickly discover it's not. Clive and Helen are hovering by the kettle in the small room where staff (of which they constitute the full complement) and volunteers (known as 'Friends') congregate for lunch and tea breaks in between gardening tasks. Full of excitement about my impending trip to Italy, the start of my long-dreamed-of botanical odyssey, at first I fail to notice anything amiss. I introduce Clive, the garden's manager, who has many years of horticultural experience under his belt, to my ailing antipodean lilies. He very sweetly doesn't laugh. I don't understand what he means when he says he'll look after them for 'one year'. It sounds like an oddly formal contract. He goes on to explain that they've just heard that the University, for financial reasons, has made the decision not to renew their lease with the Freemen of the City and to close Moorbank. Beyond a year it might no longer exist in its present form. I don't know what to say, uncomprehending, shocked.

My numbness soon gives way to anger and sadness, a stream of unanswerable questions. How could they justify closing this oasis of a garden, so unique, important and beautiful? What would be gained, apart from a few hundred thousand pounds a year, a tiny portion of the University's purse? Would it be able to survive without the knowledgeable and committed care and attention of Clive and the volunteers? How do we begin to calculate such a garden's value? Or the cost of its loss? How much is feeling like we belong in nature worth? Without that grounding, how might our children grow up to pass on the stewardship of the planet and its plants to their own children? What's the effect on a living city when it loses one of its green vital organs? What happens to the hearts and minds of those people who have spent time there, who have tended and loved it?

This news was totally unexpected. I could have better dealt with my conservatory falling down in the night. Or all four of my last renga lilies being eaten entirely away. Losing something in front of your eyes is easier to understand than anticipating the slow disappearance of a whole garden over the course of a single year, bearing witness to a gradual process of unravelling.

I felt distinctly unravelled myself as I slipped out through the back door to walk round the garden where I'd been so happy, peaceful and creative, over the previous few years. Steep steps led through a small rockery (notable in my mind for a plant its label called a voodoo lily but I had never actually seen in bloom). This is where Clive and I had once glimpsed a fox lingering one day, vivid and slinky, amongst the plants. The tall limestone wall blocked out the traffic sounds but not the barking coming from the cat and dog shelter next door. That top end of the garden was often strident with piercing cries, a constant reminder that any sanctuary was notional, rather than absolute. Behind a padlocked metal guard, two beehives housed thriving colonies of bees, free to come and go and graze the pollen-rich flowers, shrubs and trees in this densely planted three acres.

Three acres, or one and a half hectares – not so much bigger than Newcastle United's football ground, St James's Park, within roaring distance across the Town Moor. The footballers who come from all over the world to play on that revered green rectangle always made me think of the miles travelled by many of the plants to Moorbank – pampas grass from Argentina, bromeliads from the Ivory Coast, aloes from Senegal.

At the beginning of October, the many unusual tree specimens are the garden's star players. A miniature grove of maidenhair (*Ginkgo biloba*) stand next to a dawn redwood (*Metasequoia glyptostroboides*), discovered as an eight million year old fossil tree and introduced to this country in 1948, where it's shown itself to be hardy and vigorous. There's also a not entirely happy tulip tree (*Liriodendron tulipifera*). Another was planted outside the Civic Centre to commemorate the visit of Jimmy Carter in 1973, where it does slightly better. The starry grey-blue-green needles of the Atlas cedar (*Cedrus atlantica*) give the impression it's already dreaming of winter. Further down the slope, just above the course of the old Pandon Burn that trickles through the city underground, all the way into the Tyne, there's a 'coffin tree' (*Juniper coxii*), collected from Burma in 1919 by plant hunters Reginald Farrer and Evan Cox. A giant redwood (*Sequoia gigantea*) is still young, planted in memory of a talented student called Emma Morecambe who died in 2007 at the age of twenty-three. Tibetan cherry, Himalayan birch, manna ash, larch, willow and sweet gum – I tick them off as I complete my circuit, reassured by their presence. Every so often I catch a smell in the air as if a person I know has just walked past; something that would often happen to me in this garden, where everything was somehow both exciting and familiar at the same time.

Ever since I'd come across the Japanese tradition of *shin-rin-yoku*, wood-bathing, I'd taken to spending as much time outside as possible, breathing in the 120 largely unquantifiable volatile chemical compounds breathed out by the trees. Although only able to identify seventy of these, scientific research has shown that they have the capacity to lower blood pressure, pulse rate, the stress indicator cortisol and blood sugar levels in people with diabetes.

Autumn was always gorgeous with the leaves changing colour at Moorbank. It gave me the chance to 'revise' photosynthesis, half- remembered from O-level Biology lessons, the key to life on earth. Trees 'know' the days are getting shorter and begin to prepare themselves for winter when there will not be enough light or water for photosynthesis to occur. During the fallow time, they rest, living off food stored over the summer months. As the stronger green chlorophyll fades, the yellows and reds that have been there all along are revealed. Sunlight, cool nights and trapped glucose produce the vivid red of the sweet gum leaves (*Liquidambar styraciflua*). Their turning brown signifies all that is left are tannins, a waste product of the cycle.

My first autumn was particularly spectacular with a stunning kaleidoscope of colour. It was followed by an unusually cold winter, with record falls of snow. For over two weeks the garden was out of bounds, hidden beneath a thick blanket of white. Snowed *out* of my house, I had to stay in town for a week. One bright day, I managed to drive to within half a mile of my house, where I was snowed *in* for another week. When everyone emerged from the whiteout and went back to the garden, unsurprisingly, they discovered extensive snow damage. The worst casualty was the beautiful strawberry tree (*Arbutus unedo*) that had graced the garden's entrance. I'd been intrigued by its panicles of bell-shaped flowers, with dainty pink frills, pollinated by bees, hanging alongside small, seedy, strawberry-shaped fruits. Not as sweet as their namesakes (hence *unedo*, 'I eat only one', coined by Pliny) but rich in Vitamin C, they are good food for birds, or traditionally used to make jam and strong liqueur, particularly *madrōno*, which lends its name to the city of Madrid. Most famously, a strawberry tree appears in Hieronymus Bosch's *The Garden of Earthly Delights* triptych hanging in the Prado.

Moorbank's specimen became the fallen hero of its own legend when several of its boughs, weighed down with snow, were snapped right back to the trunk. As soon as they could, ground still patched with white, the redoubtable gardeners sawed off the torn stumps of branches and made a bonfire of the wood, slow to burn and smoky in the freezing January air. A practical and optimistic tribe, they decided to cut the tree down to its base so that the bed it grew in would enjoy a new lease of light and, come Spring, could be planted with a fresh scheme. Still mourning the loss of this wondrous tree myself, I was impressed by how quickly the gardeners had come up with a constructive solution to the tragedy. But the happiest ending was seeing the strawberry tree throw up new shoots and transform itself, nearly waist high and flowering, just a year later. What would become of it now? The thought makes me feel panicky and powerless.

Spotted Woodpeckers
GRAHAM MORT

From the Bramley to the rowan
        to the black cherry to the svelte air
over the valley, its pelt of dew

slung upon stone shoulders.
        The sparrow hawk goes over or a
 cuckoo – we guess at silhouettes –

their hardy throwing back of
        atmosphere and early morning
shade. Now these light-spun

pendants glitter in the apple
        tree – jet, ivory, ruby – sleekly
hatchet its seething bark.

They hunt for grubs when
        stalking the hot, cloacal sex
that birds have, their feathers

trembling with mites. Tonight
        little owls will smooth dark's
mass into the valley with

calls that bring stillness as
        their aftershock. Then brightest
planets swing close, radio-

active pearls on a swart
        breast: Jupiter and Venus, their
counterpoint before dawn

when the mind is a temple
    of self-worshipping doubt –
thought's poison sheaf laid

bare as mistletoe in a sepulchre.
    We'll know them if morning comes
and they return, breast to

breast, their jewelled bodies
    lapped by flames, their longing
wings, their hollow bones.

The Ancient Land of Borsdane Wood

DANI COLE

We're following the ghosts and relics of the past in Borsdane Wood. Our small troupe is being led through the trees — silver birch, oak, beech, sycamore — by Mick Davies, who seems to know every inch of leaf-littered ground. He has the air of a sage, dressed in a cap and sleeveless jacket, and bearing a bulky camera bag.

During the week, Mick, 60, is a laboratory manager for a food company, sometimes putting in 12-hour shifts. When he's not working, he takes "a hell of a lot of bird photography," and Borsdane Wood has been one of his regular haunts since he was six years old.

This narrow 1.5-mile stretch of woodland sits in a steep-sided valley in Hindley, Lancashire, and is Wigan's most extensive ancient woodland. When I phone Wigan Council's biodiversity officer Kieran Sayer to ask if he could walk me around the wood, he tells me he'll bring Mick along, as well as Dave Hanbury, of Borsdane Friends Group, who care for the woodland in partnership with the council.

Kieran is 25, Dave is 71, and we would look like a motley crew if there was anyone here to see us. As we head deeper into the wood, meadow gives way to green, dappled canopy, and some of the mossy branches of the trees resemble the shaggy tines of stag's antlers.

The three men settle into a comfortable back-and-forth about the jobs that need doing and the birds they've seen here — the kingfisher is the ultimate prize. "It's the closest thing we'll get to a tropical bird over here," Mick says. Kieran tells me about a goshawk that was spotted flying through the wood a few weeks ago. "It's like a sparrowhawk on steroids."

Mick stops us along a section of the Borsdane Brook, the river that cuts through the wood and separates Wigan and Bolton. Though it straddles both boroughs, Wigan Council has managed the wood since 1974. Here the brook is shallow, and there are a series of man-made weirs. It was diverted to channel water to feed Hindley Mill, a steam-powered corn mill that was later converted to a cotton mill. This part is known as 'Flag Bottom', and Mick points out the natural flagstone jutting up. We all scramble down the bank to the pebbled riverbed to see the old channel that veers off the brook's course. It's no more than a depression in the ground, a ghost-river.

Then he fishes out two clear plastic bags packed in with his camera equipment. Out of the first, he takes out what I initially take to be knapped flint – it has an angular, glassy sheen. It's surprisingly light and smooth in my hands. "There are two things this area is known for," he says. "Cotton and coal." Wigan's coal mining can be traced back to around 1450 and continued into the late twentieth century, with the last coal mines closing in the 1990s. The valley's shape exposed bedrock and the coal seams that were close to the ground's surface. Under the headline 'Mining no threat to woodland', a Manchester *Guardian* article from May 1, 1950, reported:

> *Local authorities have been told by the National Coal Board that there is no threat to Borsdane Wood near Bolton, though there is a possibility of coal mining in the area. It was stated there might be enough coal in the neighbourhood to employ 200 men for 10 years.*

Mick tells us that because of pollution, the water used to run "all sorts of colours," but efforts to clean it up over the years have been rewarded. "It's full of trout. Big trout," he says. The second bag contains something more intriguing. "What do you think that is?" he asks, holding up a brown lump. I make a guess. "Dinosaur poo?" Wrong: it's a fossilised freshwater mussel bed. The rock is cleaved in half, and he opens it, as you would with a clamshell, to reveal a delicate whorl of patterns inside. "This is where the history of the wood starts," Mick tells us.

A Vestigial Forest

Ancient woodland makes up just 781 hectares (around 3 square miles) of Greater Manchester, as identified by the Provisional Ancient Woodland inventory. The definition of ancient woodland is native woodland that has been present since at least 1600, a date that reflects the emergence of the first reliable maps (such as tithe maps), and the fact that there was little recorded planting of woodland before the seventeenth century.

Britain's post-glacial landscape would have been a scrubby, wind-scoured tundra, interspersed with groves of trees and cropped by herbivores. As the climate warmed, during the Mesolithic era, trees – birch, hazel, lime, elm, hornbeam – started to appear. True wildwood, which covered Britain after the Ice Age, no longer exists. The wildwood in the North was predominantly lime, but Borsdane Wood is perhaps the "nearest natural" remnant of these wildwoods. Because it sits in a sharp, river-carved valley, it's been left relatively unchanged by human activity. Woodland has long been a resource, exploited for food, fuel and timber. Borsdane is a vestigial forest, a fragment of Britain's prehistoric landscape.

A large barrow called 'Boar's Den' – a type of prehistoric mound that served as funerary monuments – near Sprodley Brook in Wrightington is commonly thought to be the origin of the woodland's name. During Saxon times, drifts of pigs owned by serfs would have roamed the wood, also adding weight to the theory. But in *The Place-Names of Lancashire,* Eilert Ekwall attributes the first instance of 'Borsdane' to 'Ballesdenebroc', (Borsdane Brook) in 1215, derived from Old English for 'Boell,' a name, and 'dene' taken from the Old English of 'denu' meaning 'valley.'

From the fourteenth to the seventeenth century, the wood was part of land belonging to the Langton family of Lowe Hall. J.A. Hilton in *North West Catholic History* writes that after the Reformation, Hindley was in the "debatable land" of Catholic and Puritan Lancashire. In 1628, Abraham Langton was a "Catholic recusant" and in 1652 he was charged with treason as a "papal delinquent" and his estates – including Borsdane Wood – were sold by parliament. From then, it is thought to have been common land until it passed into the ownership of Hindley Hall Estate, which is now a golf club.

'ALL YOU CAN HEAR IS BIRDSONG'

This is a broadleaved woodland, which is classed as a "scarce habitat" in Greater Manchester. It's one of 40 sites in Wigan managed by Kieran and his manager Martin Purcell. Kieran's path into conservation stemmed from his interest in nature photography. He volunteered with the Lancashire Wildlife Trust and later went on to study ecology and conservation at his local college. "I want to do my bit to try and preserve things," he says.

"Each habitat supports a different range of species," he tells me. "It's the only ancient woodland in the borough." The ground floor is carpeted with pungent swathes of wild garlic and wood anemone, both ancient woodland indicators. Ancient woodlands like Borsdane – which has 26 species of mammals and 176 species of birds – are incredibly rich with flora and fauna and are habitats for rare and threatened species.

Among some of the fungi species are the amethyst deceiver, cinnamon porecrust, which darkens from yellow to rust-brown and grows on deadwood, and fly agaric, the distinctive red-and-white topped mushroom often depicted in fairy tales. The abundance of fungi in the wood lures in foragers, which carries risks. "You get people who come and say 'I can find stuff to cook for my tea,'" Dave says. Mick tells me about the destroying angel which he saw in another wood – it's a snowy-white mushroom with pale, crowded gills. Once ingested, death can occur within days and there is no known antidote. Fortunately, you won't find it in Borsdane.

The wood is home to the lesser spotted woodpecker. Since 1970, the population is estimated to have fallen by 83% with no more than 2,000 pairs thought to be left in the UK according to the Woodland Trust. The "ongoing loss" of ancient and mature woodland is a "key factor" in its decline, the organisation says. Other rare bird species include the willow tit and the spotted flycatcher. In 1934, a wild bird sanctuary was established in Borsdane Wood, the third in Lancashire at the time. A feeding house with a thatched roof was erected, and it was supervised by wood keeper Herbert J. Evans, who was known for chasing out naughty children who ignored the "no cycling" rule.

Today, errant teenagers are more likely to leave cans and set fire to bins, which is where Borsdane Friends Group step in. "There are some very well-off youths here," Dave jokes. The community volunteer group was set up in 2009, and they help monitor and maintain the wood, organising educational nature walks and litter picks. Japanese Knotweed and Himalayan Balsam, two invasive species, have crept in between the trees and part of the group's work now involves balsam bashing. "You can see by the sheer height, nothing has a chance of growing," Dave says. "It's so dominant." Before he retired, he was a mental health nurse working with dementia patients. Borsdane holds great value for him. "It's a sanctuary – everything is so peaceful. All you can hear is birdsong."

In 1986, Borsdane Wood became Wigan's first Local Nature Reserve. This led to the planting of tree species such as Japanese cherry, and western hemlock from north-west America, "like more of a park." These days the council is focusing on native trees and is considering which species will be climate change resistant. "The biggest risk imported trees have is that they could have pests," Kieran says. "That's the major thing. Any trees that have to be imported need to be sprayed and quarantined."

Restocking and managing the wood is a "massive task" and the stakes are high because ancient woodland is irreplaceable. Centuries of growth and the accumulation of leaf-litter, mosses and lichens have created a complex network of habitats that may never recover once disturbed or impacted. Careful thought needs to be taken to ensure it can thrive for generations to come.

"We're getting to the point where old trees are beginning to fail," he says. In their place, new trees will be planted, and these will have to cope with pest disease, drought, and changes in temperature. He points out a horse chestnut that has a fissure twisting up its trunk: this is potato blight. "They get black lines up the main stem," he explains.

The affected trees will be cut down, but their stumps will be left as deadwood. "It's part of a functioning woodland that trees die," he reassures me. "Ecology is never black and white." There are other challenges to consider. Young trees planted at other sites in Wigan have been targeted by vandals who have uprooted them. "It's a lot to think about," he says. "We're trying to stick to as much heritage as we can."

There is also ash dieback – caused by a devastating fungus, *Hymenoscyphus fraxineus* – in the wood. The spores are carried in the wind, and one estimate predicts it will kill four fifths of the ash trees across the UK – a species that is sacred in Celtic and Norse cultures; the mighty ash Yggdrasil is the World Tree in Viking mythology. In British folklore, the ash possessed healing and protective properties against witchcraft. Newborn babies were given a teaspoon of ash sap to ward off ill health.

The tree is considered a good omen and also had its uses in deploying charms. In Lancashire, a woman who wanted to know who her husband would be pulled an even-ash leaf from the tree and incanted: "Even-ash, even-ash, I pluck thee / This night my own true love to see." But there is some positive news: "Some of the ash seems to be resisting," Kieran says. He's come along with a pair of binoculars, and every so often lifts them up to look at a tree to see if it is suffering from the disease.

We've reached the end of the walk. We say our goodbyes on Hindley Mill Lane, and I walk away with the feeling that I've spent the afternoon not just in a woodland, but in the far-distant past.

First published: The Mill, manchestermill.co.uk, as 'The Ancient, Magical Land of Borsdane Wood'

Lockdown in Wigan and Leigh
CLARE SHAW

When the traffic stopped, birds started.
There were owls in the darkness.
Birds woke us early with the sun
they told us we were not alone.
The sky was bigger than we'd remembered
and very blue.

RESTORATION

Then the parks became meadows,
there were flowers.
The gulls sang a memory of ocean.
and the magpie shouted *stay home*
There was suddenly so much thyme.
In the night, we heard foxes scream.
When the hospitals filled with our sick
we looked to trees. Oak breathed for us
and the chiff chaff insisted *stay safe*.
Then we sang from our lonely rooms
like the birds
and we felt our hearts break and ease
and the robin was river
and though it was the end of the world,
a snail climbed up our window –
we watched it.
There were seeds on the ledge –
we saw them grow.
We grew used to being afraid.
The grass in the cobbles was untroubled
and the wren poured its comfort on the air.
There were deer
and the breeze through the door was a memory
of wide fields rippling like sea.
Doves consoled us. Poppies shone for our fallen.
The pavement was home to clover,
buttercups grew in the cracks. Months passed.
Self-heal grew tall on the verges
and though the news was a dream
we could not wake from
there was pollen, there was nectar,
there was bee.

The Healing of Little Woolden Moss

CLARE SHAW

There's beauty in what is repaired,
in old wrongs softened
in moss, and all of its colours.
Though not everything can be restored
here there are dragonflies
and their wings are bright windows –
they lift you.
Here, healing is still in progress
and it sounds like summer.
It is skylark and curlew, buzzard –
the wide sky
where all things are possible,
and the earth
which holds its stories within it
and tells them through curve and ditch
because this a place of purpose
where hard work unmakes mistakes
and though the ground is unstable,
it is soft,
and a man will stand here for hours
to name the birds
and where once there were wounds,
there are scars
and they shimmer
and in summer
the swifts and the swallows return.

*Clare Shaw's poems were written in 2021 when she was
Carbon Landscape Poet, commissioned by Manchester
Literature Festival and Lancashire Wildlife Trust*

Walking on Blades

MARK CARSON

I play to the camera, swing across the field of view
at speed – for it's a heavy bastard and I need the lift –
crashland it squarely on the margin of the nest;
it shakes the structure with a splintering of sticks.

The missus picks her way across; it's nice to see
her dainty choice of gaps to place her killer claws,
(I hear the camera zooming in) the youngsters ducking
to and fro, avoiding early death by puncture.

Such a gorgeous salmon – yet she never smiles
at me, her face a botox mask, incomprehensible.
Tearing herself a chunk she throws the head aside,
the fledglings lining up; *it's one for you, and one*

for you, maybe one for you. They're satiated,
all of them; the kids disperse about the nest
and burp and fart and squirt their filthy faeces
at the camera lens. I seize my chance

and grab the fish-tail, kicking off with it.
At least I get to do the osprey thing alone,
trolling the estuary, strafing the oyster-catchers,
scaring the redshank silly from the shallows,

screaming down the wind, my feet outstretched
with talons sharp as scimitars to grab the lazy
surface-feeders as they trap the flies. This could
be my day! Perhaps I'll catch a sea-bream or a trout.

Kirkdale Cave, North Yorkshire

AMY-JANE BEER

The entrance to the cave is a low slot, 3 metres up the former quarry face. To reach it, we climb rock smoothed by many hands and feet. Inside, the muddy floor is similarly worn, dished and dimpled.

My son moves easily, but I'm on all fours from the off. When I see the roof is decked with small globes of silk I crawl lower still, to avoid dislodging any. They are the nursery webs of cave spiders, *Meta menardi*, each hanging from a mere half-dozen threads. I comment on their delicacy, but the boy assures me that a rope of spider silk can support the weight of a jumbo jet.

The ceiling glitters in torchlight as we go deeper – each gleam is a bead of condensation. In wetter parts, water drips from nipples of calcite. The butterscotch-coloured flowstone on the walls has been buffed ivory here and there by the passage of bodies.

It was beneath a layer of this deposit, now dated to 121,000 years old, that the 19th-century geologist William Buckland catalogued the bones of hippos, bison, deer, rhinoceroses, elephants and hyenas. This ancient ossuary is now held by the Yorkshire Museum, but fossil poop in among the bones identifies the hyenas as the original curators.

The feeding remains here now are smaller: scatterings of moth wings, several in the black-banded mustard livery of large yellow underwings. These must have been dropped by bats feeding last autumn. We can thank lockdown for them not having been swept away by other feet and knees. Around the point where daylight no longer shows, we finally find the web-makers.

Their ebony legs are needle-thin and the females have red-gold abdomens with swirling patterns like those on the surface of Mars. Some are suspended on threads; these ones pirouette in the disturbance of our heat, breath and LEDs. Others step along the walls, toe to toe with their shadows – a precisely choreo-graphed dance in which the projected partners billow and swell to gothic proportions in the lurching torchlight.

Crawling out again, we meet the first of the babies – tiny, newly hatched and making their way resolutely towards the light, where they will wait for an auspicious breeze, then spin a long thread to lift them up and out, into the bright unknown.

First published in *The Guardian*, Country Diary

Oh Wherefore Art Thou, Arctic Tern?
STAN L. ABBOTT

'The Sandwich terns have flown over and recced the island, which is encouraging,' says Sam, the National Trust's assistant warden on Inner Farne, an island a couple of miles off the coast of Northumberland whose public reopening has been delayed by strong winds and high seas. 'We've cleared vegetation and laid gravel beds to encourage nesting,' she continues, as upbeat as possible, though in truth, an aerial recce by Sandwich terns is an indicator only of the likely return to the island of Sandwich terns, not of their smaller relations, so I nudge the conversation towards the elephant in the room: the exodus of that diminutive global wanderer, the Arctic tern, during the previous breeding season under Covid lockdown.

It's mid-April, and Sam's first season on Inner Farne, which is no doubt a far fresher challenge than her previous assignment in the balmy south-west of England. I can tell she's putting a brave face on things, hoping that the Arctic terns, those fierce and feisty migrants that are right now journeying north from the Weddell Sea off Antarctica will arrive back in a few weeks' time. The Arctic tern is the more compact and elegantly fan-tailed cousin of the larger Sandwich terns that are right now hanging around the outer islands. Around 250 pairs are expected to begin nesting near the centre of Inner Farne any day.

No-one can be but amazed at the remarkable and epic journeys made by the tiny terns, which weigh only about 100g, or the same as a quarter-cup of sugar. And there are enormous differences between populations in the routes they take. The Farne Islands Arctic terns are at the southern end of the species' breeding range. When they migrate to Antarctica, they cross the UK to the Irish Sea then travel down the West coast of Africa before wandering east across the Indian Ocean – as far as New Zealand. It is only here that they finally turn south towards Antarctica. The terns that breed further north, on the Arctic archipelago of Svalbard, for instance, head straight down to the Weddell Sea adjacent to the Antarctic Peninsula. This is probably because the breeding season is later in the High Arctic, and so migration south needs to take place at a time when the ice conditions will be favourable. But from whichever breeding territory, at each point on their journey the birds take advantage of both prevailing winds and optimum food-gathering conditions.

More recently, thanks to geo-tracking technology, ornithologists have found that one Arctic tern travelled *at least* 60,000 miles in a year (equivalent to flying to Australia five times), leaving the Farnes in July and returning to breed late the following Spring. This individual took a month to fly to the tip of southern Africa from where it took a loop east, eventually flying west along the Antarctic shoreline to the Weddell Sea, from where it would eventually take a more direct track back north to its breeding ground.

I leave Sam at St Cuthbert's Chapel and head towards the high point of this cheese wedge of an island. I can see that she and her colleagues have been busy since moving into their seasonal accommodation in the old pele tower and the lighthouse, clearing vegetation and repairing boardwalks. But the island nonetheless exudes a slightly forlorn feel and, perhaps it's the idea of potentially unrequited anticipation, but I can't dispel from my mind an image of the sparse stage setting of *Waiting for Godot*, with its leafless tree and lone bare rock. Buffeted as it is by briny winds off the North Sea, of the former, Inner Farne has none; of the latter it has plenty, with only a thin covering of guano-enriched soil over the dense basalt of the Great Whin Sill. This distinctive intrusion of igneous volcanic rock emerges in places across Durham and Northumberland from High Force in the south to Hadrian's Wall in the North. Here on the coast it manifests in fortified outcrops surmounted by the dramatic castles of Dunstanburgh, Bamburgh and Holy Island, all three of which I can see as I cast my eyes back to the mainland from the Farne Islands, this easternmost Whin Sill bastion.

The February storms have ripped skylights and windows from the wooden building that was, pre-pandemic, the modest visitor centre in which daily bird sightings would be recorded on a blackboard. The unguarded structure was then invaded by pigeons and repair schedules are at the whim of scarce contractors and fickle sea conditions. The chapel too could do with some TLC, but the gravel beds are ready to lure the tiny travellers back with the promise of a five-star welcome.

While making the short crossing on *Glad Tidings IV*, just a little earlier that day, we'd paused to crane our necks towards the highest cliffs on Inner Farne, each eighty-foot rocky turret seemingly topped by a single shag, like elaborately carved pieces from a giant chess set. Beneath the shags – on the columns bleached white by tens of thousands of nesting birds – guillemots are staking their individual claims on narrow ledges.

Back atop the island, I have reached the thick end of the wedge and passed the lighthouse and am now looking down upon that same scene from above. Only a thin steel wire stretches across between me and squawking, chattering mass of birds below. Seen in close-up like this the shags are no longer black, but rather a shimmering mix of petrol blues and emeralds, from which green eyes peer out above the mottled yellow patch behind the bill. In the way of birds' eyes, they seem to shine as tiny LED lights rather than passively absorbing my presence and the level of threat I pose. As island residents, the shags are early layers and the nearest bird appears ready to guard a single off-white egg, though there may well be more in the nest of rough twigs beneath her body. I spread my gaze wider and see a single razorbill standing out from its similarly sized guillemot neighbours, thanks to an artist's lightly drawn white stripe on its blunt-ended beak. A metre away from the shag and its egg, two impressively white and black guillemots are mating to the distinctive cry of kittiwakes (*Kittywake! Kittywake! Kittywake!*) and before long the entire menagerie will be rearing a new generation to the incessant echo of neighbourly squabbles. The guillemots (which look like overgrown puffins, minus the coloured bills) will lay their eggs on the bare rock, from which they are audaciously protected from rolling off by their carefully evolved elongated oval shape.

I scan the fluctuating mass of wings that is fanning the acrid stench of ammonia from decades of guano deposition, hoping to spot the distinctive white face and body of an ocean-wandering fulmar, our 'northern albatross'. Neighbours of fulmars need to be wary. A chick that finds itself alone and under threat in its narrow twig nest will regurgitate the foul contents of its stomach, releasing a projectile plume that can glue a predators feathers together and thus be potentially lethal. Turn that the other way round, and perhaps having fulmar neighbours will protect your own offspring from predatory gulls. The fulmar colony on this part of the island is lower down, and so no nests are visible from the clifftop, where, at some distance, the other birds appear concerned neither by my presence, nor by that of the more professional watchers, making this a fine vantage from which to capture the perfect image.

RESTORATION

I continue my circumnavigation of the island: early puffins are checking out burrows. It's nice to see them at their leisure, arriving on the wing relatively slowly, landing elegantly and then poddling around like mislocated penguins, popping their heads into last year's burrows or perhaps the odd recently abandoned rabbit hole. By and large, puffins will return to last year's burrow, where they'll raise a single puffling. From then on, their onshore arrival will be altogether different as they zoom in fast and low with silvery sand eels lined up in their beaks like plastic Dracula teeth. The objective is not to be mugged by the superior-sized herring or black-backed gulls that are ever ready to steal your catch. Puffins have been just about holding their own on the Farne Islands, though the population is vulnerable to changes in the availability of sand eels – the only safe food for pufflings – as these the availability of these tiny fish has become less predictable in some locations. This unpredictability can leave adult birds no option but to travel widely in search of food. In a good season, though, in less than three months the successful chicks will vanish with their parents into the vastness of the world's oceans. Inner Farne may be the only piece of land their tiny orange 'duck feet' will touch in their entire long lives, returning each year to breed.

The boardwalk continues to the north, then east, as it swings back towards the pele tower. Off the more gently sloping eastern shore grey seals bask on a shingle bank on the islet of Wideopen, while eider are beginning to pair up and have come close to shore in readiness for building their simple nests – nests which the female eider will line with her own fluffy down. The white and black plumage of the males only slightly breaks up their silhouette against a now turquoise 'Mediterranean' sea, which echoes the splash of colour on the birds' heads and necks. In these parts, eider are often called Cuddy's ducks, after St Cuthbert, patron saint of the Saxon Kingdom of Northumbria, whose seat was just over the water at Bamburgh. The saint spent the last decade

of his life alone on the island in a tiny hut. He liked to be surrounded by the nesting birds at his feet. I have only once been
on the island when the eider are on the nest; they are early to
lay and early to hatch. The mottled brown females remain glued
to their eggs and seem oblivious to human presence. Once their
chicks are hatched and ready to take to the water, *en famille,*
closely related birds will join forces with a 'raft' of chicks protected by their mums and aunties.

And so to the missing piece of the avian jigsaw, the one whose
arrival we await as for Godot: the Arctic tern. In August 2021 I
learned about the exodus of the entire breeding colony of close
to 1,000 pairs. Stepping ashore that summer's day, I had found
it eerily quiet; the vegetation untidy and overgrown. Being that
late in the season, I knew we were unlikely to see any Arctic
terns, but nor was there any evidence of any breeding success
for these chattering little globetrotters, whose migration is the
longest in the avian kingdom and belies their seeming frailty. I
bumped into one of the wardens: my heart paused and my flesh
chilled. 'It wasn't that all the birds had left,' he said: rather, 'they
hadn't come here at all'.

The early lockdowns of the Covid pandemic had brought
us the odd lighter animal-inspired moment: goats pacing the
streets of Llandudno and fallow deer on zebra crossings in
London. What had not been apparent back then was that the
Arctic terns, which have developed the harassment of day-trip-
pers on Inner Farne to something of an artform, nonetheless
actually depended on a human presence for their breeding
success. Before Covd struck, you'd step ashore and pick your
way up the hill towards the chapel, taking care not to trample
any of the ubiquitous Arctic tern nests, each with its carefully
numbered lollipop stick marker. Wandering amongst ground
nesting birds like this is a rare enough phenomenon here in the
British Isles. Covid changed all that and, as I write, we can but

guess if the change is for ever or if word will have got round the tern community as they begin to return north: 'Hey guys, the humans are back!'

In a successful breeding season, to get up close to the puffins or the high-rise cliff-dwellers, you must run the gauntlet of many more Arctic terns... and there's no excuse for not coming prepared. 'Bring a hat!' urges the National Trust website, a message reinforced by the captain of your boat on the short crossing from Seahouses.

On my most recent visit in 2019, my first encounter with the well-travelled 'sea swallows' came even as I left the jetty; some birds had nested right on the path itself. One rose from its nest and hovered jerkily at my eye level on its slender white and grey wings, cackling manically like one of Macbeth's witches. 'I've been to places you can only imagine,' it goaded me. It was almost close enough to reach out and touch and I could just about look into its beady black eyes as it assessed whether it should bother with me, happily returning to the nest once I was a yard or two beyond it.

Above the little cobbled courtyard by the chapel the birds get really feisty: feisty enough to actually draw blood with their sharp-tipped crimson beaks. And this is the puzzle: if the birds devote such energies to terrorising human visitors, surely they should have welcomed our absence and that of the wardens during the pandemic. I talk to Chris Redfern, Emeritus Professor at the School of Natural and Environmental Sciences, at Newcastle University, who knows about as much about Arctic terns as there is to know: he's been following the Farnes colonies since childhood and tells me that the occasional dive-bombing mission is just a 'behavioural response'. As often as not the birds may make a lot of noise but will recognise that visitors don't pose a threat and may often stay on the nest, even with people gathered around them. Perhaps counter-intuitively then, on a mainland site, a human incursion might well lead to the birds abandoning their nests altogether, for which reason there is no public access to the colony down the coast at Long Nanny, something that suggests arctic tern colonies develop their own particular 'niche' behaviour according to some rules we humans are as yet unable to de-code. The bird's tolerance of humans is therefore what makes a trip to Inner Farne so special.

Chris tells me: 'Early in the season in 2021, about May and after lockdown, some people had taken photographs of Inner Farne, from which it was apparent that the terns had abandoned the island, now overgrown with vegetation. But when I went out last year to Brownsman Island it was pretty clear that there were substantial changes there too.'

Less frequented Brownsman doesn't have the visiting day boats of Inner Farne, but it too has a modest complement of National Trust wardens who spend the summer in the old lighthouse keeper's cottage there. 'Last year there were no Arctic terns nesting immediately around the cottage as they had done in previous years,' continues Chris. 'They had moved to the other side of the island into deep vegetation, and there was very poor nesting success. The chances are that the group that's moved from Inner Farne will have done quite badly too.'

In fact, although a few ringed Arctic terns from Inner Farne were later located on Brownsman, most of the Inner Farne colony appeared to have dispersed more widely – some to Staple island in the outer Farnes, others some twenty miles south to Coquet Island (home to the country's largest colony of threatened roseate terns), while others had flown much further afield to the Isle of May, some fifty miles north off the coast of Fife.

'At the beginning of the season last year a lot of people were blaming the National Trust for the abandonment. That's a bit unfair. The Trust responded to the pandemic in the same way that other organisations did and they really had no option but to withdraw their staff to the mainland. But it's given us an important lesson which will help in future planning for the management of this island colony – that it's important to *have* people there.

I spoke to Gwen Potter, the National Trust's Countryside Manager for the Northumberland Coast, who goes slightly further and suggests that the birds even follow the wardens around. She's upbeat about the terns' possible return and tells me about significant investment in new ways of managing the vegetation, as well as a strong warden presence early in the season to deter predators. Decoy terns may also help bring the birds back as they arrive from their long journey from Antarctic seas.

Perhaps, like Godot, the Arctic Tern derives its attraction to us precisely because of its enigmatic behaviour, and like eminent literary scholars who pore endlessly over Beckett, Chris Redfern and others have devoted their lives to the body of knowledge on the Arctic Tern. Despite this, it retains many mysteries. And while we know that Godot will never come; Chris, Sam the warden and many more, myself included, live in the hope that the Arctic tern shall, once again, do so.

A NOTE ON AVIAN FLU: A modest number of Arctic terns were reported to have returned to Inner Farne by the end of May 2022, with pairs nesting in the courtyard by the pele tower and alongside the boardwalks. With the first egg laid on May 19, there was optimism of an eventual more comprehensive return in coming years. And there the story should have ended on a positive note. However, avian flu returned this year – with a vengeance – posing a significant threat to a widening number of species. I returned to Inner Farne on July 1, 2022, where I saw several dead kittiwakes. Guillemots are also suffering and, further north, the Bass Rock and Shetland gannet colonies. The day following my visit, the islands closed to the public. Hope remains that the impact on puffins and Arctic terns will remain modest. Sand eels appeared plentiful and the Arctic tern colony was estimated at about two thirds its pre-Covid numbers, showing good numbers of healthy chicks. It is of course hoped that all birds affected will show some form of resilience and return next year.

Mersey River
JENNIFER LEE TSAI

Listen   some shattering in the void of my form
I hear your song   borne on the cry of a seagull
the river flows   entranced
by the operatic language of the sea   which beguiles
a geography of otherness   This otherness
becomes me   I swim towards the coastline
clasping mementoes   from my grandfather
a Chinese passport   papers from the Blue
Funnel Line   photographs in sepia
grandmother's jade pendant   translucent white-green
Blemished entities   rise and dissipate
twist and untwist   speckles split
the coastline   Beyond waste chemicals
breaking stabilities   on the scaur
like phonetic entities   one pulse
through the murky field   alluvium birls
Listen   I want to hear you speak to me
I do not want the city   to forget you
or the other Chinese sailors   of Chinatown

Walney Island
KATE DAVIS

'The land was ours before we were the land's...'
'The Gift Outright', by Robert Frost

A ribbon curving the tip of this dead-end
peninsula; glacial clay and terminal moraine
laid down under the last liquefying gasp
of a thousand yards of ice. This place

did not invite us; we came,
hunter-gatherers dream-time dazed, to pile shell
on emptied shell, to cut and burn,
to tear up its precious buried things.

And still it bears the great weight of us,
puts up with our grimy paraphernalia.

But there are nights and sea-mists
and days of plundering wind when we hear
the far cry from its iron core:
No-one owns the land – the land owns you.

Bores on the Solway

ANN LINGARD

The tidal bore on the Solway approached "with a hoarse and loud roar, and with a brilliance of phenomena and demonstration, incomparably more sublime than if the wide sandy water were densely scoured with the fleetest and the most gorgeously appointed invading army of horsemen; before the first wave can be descried from the shore, a long cloud or bank of spray is seen, as if whirling on an axis, and evanescently zoned and gemmed with mimic rainbows, and the rich tintings of partial refraction, sweeping onwards with the speed of a strong and steady breeze."[1]

So wrote a possible observer in 1848, seemingly carried away with the eloquence of his prose. Fifty years later, George Nielsen described the tidal bore approaching the River Eden "with great speed"; "the wave is white with tumbling foam; a great curve of broken surf follows in its wake; and the white horses of the Solway ride in to the end of their long gallop from the Irish Sea with a deep and angry roar". And indeed, there are much earlier accounts of people being swept away and drowned by the bores as they swept up the rivers: in February 1216 followers of the Scottish king Alexander II, laden with spoils from pillaging Holme Cultram Abbey, were crossing the ford on the Eden when the incoming tidal bore overtook and drowned 1,900 men.[2]

The first time I experienced the Solway bore I was actually out in the firth just to the West of Bowness – standing chest-deep in the water, in a line of haaf-netters, fishing for salmon. Distant Criffel had been blotted out by the rain that was beating in our faces, but a dark line with a wavering white crest appeared on our seaward side, moving upstream towards us and accompanied by a low roar. There was laughter, and a shout of 'Whose idea was this, then?', and we all hastily waded for the shore. It was not a large bore, perhaps only 30 centimetres high, but it seemed animate in its purposefulness, pushing on up the Firth. Behind it, the brown water rose quietly up the mudflat and spilled silently, frothy-edged, into the creeks. After the bore had passed, we carried our nets back into the water and resumed our fishing, shifting positions in the line as the incoming tide rose higher. The second time I saw a bore was at Grune Point at the edge of Moricambe Bay: it's only in retrospect that I understand what I saw – I was sitting on the edge of the saltmarsh with artist Lionel Playford, and as he sketched we were chatting about the patterns of stillness and turbulence on the water as the tide slowly rose in front of us. A shallow layer of water had covered the mudflats and was calm and glossy, when what seemed merely a low wave less than 10 centimetres high curved around the point and, itself unshowy but silvery, over-rode the smooth surface. It poppled against the saltmarsh's edge and carried on past us up into the creek.

There are perhaps a dozen estuaries in Britain where a tidal surge, bore or aegir occurs, and even then they are not easy to predict, but the main requirements are that the incoming tide is funnelled into a narrowing estuary; a big spring tide is due; and there should not have been much rainfall to swell the outflowing rivers. The Severn bore is the most famous, but others include bores at Arnside on the River Kent by Morecambe Bay, and on the Rivers Eden and Nith that empty into the Solway.

On the weekend of October 17th and 18th, 2020, spring tides with ranges of about 10 metres were predicted, and rainfall had been (unusually) low for Cumbria and Dumfries & Galloway. By Sunday social media were already showing photos and videos of various bores on the Upper Solway – by Burgh Marsh, and on the River Eden and the River Wampool.

So on the Sunday I too visited the Wampool and was thrilled to hear and see that bore for myself. The river was low, and a flock of gulls was resting and arguing on a sandbank down-river. Suddenly there was the sound of sighing and shushing, and the gulls flurried up onto the surrounding fields. And then it came – a glinting line of water, rushing inland. It wasn't a single wave, but a train of several smooth wave-forms chasing the front-runner in orderly fashion. The leader hit the supports of the bridge, and split around them, then its edges swashed and broke noisily along the banks. But all the while the waves kept pace with each other, even as the front poured and rattled over a small shingle bed below the bank. And, as on that Solway bore, the front pulled the tide behind it so that the water reached up the banks in minutes. Comparing the height against the bridge supports before and after the bore passed, nearly two metres of height had been gained in 10 minutes. And the current, brown with sediment, raced on upstream, with lumps of tree-trunks and timber swirling on its back. Brown foam spun in eddies below the bank and the sound now was of rushing, splashing water. How far inland did it travel? I wish I knew where its energy had fizzled out. It would be a fine thing to fly in a gyroplane on a day when a Solway bore was expected, and to watch the Upper Solway fill and spill into the rivers.

I'd naïvely thought that the bores would happen shortly after the tide turned, but this is not the case – and when you look at the map and know the areas that the Upper Firth includes, it begins to make more sense that the bores often occur much later in the tidal cycle, sometimes just before predicted high tide. To confuse predictions even further, the tidal cycle in the Upper Firth is far from cyclical – the ebb takes up a disproportionately long period compared with the flow. At Torduff Point on the Scottish side, for example, there are only two-to-three hours between low and high water; the rest of the near-six-hour cycle is taken up with the ebb. But at Carsethorn on the mouth of the Nith, and at Silloth on the west side of Grune Point, the six-hour cycle is fairly standard.

To imagine the Upper Solway basin filling up evenly, like water in a bath, is wrong: there are the river channels, the sandbanks, the vast disc of Moricambe Bay, the friction created by the shallows and the scaurs, the hollows and channels around Port Carlisle … Knowing the time of low water at Silloth, I've waited at Grune Point during the big spring tide, waited for the tide to flood – and slowly, very slowly, a glimmer appears in a distant channel nearer the Scottish side; after two-and-a-half hours the sandy, muddy expanse of Moricambe Bay is still exposed, even though it's only 'just around the corner' from Silloth. Then suddenly, after about three hours, the tide arrives, and rapidly fills the bay, bubbling and hissing at the edges of the sculpted mudflats and the small cliff-edges of the saltmarsh. And still it floods in, until at least an hour-and-a half past Silloth's high water time.

It is at that late stage that the dammed-up pressure of the tide suddenly overcomes the force of the outgoing fresh water from the rivers – and breaks through. So the bore on the Wampool exploded up-river at about the same time that high water was due at Torduff Point; the bore on the Eden – further to the North-east, also roared up-river at about the same time.

And as that bolus of water pushes up the river so it forces the river's flow to temporarily reverse; the turbulence at the edges sweeps up the sediment; sometimes the bottom of the leading edge is slowed by friction against the river bed so that the peak of the wave topples over into an aerated white crest. The dynamics of every bore, even in the same river, are always different, dependent on the relative flows of fresh and salt, the heights and the weather. It would be so easy to become addicted to looking for bores, to become a 'bore bore' …

The Valley
MIKE BARLOW

This valley starts and ends where you can see it.
There's nothing else. Beyond could be a Christo work,
wrapped in mist, draped in rain or summer haze.
Sometimes the main road whines like toothache,
or a train trundles over a nerve or Mason's
milking parlour hums a low level tinnitus.

From Furnessford bridge to the falls where we watch
trout leap towards their spawning ground
we are defined. Broadband, though, is with us,
the unimaginable entering unimagined fields
where a ginger-flanked buck grazes amongst geese
and a parliament of rooks unsettles the woods.

Stacking logs beneath a daylight moon, the silent
flight of a summer owl's just something
one of us means to tell the other but forgets
while headlines on a lit screen seem no more
than flimsy narratives foisted on a world
already at ease in its own mind.

Clavicle Wood

Andrew Michael Hurley

It's nothing to look at, Clavicle Wood. A half-mile, L-shaped strip of trees that first parallels a railway cutting and then dog-legs along a stretch of Sharoe Brook, a cloudy urban stream which twists its way through the north side of Preston. But when the Covid pandemic struck and we were forced to find natural spaces closer to home, it became something of a sanctuary, a place where the long weeks of lockdown could be charted not by the graphs of cases and casualties but by the progression of floral changes: snowdrops to celandine to bluebells to the swirl of downy cottonwood seeds let loose on a warm afternoon in May, making it seem as if it had snowed.

Its fate, however, might already have been spelled out. During the building of the new housing estate further along the rail-way line, all the poplars that once bordered the embankment were ripped out (a vicious process, I remember, in which cranes yanked at the trees as if they were stubborn teeth) and a high wooden fence put there instead to deflect the noise of the pass-ing Pendolino trains.

In the same way, the land next to Clavicle Wood – part of an old golf course turned to wild meadow – has long been ear-marked for development (that vague but ominous word), and so at some point the maple, beech, hawthorn and sycamore here might well be deemed just as unimportant and inconvenient too.

It brings to mind Blake's line, 'The tree which moves some to tears of joy is in the eyes of others only a green thing that stands in the way.'

For those of us who love and need these natural spaces between the bricks and concrete, the thought processes that might lead a person to be so unconcerned about the destruction of a wood are unfathomable. It's baffling that the same place can, to someone else, have no *meaning* at all. But then if there's a profit to be made, meaning can be expunged from pretty much anything.

On the plans for Beech Crescent or Cottonwood Close, or whatever name they give to the roads that might eventually replace and recall the trees that are uprooted, the wood will no doubt be nothing more than a set of measurements. So many acres to be cleared away. There will be no note of the name we've given it, nor of the memories that it holds for us, or for anyone who has spent time here. It will be 'valueless' in that sense.

Although it will be upsetting to be reminded of this year, it's important that the wood remains. Because once life experiences, good or bad, are tangled up in a particular place, that place becomes precious, or at least significant. It's the site where some of our roots are planted, somewhere which shows us that we have lived and what we've lived through.

In his book *Common Ground*, Rob Cowen talks about this 'emotional intertwining' of people and locality, and explains how 'time spent in one place deepens this interaction, creating a melding and meshing that can feel a bit like love'.

I'd always thought this sort of idea more than a little quixotic, the preserve of the minority who'd spent their entire lives in timeless rural places, but by retracing my footsteps through the wood during lockdown, in various states of numbness and apprehension, I began to see how that reiterated path-making might begin to bind emotion to physical space. When so much thinking and feeling has occurred in one place, it's hard not to be reminded of those contemplations on future visits.

But memory is a diminishing return, of course, and recollections come to us rosy with nostalgia, or perhaps wholly inaccurate. Yet we expect that. It's the ability to feel that our emotional lives are associated with and expressed by place that matters.

It's a feeling that John Clare voices in his poem 'Remembrances', one of several penned in opposition to the Enclosure Acts:

Summer pleasures they are gone like to visions every one,
And the cloud days of autumn and of winter cometh on:
I tried to call them back but unbidden they are gone
Far away from heart and eye and for ever far away...

The memories he speaks of here have not only been made to seem distant by the passage of time but, we discover, by the wide-scale devastation of the landscape in which they were formed. Clare talks of seeing places special to him torn up by the 'never weary plough' and describes how a beloved tree 'To the axe of the spoiler and self interest fell a pray.'

The feeling of 'belonging' that we're talking about here requires that the physical appearance of a place doesn't change all that much; that the past – collective and personal – feels alive; that it remains embodied in the landscape and decipherable by those who live there. Yet, this is almost impossible in suburbia, the edges of which are always being added to, and where the past, especially the recent past, is usually removed in its entirety. Once work on a new housing estate gets going, it's hard to picture what the land used to look like before, and the speed of it all doesn't give us enough time to process what's being lost. This is why during lockdown, when there was a hiatus in building work, it was possible to see more clearly the importance of preserving somewhere like Clavicle Wood, in words if nothing else.

INTERIOR
It's a damp afternoon in early September, and now that things have returned to a semblance of normality, the main road by the wood is back to a constant flow of cars and lorries.

But step into a wood and everything changes, every sense is altered.

The immediate and unexpected feeling for a place as small as Clavicle Wood is enclosure. It's all trees. Suddenly. A few paces in and they've sprung up behind me in a tousled screen: syca-more, elder, hawthorn, sapling oak and sapling ash and the huge cottonwood trees above them all. The effect is so complete that even though the wood is only twenty or thirty feet wide here, I can't see the road or the houses of my estate anymore. There is only the BMX track that did for my son's collarbone winding between the trunks, the trees that came down in Storm Ciara in February incorporated ingeniously into the course.

The birch that I'd watched from my house being decked by the wind still lies where it fell, however, too heavy to move, its splintered trunk rotting and soft and covered in bracket fungus. Other trees have toppled more recently, making it necessary to clamber over them or under them. But the blockade invites touch: smooth skin, hard, rutted bark, knotholes, splits, forks. I'm close enough to sniff the different trees. None of them are as fragrant or pungent as pine, but there's something almost home-opathic about the smell: a faint hint of vegetation at the back of a water-pure cleanness. It's potent enough, whatever it is, to subdue the exhaust fumes from the road outside.

A few yards on the clamour of the traffic is starting to be replaced by the sound of the treetops moving in the wind, of the rainwater pattering down through the leaves and branches as if from broken taps. A robin sings above me and is answered by another further off. I walk on, stop, walk a little further, trying to pinpoint the moment where the sound of the road disappears completely.

During lockdown, it wasn't only how far we could go that changed by how we *moved* too. In taking our allotted daily dose of fresh air, we were urged not to linger but to simply exercise and return home. The wood was then a place to pass through; now, there is a certain freedom to be still and loiter. Which I do. When all man-made noise ceases, I stand and close my eyes and try to listen only to what's here, what *this* space and no other contains. If the wood offers us meditative seclusion, then it seems proper to accept. As Thoreau says, 'What business have I in the woods, if I am thinking of something out of the woods?'

There's a tone of veneration in his words that alludes to the ancient analogy of the wood as sacred, the wood as temple. And certainly in April and May, when it seemed that every day here, there was something new and vibrant growing, it was easy to understand how the arrival of the summer might have once been considered a visitation from the divine.

It's that the interior of a wood, like that of a man-made place of worship, is differentiated from the outside by a feeling of closeness with some (more powerful) *other*. Immersed in a wood, we can describe its contents taxonomically, we can explain biological processes, but the experience of *being* for the living things here is utterly incomprehensible to us. Trying to imagine what it is like to be that robin in the branches, how it experiences the wood, other creatures, its own song, the air, is like trying to imagine a different dimension. We simply cannot grasp how the things of the natural world conceive themselves.

Even the idea of self-conception is misleading. An ego is a human burden. The 'harmony' that we seem to notice in nature is achieved through an intelligence or a knowing that's beyond us.

The Private Life of *Lepus lepus*
JANE ROUTH

i. at his toilet

If he had not been so particular...

the meadow still, morning light in the dew
Nothing moves

a black   flickering

RESTORATION

something about his left ear
he scratches scratches scratches
with his hind leg

a quick change of sides,
right leg behind right ear to even things up
then flicking the left again and again

He sits up

paddles his front feet in the dew
rubs them together, rubs and rubs
then washes his face

paddles in the dew
rubs his paws together and together
and washes his face

Did I see him spit on his hands?

ii. sleeping

Only because I already knew...

there: in the slight south-facing dip
before the meadow curves down to the wood

that last molehill in the run,
the soil slightly lighter (ears flat-packed along his back)

Day after day in his form
blades of grass just so

Is he dead?
Watch

sometimes a deep breath
– the molehill heaves.

NORTH COUNTRY

Day after day
I watch at the upstairs window.

iii. about his business

Hare gone dandying
down in the woods
His fields, not mine

I can see where he lay

O I want to walk out
in his field
and touch his form

I know every blade
could walk straight there
three paces left of those rushes

iv. betrayed

After the gale, making notes:
which trees to be felled, fences
to be tightened, and a short cut

unintended
close by his form
its deep slot, angle of thigh

Old man hare lolloping by
along the berm
treats me to his disregard

He saw me
        looking
Won't be back

The Chevin, Otley

CAREY DAVIES

It's a bright and blustery October day, and I walk up the Chevin escarpment through an autumn soundscape: the dry, susurrous rustle of crisping oak leaves in the wind; the rattle-cackle of fieldfares as they raid a hawthorn for its red bounty; the delicate chatter of a flock of linnets, newly banded together for the months ahead.

I walk into a swathe of woodland I used to love as a kid, full of millstone grit boulders and makeshift rope swings. It is dominated by hundreds of beech trees, some perhaps 30 metres tall, creating a high, cathedral-like canopy. The dark, slate-grey trunks are spaced far enough apart that you could slalom a bus through them, and they have a kind of gothic grandeur: stone columns supporting a huge, vaulted roof of green and gold.

Today, when I walk into this hall of beeches, the wind recedes to a high whisper, and there is an oddly comforting sense of both enclosure and spaciousness. But at the same time the light darkens, and as always I am struck by how bare the forest floor is. That dense foliage – and the carpet of beechnuts that it sheds – has the effect of suppressing growth in the understorey.

Beech is classed as non-native outside southern Britain due to its absence at the end of the last ice age (although recent scholarship in Scotland has challenged this), and is sometimes removed by foresters. But to contextualise beech, I wonder if we need to look back even further. In the forests of the deep past, where beech evolved (along with all our woodland species), the grazing, tramping and disruption inflicted by now-extinct megafauna – including elephants – would have fostered diversity by constantly creating dead wood; paradoxically, one of the best ingredients for new life.

Woodland ecosystems evolved to adapt to this creative destruction, and it remains the case that the best way of encouraging biodiversity in forests is to recreate the sort of messy havoc these giant beasts would have inflicted – but we tend to be averse to untidiness in our natural spaces. In looking at empty forest floors like this, perhaps we shouldn't see a tree species that "doesn't belong", but more a failure of our own imagination.

First published in *The Guardian*, Country Diary

Alport Castles
for J.W

HELEN MORT

The wind let the landscape move
how it always wanted to,

leaned us together
like ferns, or upper branches

and we walked the slope
believing we were part of the scenery

talking about music and summits,
places we'd never go again.

Then the rocks finished my sentence -
tall and architectural:

their moat of grass
their keep of clouds,

more intricate than any human fort.
We sat up high and praised

like two off-duty gods
as if a view was something

made. And the clouds
over Derwent mended

and we were briefly glorious,
though neither of us had

built, would build a single thing.

Commonality

POLLY ATKIN

Every evening now we walk on the common. We walk clock-
wise, checking the duckpond for frogs or herons, before moving
slowly up under the trees, past the metal bench without touching
it, and along the last strip of tarmac to the end of the overgrown
tarn we call Heron Pond, though the maps and guidebooks insist
it is White Moss Tarn. In the wet months the heron is always
there, stalking through reedy water, or pretending to be invisible
behind the cloche of the willow or wall of rhododendrons.

Here we turn off the main route, following a thin indentation
that curves up and back almost parallel to the way we have just
come. It takes us onto a boggy moor with craggy knolls dotted
over it like sleeping trolls, and paths winding between scattered
trees. Sometimes we climb a troll and look down towards Rydal
Water, which has been creeping further and further away from us

these last weeks as we move only on foot. We follow one path, or another, skirting the crags as if circling a moat, and emerge back onto the road from behind the wall of an enclosed wood.

Every walk is the same. Every walk is different.

Sometimes we are especially tired or the weather is bad, and we only go as far as heron pond, and return parallel to the tarmac, on a path raised and half-hidden in the trees, that once was the road. The ponds alongside it have dried up in the strange drought of this first pandemic Spring. They are leaf-pits now, strewn with weed which dripped from sodden branches in the ceaseless rain of February, and has dried into grey-green curtains of moth-eaten lace. This path is always Autumn underfoot; old leaves and beech mast all year round. As the weeks roll by we have to stoop lower and lower to creep under the branches of the big trees as they green.

We are not alone when we walk. We cross paths with neighbours and greet them from a distance. We see red squirrels leaping from one side of the road to the other, or chasing each other up the garden trees in their cloisters or the feral trees on the path. There is a tawny owl who hunts along the same route we take. We disturb it day after day without meaning to. Sometimes it sits in a tree and blinks down at us; sometimes it keeps three trees ahead of us. We meet herdwick sheep who have fled their fields to exercise their historic grazing rights on this land that used to be theirs, who watch us cautiously, checking whether we have come for them before they relax. We see birds we are learning to identify with a bird song app that records their voices as we stand and listen, trying to fix cadences in our minds. We see ones that we cannot mistake: fighty jay, shouty wren, cuckoo cuckoo cuckoo.

Sometimes we disturb a deer grazing one of the gardens of the empty second homes along the road or the dell that sinks and rises behind the duckpond. This dell, like the duckpond, was created when one of the large houses was built in the late 1880s. Trees were felled, and the fell-side scooped out for the house and its walls. It is waste-land that has re-greened itself into segments of meadow and swampy grove, perfect for deer to hide themselves in. One rainy evening we see a roebuck standing there, next to a tree we once watched a barn owl hunt from until it got so dark all we could see was its white face like a moon. The roebuck watches us watch him and does not run.

When I find an antler on the path one day I say this is it: once I find the other that's me gone out of this shell and into the woods. I half believe it.

*

The first winter I lived in Grasmere I got lost on the common in the snow. I followed a path which vanished into untrodden commonality, as so many paths do. It went everywhere, or nowhere. I was less than a mile from home. But even then, in those days when I thought I had left sickness behind in town somewhere, I knew my limits: my aptitude for falling and for breaking. I thought of Lucy Gray. I thought of my colleagues on call for mountain rescue. I turned back, retraced my steps. I hated to retrace my steps. I thought to return the same way I went out was a kind of failure. I had a lot to learn. The common helped teach me.

The second time I took that path the foxgloves were out. It was raining, heavily. I had not accounted for how the seasons change everything. Paths that seemed confusingly various in the snow had vanished completely into waist-high bracken. I got turned around again.

I would not know for many years the range of the common, the vastness of it, how many small and various worlds it encompasses. I had only wanted to walk out but stay close to home. The path sent me home, but never the way I planned.

*

It may be impossible for me to write about my relationship with Grasmere without plagiarising or self-plagarising, parody or self-parody. I tell people I came to Grasmere by mistake.[1] I went to Grasmere to live deliberately.[2] I went to Grasmere to research other people living deliberately, and learnt to live deliberately. I retired to the mountains to make work that might live.[3] I retired to the mountains to live. I had a mysterious sense of pre-existence of a life I might lead there, a prophetic instinct of the heart.[4]

I moved to Grasmere to study how the Wordsworths made it their home, how they called into being a myth of home so powerful it has shone through the centuries like a beacon, luring others to the hot centre like moths.

I theorised that one of the ways they made Grasmere home was through repetitive local walks, looping the 'huge concave' of Grasmere's 'circular vale'.[5] I wrote of walking as a way of knowing and getting to know. I began, little moth, to do this myself.

*

The common is a diversion, a nothing-place. A place to stop because you can. There are no gates, no stiles, no fences to cross.

You could look at it and think it a wild place that has always been wild, but it is edgeland, industrial wasteland, domestic margin.

In 1829 De Quincey describes it as 'that rocky and moorish common (called The White Moss)',[6] a place of 'swamps', apparitions of the air, and the 'silence of ghosts'.

In 1802 Dorothy Wordsworth describes it as 'this White Moss a place made for all beautiful works of art & nature, woods & valleys, fairy valleys & fairy Tairns, miniature mountains, alps above alps.'[7]

In 1802 it is an inhabited fairyland, useful and used. Not an empty world or a private one, as Dorothy's next sentence shows:

RESTORATION

'Little John Dawson came past us from the wood with a huge stick over his shoulder.' She writes about being driven from walking on the path 'by the horses that go on the commons.'[8]

People worked there, slept there, wandered there, camped there, begged there, let loose their horses and got fines there. People fell into the quarries and died there. People lost their eyesight to quarry blasts there. A man was stabbed in the leg by a young girl there. People foraged and harvested the growth of the land. Commoners fought for their rights and landowners pushed at the common's edges to make space for themselves and their plans. You might be trespassing on some temporary home when you cross it, some borrowed belonging.

Walk there now and you may see none of this. Only fairy wilderness. If you look closer – fairy ruins.

*

In 2015 my partner and I move into a cottage opposite the one I lived in when I got lost on the common eight years earlier. In that eight years I have got iller, the distance I can walk shorter.

I begin to walk on the common because it is close to home; because it feels far when I cannot go further.

I walk there particularly in winter, when my energy levels are lowest. As the bracken dies back in the autumn the paths rise out of it. I learn their ways in winter so I can keep them in my mind in summer. In wet seasons they sink into bog. In dry seasons they reappear like scars.

I love the common because it leads to nowhere but itself, but will never lead you quite the same way twice. I love it because I trust it. I know which paths are safe in which weather. I know how to go there and not hurt myself.

For a long time after I begin to walk there I only go so far, and turn back. When the ground feels uncertain, I retrace the path I know. I keep safe.

Though I'm sure there is a way to cross from the tarn-side of the common to the lake-side, I can't find it. One winter afternoon I think I have it, following a wall which I know meets the road, but I lose the way in the undergrowth, the overgrowth spilling out from the garden of the big house over the wall. The big house is empty most of the year – its garden belongs to the birds and the animals – red deer, red squirrels.

It is a deer who shows me the way. A roe deer, who I meet on the old road one November afternoon. I watch where she goes, how she turns to look back at me. I wait until I can't see her anymore, and I follow her hoofprints in the wet earth.

This is how I learn the circle; how to go through.

*

In early March I go looking for frogs in the tarn. Something shiny catches my eye. I poke it with my toe. Green glass, goblin. I dig with a stick, then my hands, and a bottle emerges, then another. Victorian gingerbeer bottles, marked W.W. Hodgson, Outgate, Ambleside.

Everywhere we walk during these locked-down weeks we find treasures of old waste. A lemonade bottle. Shards of porcelain. Thick glass annealed by fire. Glazed pottery. One path is so strewn with fragments it looks like mosaic.

In December 1890 the *Lakes Herald* ran a story headlined 'An Interesting Boghole', decrying 'obnoxious refuse' marring the landscape of The Lakes. The Lake District Defence Society argued for 'the necessity of keeping the roads free from heaps of rubbish [...] so obnoxious to tourists'. The 'interesting boghole' is White Moss Tarn. To the council it was a nowhere to sink waste in. But to others it was interesting – a boghole with Wordsworthian associations, with plant-life of particular note. A promise is made to move the dump for posterity and tourism. The rubbish is dug in further, covered-over. The boghole becomes a destination in itself.

RESTORATION

130 years later, the rubbish is still resurfacing: proof of lives.

*

To live with illness is to live with uncertainty. To live with illness is to live with disruption. The only certainty is that disruption will come. All planning must circle contingency. Everything circles.

I am realising fully in a way I never have before – not in my body, in the risky fringes of the body – that there are people who have never had their life disrupted by illness. Who have not been forced to accept uncertainty as one of their life's guiding principles. They have never known the boredom of illness, or the repetition. How living with illness is living with a different relationship with time.

I try to remember how I felt as a teenager to realise my body would take priority over any plans I made for it. How every time I broke a limb or ligament I would cry with frustration, convinced my life was over because it was on hold for six weeks, eight weeks, twelve weeks. Months spent at home, half-years lost waiting for tests which yielded no useful results, half-decades lost chasing wrong diagnoses. I remember all this – how it felt to think halting the usual progression of my life for a mere weeks was equivalent to ending it – and try to feel empathy for those that feel that way now.

I remember how it felt to finally find out why my life was like this. I hadn't been imagining it, or wishing it, as I had been told so many times by so many doctors. It was genetic, in me at the very core and the very smallest parts of me. I could stop pretending to believe I could manifest a life uninterrupted by sickness. I could learn to live with disruption, diversion, repetition.

I think of all of this as we circle the common, as I stop to catch my breath, or watch a bird, or click a joint back into place, or to rest, or to listen for the deer whose unseen watchfulness has raised my hackles. I try to find toleration for people's anger at lockdown.

Together, we talk about risk, how ill and disabled people must account for risk and plan for contingency and can never forget it.

In early May, Miranda Hart compares living with Chronic illness with living in lockdown:

'Chronic Illness is lockdown, it is quarantining. Anyone who is finding lockdown hard, imagine being the only one in lockdown [...] Imagine having dreams for your life, then being told to go into Lockdown: that is Chronic Illness.'[10]

Chronic Illness for many is a kind of permanent lockdown, but the lockdown most people experience in 2020 is nothing like Chronic Illness. It's more like breaking a bone. It's horrible, it's inconvenient, it changes your short-term plans, but it won't last forever. Many people found themselves limited to home or a short circumference around home for the first time in their lives. As lockdown eases, their boundaries will expand. For me and millions like me, they won't. They will shrink back further, as the risk of moving through the busy world only increases. I struggle to imagine any ground we could share – any common land that could take us all. If we are in any thing together then it must be as mutable as the common is, as personal to each participant. I tweet I've been in plaster casts that have lasted longer than this lockdown. I try to imagine how it would be to fear the itch more than the falling.

*

As the evenings lengthen we go out later, shifting our wandering hour with the deers' and the daily covid briefing.

Sometimes we follow the stony bridleway down past the old quarries, to amble back along the river to Grasmere through the mossy woods, bluebells ecstatic in the low light. Halfway down we stop and look for evidence of the hutments that once stood there: a shanty town that housed workers on the Thirlmere to Manchester aqueduct.

RESTORATION

In January 1886 various papers ran the same bulletin:

The plant for commencing the Thirlmere Waterworks is rapidly entering the Lake District. During the past few days cabins for the navvies have been constructed on White Moss Grasmere, and labourers are swarming into the district.

Photographs show the hutments bare and functional against bare crags; Dunny Beck at the lower boundary; a pale rough road leading up from them towards the tarn, the tarn itself unseen. White Moss Common looms over the hutments. It's hard to place now, standing at the same point. The tree growth is so immense, it seems a different landscape entirely.

We stand on mossy cushions on rocky outcrops and try and picture the huts; the scene un-greened, un-treed. We examine remnants of wall, smashed pots and glass bottles along the beck. Evidence of habitation. Of working lives.

In 1890 it is estimated there are 450 of 'the pipe track people' living in Grasmere.[11]

Many, though not all of them, would have been living in the shanty town on the common, where now bluebells sway under pine trees broken by their own weight, and deer weave between beeches and birches, and squirrels skitter from high in oaks that sprout out of rocks and look as if they have always been there.

They haven't. This is an ancient wood, and a new one. Cleared centuries ago, regrown through generations of un-use, of abandonment. Natural and not at all.

*

There is one crag – the highest and largest of the common's sleeping trolls – that gives a panorama of Grasmere and Rydal. It is low enough and high enough that you can see both lakes, the angles implausible. Its sides fall into slopes and terraces that feel at once man-made and geologic. The top is a natural or unnatural stage, with a boggy centre enclosed by a walkway of stone. It has an uncanny air – peaceful and watchful – of being occupied a very long time ago, and occupied still. Every time I sit there, on a chair formed from rock, I think I might never be able to turn my eyes away and leave.

Dorothy wrote about the light there, the particular perspective:

> *'There was a strange Mountain lightness when we were at the top of the White Moss. I have often observed it there in the evenings, being between the two valleys. There is more of the sky there than any other place. It has a strange effect sometimes along with the obscurity of evening or night. It seems almost like a peculiar sort of light.*[12]

It is the summit of the common, and the peculiar sort of light there, that makes Dorothy feel 'more than half a poet' one Spring evening in 1802. She records:

> *'night was come on & the moon was overcast. But as I climbed the Moss the moon came out from behind a Mountain Mass of Black Clouds – O the unutterable darkness of the sky & the Earth below the Moon! & the glorious brightness of the moon itself!*[13]

I read this passage so many times without noticing where she was when had this revelation, but once I did, I understood. Anyone who eats the moonlight there could never be the same again.

*

I love the safety of the common and its familiarity. I love the strangeness of the common, its uncanny uncommonness, its particularity. How it is both open and closed. How it opens and closes around you. I love its communality – how it is shared – but also its refusal of the communal. It can never be shared, not even with yourself. It is a different common every time you go there.

RESTORATION

I could walk the common for a thousand years and never know it. I could walk the common for a thousand years and always find a new path, which will lead to a tree, a view, an angle on the village I've never seen before. A pocket of land that seems to have opened up from rock. Sometimes I think I have been walking here a thousand years already, that we're long lost to the woods. Who will recognise us when we meet them on the old road, in the gloaming? Will we still have something in common?

Grasmere, May 2020

Spar Boxes, Northern England

PETER DAVIDSON

North Pennines: high, rain-glimmering roads, precipitous valleys, gritstone chimneys and shafts abandoned among the cotton-grasses of the moors. Washing-floors and waterwheels by upland streams, stone portals in the flanks of the hills. The landscape of W.H. Auden's earliest poetry:

> *Head-gears gaunt on grass-grown pit-banks, seams abandoned*
>   *years ago;*
> *Drop a stone and listen for its splash in flooded dark below...*

The seams of coal and veins of lead below the moors are rich in prismatic minerals as well as in metalliferous ore. Auden wrote in the 1930s of lead mines in decline: ghosts of industry in remote country. But, in the nineteenth century, lead extraction had flourished in Weardale and on Alston Moor as part of the mining which stretched across the north of England from County Durham and Northumberland, to West Cumberland and the Isle of Man.

NORTH COUNTRY

In the same region there flourished the making of spar boxes: glass-fronted cases filled with assemblages of the minerals found among the veins of ore, sometimes an abstract arrangement, sometimes representations of street scenes or fantastical parks or caverns of crystals and shards of coloured minerals. Sometimes a free-standing arrangement of minerals was made to stand under a glass dome: an arch of specularite and quartz, or a glittering tree of fluorspar and crystal needles. So far the history of this art is little known. A few experts are beginning to piece its history together; records have been recovered of spar box competitions in the North Pennines in the late nineteenth century; and there was a spar box of some two thousand mineral specimens, cemented together by a miner, Isaac Robinson of Nenthead, shown in the Great Exhibition of 1851. It may be assumed that the majority of the makers of spar boxes were the miners of Man, Cumberland and the North Pennines, who had access to the minerals as well as slack periods in which to make the arrangements. This would be wholly consistent with the culture of the northernmost counties in England, with their long traditions of bold designs and technical perfection in many crafts, particularly in the making of quilts and rugs.

At first sight the spar boxes appear to be uncomplicated instances of *arte povera*, a cheap art as specific to place and conditions as is arctic carving on bone or walrus ivory. Fluorspar, quartz and galena are found in the Pennine mines, hematite and smoky quartz in the mines of west Cumberland. Coming upon these minerals would be a part of the miner's daily experience. For most of the nineteenth century it would seem that they were available to the miners as a bonus, although with the steady rise of Victorian mineral collecting, some mine owners came to consider the minerals as a profitable sideline for themselves.

The northern mines are often situated in remote country and high among the moors, thus creating the juxtaposition of rough country with the gritstone buildings of small-scale industry which haunted Auden's imagination. In adverse weather it was often impossible to reach the high entrances of the mines. The assumption therefore is that the Weardale spar boxes are the simple product of this enforced leisure: a craft of expediency practised in the miners' sparse and irregular leisure hours. Assemblages of what the men themselves called the 'bonny bits' from the mines, they prolonged into the twentieth century something of the appearance of the spar and crystal garden grottoes of the eighteenth century. (But no such grotto seems to survive in the mining counties.) There are significant reports, in this context, of a nineteenth-century spar box clearly continuing the grotto taste: shells and coral as well as what were described as 'Cornish minerals' formed the decoration. Yet the chief development of the Victorian heyday of the spar box was the construction of the street scenes or scenes of fantasy which combine the grotto-aesthetic with something of the atmosphere of the transformation scenes, 'the radiant revolving realms', which traditionally concluded Victorian pantomimes. The Victorian peepshow, which often contained street perspectives, may also have been a decisive influence.

It is possible that the link between the spectacle of the Victorian minor theatres, peepshows and the spar box is documented by a unique example, now in a private library in Norfolk. Known affectionately to its present owners as 'Little Bo-Peep in the Vaults of Death', it combines minerals, shells, mirrors and figurines into a tableau of a dim grotto with an interior pedimented structure outlined in shells. Inhabiting this ambiguous space is a dressed porcelain figure of a shepherdess. It is not wholly easy to conjecture a date for this artefact, but the middle of the nineteenth century seems likely.

The other sources which may be safely conjectured for the spar boxes is the appearance of the mineral-bearing cavities themselves. John Postlethwaite's *Mines and Mining in the English Lake District* (1913), a copy of which was owned and annotated by the adolescent Auden, describes this exactly:

> *Cavities, called 'loughs', lined with crystalline quartz and other minerals, are frequently met with in veins, some of them not larger than a nut, and others sufficiently capacious to admit several men. The interior of some of the larger loughs, when first broken into, form a spectacle of unrivalled splendour. The walls of the cavity formed of crystallised quartz, aragonite, dolomite, fluor spar, iron pyrites, blende, galena, and other minerals, arranged in the most grotesque order and reflecting the light in a variety of colours from thousands of prisms, produces an effect that cannot be described.*

There were no discernible rules for the construction of spar boxes. They seem to have been a genuinely spontaneous art, existing on the line between popular tradition and the small industry of mineral-dealing. One mining couple from Garrigill near Alston, John and Sarah Walton, founded a modest dynasty of mineral dealers. An indication of the confluence of mineral-dealing with the world of the spar box is given by the advertisement of John Eggleston, who was active in the 1880s as a mineral dealer in Sunderland, but also dealt in 'Birds' Skins, Birds' Eggs, Butterflies, Moths, Shells, Cabinets, Fossils'. A.J. Eggleston of Fairhills exhibited at a geological exhibition in Weardale in 1887, while the greatest of spar boxes was made by an Egglestone, and contained two stuffed birds among its other assemblages. It has been suggested that the aesthetic subtlety of some of the Cumbrian spar-columns is such that more professional artists may have been involved in producing them, perhaps for the mineral shops which then flourished. It also seems likely that the miners from one area themselves occasionally bought in (or exchanged) minerals from other areas for their spar boxes. Certainly, there were exhibitions, and competitions in the 1880s and 1890s in St John's Chapel in Weardale, with competition classes for both spar boxes and for spar models, which could take the forms of columns, arches, rotundas with columns, pyramids or trees.

Papers in the case of a spar box recently sold at Leyburn in Yorkshire, establish a date in the 1830s. This may be the earliest dated English example. Similarly, a pair of small spar boxes, the cases formed as gothick follies, was sold in 2012 by Thomas Coulborn. Conjecturally dated to the 1840s, they seem to look back to the often beautifully crafted mineral souvenirs sold at Matlock and other Peak District towns during the boom in domestic tourism, driven by the wars on the continent, in the late eighteenth and early nineteenth centuries.

This was an art sufficiently within living memory to be revived. In the exhibition of spar boxes held at Killhope in Weardale in 2001, there was an example from the 1920s, made by a steelworker from Workington in West Cumberland which, interestingly, also included shells. Experts suggest that there may have been spar boxes being made in northern England, in continuity with the Victorian tradition, as late as the 1950s. Certainly the tradition was dormant for a short enough time for it to be revived easily, and there are again highly skilled spar box makers in the northern counties. A retired Northumbrian stonemason to whom I spoke a decade ago, remembered from decades earlier the technique of rubbing a cluster of minerals gently on the rounded end of a hammer to divide them into prisms and secure the greatest sparkle. He remembered also some traditions of design for the more elaborate boxes, including the use of multiplying mirrors in the back corners of the case. It took him little more than an evening to construct a small spar box, using tile cement as the medium of adhesion. What emerged from the surprisingly rapid process

of arrangement was a small cave of glimmering spar with sta-
lactites and stalagmites of quartz adding depth and brilliance
to an arrangement which included a receding lake of greenest
fluorspar in the most deeply shadowed corner.

Therefore, so far it seems uncertain that spar boxes were
exclusively local *arte povera*, and it is established beyond doubt
that Weardale boxes usually contain some minerals bought in
from the mines in the west of Cumberland. Records show no
fewer than seven mineral dealers in Alston in East Cumberland
in the course of the nineteenth century, so a source is clearly
identifiable. The population of skilled mining communities is
axiomatically fluid: as there are samples of Pennine fluorite in
virtually every mineral museum in the world, so it was said in
the nineteenth century that one could find a Weardale miner in
any mining community in Europe. This might possibly explain
the fact that there are in existence spar boxes from Bohemia
and Russia, although so far none have emerged from the lead
country of south-west Scotland. There are at least two pro-
to-spar boxes in the *Kunst and Wunderkammer* at Schloss
Ambras in the Tyrol. Perhaps mid-seventeenth century in date,
these cased assemblages of minerals are formed into miniature
landscapes in which small glass figures enact scenes from the
Gospels.

The spar boxes now at the Killhope Museum – the selfsame
lead-workings of Auden's early poem 'Who stands the crux left
of the watershed...' – are themselves the nearest thing there
is to a national collection, though there are also examples in
museums in Kendal and Newcastle. A description of some of
Killhope's finer examples will serve to give a sense of the art at
its most developed.

The Egglestone Spar Box is the grandest in the collection:
a substantial Victorian cabinet with two glass-fronted boxes
one above the other. It was made by Joseph Egglestone of

RESTORATION

Huntshieldford, near St John's Chapel in Weardale, in the first years of the twentieth century. Later it was taken around the local shows by his son, and exhibited for threepence or sixpence per viewing. In the upper case is an assemblage of natural wonders, eloquent of its period, with stuffed birds and mosses arranged behind a proscenium of mineral crystals. Fine pyramids of large pieces of spar stand on the floor of the upper part of the case. The lower cabinet is a superb representational spar box, with a street scene all made of glimmering fragments of minerals multiplied into an infinite boulevard by judiciously placed corner mirrors. There is a grotto-roof of spar and crystals. Little lamp-posts stand among pyramids of translucent and reflective minerals. The effect is remarkably reminiscent of the Victorian pantomime transformation scene, with a close of ordinary houses in the process of metamorphosis into a reflecting grotto.

Nearby is the beautifully restored spar box made by Robert Ridley at Allenheads in 1896. This is a work of the highest fantasy, with magnifying lenses let into the upper part of a magnificent case to give peepholes into a cave of quartz, aragonite and fluorite. The main window in the lower part of the case shows a mirrored street-scene, with two Victorian bow-fronted villas, with lace curtains, facing each other across a shimmering yard. The scene is so organised that you catch a glimpse of your own face framed amongst the transformed villas and paths and pyramids of spar. Originally, the case had provision for the villa windows to be lit by candles.

The Killhope collection has also, under glass domes, cones and arches of spar. There are a pair of rotundas of three spar columns with a circular roof, like the Temple of Vesta in translucent metamorphosis, all made of green fluorspar and white quartz. There is a vast pyramid of purple fluorite, galena and needle-crystals. There is an extraordinary stylised pine tree made up entirely of refracting and translucent minerals. This is a work of art of such strangeness, such confidence and assurance in its use of materials, that it echoes (presumably unconsciously) not so much the eighteenth-century tradition of fluorite grottoes, as the prodigious objects of the Renaissance cabinet of curiosities.

Miners working the deep seams of northern England (or the mine galleries running under the sea) sometimes hacked their way into the loughs, geodes walled and roofed in spar and crystal, stars under earth in the lights of their lamps. It must have been like breaking into a spar box, into a place of glimmering points of light, constellations of crystal.

From *Distance and Memory*

This Wild Garden
VICTORIA BENNETT

For as long back in my life as I can remember, I have used writing to make sense of this world, either through the words of others, or through my own. It has been my constant, in an often changing world. When grief took those words away, I wondered what I would become. Yet, without them, I felt unrecognisable to myself. In the face of death, I needed to see what could live.

As autumn took hold, my four-year-old son and I started digging out the rocks and rubble that made up the ground on which our house was built. A former industrial site, this soil seemed an unlikely place to grow a life, but we began to plant.

A decade on, the garden is a wild, sustainable apothecary, and the seed planted between the hours of care is almost fully grown.

A book. A child. A life.

RESTORATION

The garden does not stay still, any more than the life it holds. September is a contrary month, and my favourite. So much of it is about endings; the slow creep into winter, the darkening days, the falling back of the garden, yet it also carries a curious quiver of energy. Deeper, older, drawn from a knowing that this folding down into winter sleep is something needed. It feels like a yearning, a whisper to curl tight into its cocoon and let the small things grow within.

The harvest is a moment of remembrance, an honouring of the gifts it has brought, and what now passes away, but it is also a time of gathering, and preparing for what will come. I mark my 51st birthday. As the year turns, I gather seeds from the micro-meadow that was once a mowed green lawn. I pick damsons and blackberries for jam, from saplings and bare roots we planted. I forage elderberries and rose hips from the nearby hedgerows, my son now tall enough to reach the higher branches. Like the damson tree, he has grown tall, though I remember the feel of his small hand in mine; the years moving by so fast.

This is the wild garden I have grown. A book. A child. A life.

I do not know what the next decade will hold. It feels so unsteady right now. But to be here, at this moment — to watch my son as he grows into his adult world; to witness my story transforming into a book that will make its way without me into other hands; to see the meadow we nurtured sow its seeds for future years; to make jam from the trees we planted as saplings ten years gone — all this is beautiful. All this holds hope.

April

JEAN SPRACKLAND

machine of spring with all your levers thrown to max
clouds in ripped clothes and sheep trailing afterbirth
where last week's buds sucked blue juice from the dusk
now the branch is swollen   priapic
cherry bling and hawthorn sex-bed smell
motorway hedgerows on thrust   electric rapefields

Your levers are jammed and nothing can pull them back
not now   not front   not squall
city gutters clogged with blossom
muddy ponds spuming with cannibal tadpoles
the long blinding days   your bashed clock
the violent small hours   magpie clacking at the robin's nest

And us lying open-eyed all night
breathing in the green noise of pollen
hearing the long bones of the trees stretch and crack
wondering   will you ever power down or is this it now
wondering   what can any death amongst us mean to you
and will we make it through to summer or is this it now

ENDNOTES

INFLORESCENCE
Anne Taylor
1. Debby Banham, *Food and Drink in Anglo-Saxon England*, 2004
2. Isabella Beeton, *Mrs Beeton's Book of Household Management*, 1861
3. Peter Brears, *Traditional Food in Cumbria*, 2017
4. Geoffrey Grigson, *The Englishman's Flora*, 1955
5. Jane Grigson, *The Observer Guide to British Cookery*, 1984
6. Guide Vert, *La cuisine française*, 1982
7. Shakespeare: *Cymbeline*, Act IV, iii
8. Nancy R Thomas, 'A lion's eye view of the Greek Bronze Age', in G Touchais, R Laffineur, F Rougemont (eds), *PHYSIS L'environnement naturel*

Sally Goldsmith
1. Whitecoal kilns – small pits – have been discovered all over woods in parts of south-west Sheffield. Until the 1980s, no one knew what they were.
2. The Vernon Oak is a 200-year-old street tree in Sheffield, threatened with felling during the campaign by Sheffield Trees Action Group (STAG) against Sheffield City Council and their contractors Amey. This tree and many more were finally saved in 2018 and the Council now works with STAG and other partners under a new strategy.

Nicola Carter
1. Dictionary.com. https://www.dictionary.com/
2. Anil Seth, *Being You*, 2021
3. David Craig, *Native Stones*, 1987
4. George Eliot, *Middlemarch*, 1987
5. Al Phizacklea and Ron Kenyon, *Scafell and Wasdale, FRCC Climbing Guide*, 2014
6. Jan Levi, *And Nobody Woke Up Dead, The Life and Times of Mabel Barker*, 2006
7. Ken Wilson (ed), *Classic Rock*, 2007
8. The Pinnacle Club, *The Pinnacle Club Centenary Journal*, 2022
9. Jan Levi, *And Nobody Woke Up Dead, The Life and Times of Mabel Barker*, 2006
10. Terry Abraham, *Life of a Mountain – A year on Scafell Pike*, Film 2014. Available at https://www.bbc.co.uk/iplayer/episode/b04y4gd7/life-of-a-mountain-a-year-on-scafell-pike [Accessed 16/09/21]
11. Keith Richardson, *Joss*, 2009
12. Carlo Rovelli, *Helgoland*, 2021
13. H E Rollins (ed), *The Letters of John Keats*, 1958
14. Mihaly Csikszentmihalyi, *Flow*, 2002
15. William Wordsworth, '*I wandered Lonely as a Cloud*' (First published 1815) *The Collected poems of William Wordsworth*, 1994
16. William Wordsworth, 'The World Is Too Much with Us', *The Collected poems of William Wordsworth*, 1994
17. Simon Bainbridge, *Mountaineering and British Romanticism*, 2020
18. Alan Hankinson, *Coleridge Walks the Fells*, 1991
19. Al Phizacklea and Ron Kenyon, *Scafell and Wasdale, FRCC Climbing Guide*, 2014
20. Heino Lepp, *Case Studies – Beatrix Potter*. Available at https://www.anbg.gov.au/fungi/case-studies/beatrix-potter.html [Accessed 2/01/22]

Jack Hartley
1. In 2023, "Cumbria" will become two separate districts—"Cumberland" and "Westmorland and Furness"—reflecting something of the county's historic division which existed before the 1974 creation of Cumbria County Council.
2. A note on pronunciation: "ð" or "eth" is a scary looking little consonant but it signifies a sound which we all use on a daily basis, that of the "th" combination we find in "breathe" or "that."
3. Trod is a Lakeland dialect word of Old English / Old Norse etymology and means, path, route, way trodden.
4. This show is usually referred to as the Eskdale Show which began in 1864 and is

organised by the Fell Dales Association, an organisation which was created to foster and promote mutual support between Herdwick farmers as well as the development of the breed. The organisation and the show thus acted as an important formalisation of social and community bonds between people living in the central Lakeland valleys, whose ongoing though evolving ways of life help us to make sense of the evidence of human history we can find in the region's place-names.

5. Neil Curry (Ed), *Norman Nicholson: Collected* Poems, 1994
6. Ibid; 7. Ibid. 8. My emphasis.

RETROSPECTION

John Gough Notes from *The Dark Path to Knowledge*, edited by Michael Pearson and Ian Hodkinson, CWASS; notes reproduced by kind permission of the editors.

1. Moldavian balm is also known as moldavian dragonhead, and was first formally described by Linnaeus in 1753. It has dragon-like blue flowers and lemon-scented foliage, and is native to Moldavia (now Moldova, Romania and Ukraine).
2. Hydrophobia or 'fear of water' is a set of symptoms associated with the later stages of rabies. The person has difficulty swallowing – showing panic when presented with liquids to drink.
3. John Fothergill (1712–1780) was a physician, plant collector and Quaker. Born in Wensleydale, he attended Sedbergh School before being apprenticed to an apothecary. He went on to study medicine at Edinburgh before practising in London.
4. Ingestion of henbane may result in hallucinations and if consumed in large quantities may result in death.
5. John Wilson (1696–1751) wrote *A Synopsis of British Plants: in Ray's Method*, 1744. Extensive biographical details are included in Hodkinson (2019) *Natural Awakenings*.
6. John Ray (1627–1705) wrote extensively on botany and zoology and made important contributions to taxonomy. It is unclear which Thomson is referred to: one possibility is Thomas Thomson (1773-1852), the Scottish chemist, who founded *The Annals of Philosophy* in 1813. This became a leading scientific periodical of the time.
7. John Gerard (c1545–1612), author of *The Herball*, or *General Historie of Plantes*, Norton, London (1597) and John Parkinson (1567-1650) wrote *Theatrum Botanicum*: *The Theatre of Plants* or *An Herball of a Large Extent*, Coates, London (1640).

RESISTANCE

Charlie Gere

1. Robin McKie, 'Sellafield: The Most Hazardous Place in Europe', the *Guardian*, 2009
2. Ibid. 3. Ibid.

Maggie Reed

1. *The Queen's (now the King's) Guide to the Sands* is the royally appointed guide to crossing the sands of Morecambe Bay, an ancient and potentially dangerous tidal crossing in northwest England.

Karen Lloyd

Thanks and appreciation to Dr Josie Gill of Bristol University and to Maxwell Ayamba of Nottingham University for their assistance in this piece.

1. Also written about in *The Gathering Tide*.
2. 'The Transatlantic Slave Trade', *Visit Lancaster*, https://visitlancaster.org.uk/museums/maritime-museum/the-transatlantic-slave-trade/
3. *The Lonsdale magazine*, 1820. 4. Ibid

RESTORATION

Polly Atkin

1. Bruce Robinson, 'We've gone on holiday by mistake', *Withnail and I* (1987).
2. Henry David Thoreau, 'I went to the woods because I wished to live deliberately, *Walden*, 1854
3. 'the Author retired to his native mountains, with the hope of being enabled to

construct a literary Work that might live', William Wordsworth, 'Preface to the 1814 Edition', *Prose Works*
4.   Thomas De Quincey, 'Lake Reminiscences, from 1807-1830, By The English Opium-Eater, No.1', in *The Works of De Quincey*, Grevel Lindop et al (ed), 2003
5.   William Wordsworth, 'Home at Grasmere', *A Guide Through the District of the Lakes*, 1810
6.   Thomas De Quincey, 'Sketch of Professor Wilson', *The Works of Thomas De Quincey*, Vol 1, Grevel Lindop, Barry Symonds (Ed), 2000
7.   Dorothy Wordsworth, 2 June 1802, *The Grasmere and Alfoxden Journals*, ed. by Pamela Woof, 2002
8.   Ibid
9.   'An Interesting Boghole', *Lakes Herald*, 5 December 1890. Accessed through the *British Newspaper Archive*.
10. Miranda Hart, Instagram Post, 2 May 2020 https://www.instagram.com/p/B_r_gNuFHVR/>
11. *Westmorland Gazette*, 9 August 1890. Accessed through the *British Newspaper Archive*.
12. Dorothy Wordsworth, 8 February 1802, *The Grasmere and Alfoxden Journals*, ed. by Pamela Woof, 2002
13. Ibid

CONTRIBUTORS

Stan L Abbott is an award-winning journalist and writer on the outdoors and conservation, whose career as a journalist began in Yorkshire. He is Chair of the Outdoor Writers & Photographers Guild. His books *Ring of Stone Circles* (2022) and *Walking the Line* (2020) were shortlisted for Lakeland Book of the Year awards.

Jason Allen-Paisant is a writer and senior lecturer at the University of Manchester. He is the author of two poetry collections, including the award-winning *Thinking with Trees*.

Simon Armitage is the current Poet Laureate for the United Kingdom. He has received many awards for his poetry, and was named the Millennium Poet in 1999. He has published over 15 full poetry collections.

Alison Armstrong is a writer of prose and plays, originally from East Yorkshire and now based in Lancashire. She won a Northern Writers' Award in 2017 and a Royal Society of Literature award in 2020. Her poems, essays and short stories have been published in magazines and journals, and *Fossils* is her first book.

Jenn Ashworth was born in Preston and studied at the universities of Cambridge and Manchester. Her novels include *A Kind of Intimacy*, *The Friday Gospels*, *Fell* and *Ghosted: A Love Story*. She was elected a Fellow of the Royal Society of Literature in 2018. In 2019 she published *Notes Made While Falling*, a memoir told in a series of essays. She is a Professor of Writing at Lancaster University.

Polly Atkin is a writer of poetry and nonfiction. She has published two poetry collections, and one nonfiction book on the life of Dorothy

Wordsworth. She lives in Grasmere.

William Atkins is a non-fiction author. He has published four books, the first of which was shortlisted for the Wainwright Prize. His journalistic work has been published in the *Guardian* and the *New York Times*, amongst other publications.

Maxwell Ayamba is a journalist and academic who advocates for increased access to nature for marginalised communities. He is the founder and co-ordinator of the Sheffield Environmental Movement, and co-founder of the walking group, Black Men Walking.

Victoria Bennett is a disabled poet and author. Her debut memoir, *All My Wild Mothers* (Two Roads, 2023) won a Northern Promise Award, and a Society of Authors grant to develop from draft, and was longlisted for the inaugural Nan Shepherd Prize. She founded Wild Women Press in 1999 to support rural women writers in Cumbria, and is the curator of the Wild Woman Web project, an inclusive online space focusing on nature, connection, and creativity. When not juggling writing, full-time care, and genetic illness, she can be found where the wild weeds grow, tending her apothecary garden.

Mike Barlow is a poet and artist who has received numerous awards for his poetry and has published ten full collections and pamphlets.

Thomas Bewick (1753 – 1828) was a natural history author and prolific engraver born at Cherryburn in Mickley, Northumberland. He is best known for his illustrated work, *A History of British Birds.*

Amy-Jane Beer is a biologist, naturalist and writer based in North Yorkshire. She is a Country Diarist for *the Guardian*, a columnist for *British Wildlife* and a feature writer for *BBC Wildlife magazine*, among others. She campaigns for equality of access to nature and sits on the steering group of the environmental arts charity New Networks for Nature, and is President of Friends of the Dales.

William Billington (1825-1884) was known as the 'Blackburn poet'. Especially rare for his time in being a working-class poet who worked in cotton mills, he also wrote journalistic accounts for various publications, sometimes in local dialect. His work focused on Lancashire and its people, and his poems were published widely in broadsheets, as well as in his own collections.

Anne Brontë (1820 – 1849) was a novelist and poet, and the youngest Brontë sister. Her most well-known novel is *The Tenant of Wildfell Hall*, which is now viewed by many as the first feminist novel.

Charlotte Brontë (1826-1855) was the oldest of the Brontë sisters. A novelist and poet, she is best known for the classic novel *Jane Eyre.* She published four novels in her lifetime, which she spent in Haworth, West

CONTRIBUTORS

Yorkshire, where she was born and lived with her two sisters, Anne and Emily, also authors, her father Patrick, and brother Branwell.

Emily Brontë (1818-1948) was a novelist and poet, best known for *Wuthering Heights.* The middle sister of the Bronte daughters. Though Wuthering Heights was her only published novel, she also produced much poetry throughout her lifetime. She lived in Haworth, West Yorkshire with her two sisters, brother and father.

Claire Burnett is a writer who first learned to love the countryside as a child, living on Exmoor. She moved North in her forties, to the Yorkshire Dales, then Lancaster, and now enjoys exploring Morecambe Bay and the wider area.

Jane Burn is an award-winning poet and illustrator based in the North East of England. Her poems have been published in anthologies including *The Valley Press Anthology of Prose Poetry* and *The Anthology of Illness.*

Rachel Burns is a poet, short story writer and playwright. She has been longlisted in several playwriting competitions, and has had her poems published in various literary magazines. Her poetry pamphlet, *a girl in a blue dress* is published by Vane Women Press.

Loren Cafferty is a writer of fiction and creative non-fiction, from Cumbria. She currently lives in the Forest of Bowland.

Dick Capel was Countryside Manager for the East Cumbria Countryside Project and commissioned the Goldsworthy Sheepfolds and the Eden Poetry Path, as well as working on conservation initiatives in the region. He was previously a warden for the Nature Conservancy Council. *The Stream Invites Us to Follow* (Saraband, 2021) is his first book.

Julie Carter is an essayist, poet and non-fiction writer and an MA student at Lancaster University. Details of her books and her popular monthly 'Mindfell' Blog can be found at www.mindfell.co.uk.

Born and raised in Barrow-in-Furness, **Nicola Carter** now works as a mountain leader and climbing instructor in the Lake District. She began writing during the winter lockdown of 2021 and won a place on Lancaster Lit Fest's series of writing workshops, New Writing Northwest. Her essay 'Fragments on the Mountain's Edge' won first place in the inaugural Future Places Writing Essay Prize (2021).

Mark Carson has published two pamphlets with Wayleave Press, *Hove-to is a State of Mind* (2015) and *The Hoopoe's Eye* (2019).

Jo Clement is a writer, editor and lecturer in creative writing at Northumbria University. In 2012, she received a New Writing North award.

Mark Cocker is an acclaimed naturalist and author. He has written extensively on the natural world for British newspapers and in his own publications.

Dani Cole is a features writer and photojournalist based in Manchester. In 2021, she was highly commended in the NCTJ Awards for Excellence as Trainee Feature Writer of the Year. She is passionate about storytelling, with a particular focus on people and communities. More at www.dani-cole.co.uk

Samuel Taylor Coleridge (1772-1834) was an English Romantic poet known for launching the romantic age of English Literature alongside William Wordsworth, with their joint publication *Lyrical Ballads*. He is most well-known for his longer poems, particularly *The Rime of the Ancient Mariner*, *Kubla Khan* and *Christabel*. He spent the last half of his life in Grasmere, the Lake District.

Wilkie Collins (1824-1889) was a novelist and playwright who authored *The Woman in White* and *The Moonstone*. He collaborated with and was mentored by his contemporary, Charles Dickens.

WG Collingwood (1854-1932) was an artist, author, academic and antiquary. He worked closely with John Ruskin as his assistant, and was a long-term resident of Coniston, Cumbria.

David Cooper teaches English at Manchester Metropolitan University where he is the founding co-director of the Centre for Place Writing. He is currently writing a critical book on the immersiveness of contemporary place writing.

Geoff Cox is a retired educational designer from Sunderland, now living in the South Lakes. He started writing in 2018 and has worked in several genres. In 2020, with painter Heather Dawe, he released *Traceless*, a book on fell-running and the environment, published by Little Peak.

Kerry Darbishire is a poet based in Cumbria, with most of her poetry drawing on the region as their subject matter. She has published three full poetry collections, and two poetry pamphlets.

Peter Davidson has edited multiple poetry anthologies and has published numerous academic articles on the post-reformation culture of British Catholocism. He is currently a Senior Research Fellow at the University of Oxford.

Carey Davies is a journalist focused on the outdoors and natural history, and a writer for the *Guardian's* 'Country Diary.'

Kate Davis is a poet and storyteller from the Furness peninsula, where she was born and still lives. Her writing is an exploration of that area – its geology, landscape and sea – and of what it's like to exist in such a place when you have a disability that affects mobility. In 2018 she set up Open Mountain, with Kendal Mountain Literature Festival, to provide a space where people can talk about their experiences of who gets to go where.

CONTRIBUTORS

Charles Dickens (1812–1870) was a Victorian novelist and social critic. He is the author of some of Britain's most well-known novels, including *Great Expectations*, *Oliver Twist*, and *A Christmas Carol*. He has a lasting legacy as one of the most-read English authors.

Joanna C. Dobson is a writer and researcher from Sheffield, where she is studying for a PhD in English and Creative Writing at Sheffield Hallam University. This piece arose from an ongoing collaboration with the electroacoustic composer Julia Schauerman.

Stephen Dunstan was born in Barrow-in-Furness, studied Politics at Lancaster University and lives in Blackpool. He is married to Jane. He has a Masters in Public Administration and works as a Finance Director. A keen birder, he has co-written county avifaunas and bird reports for thirty years.

Paul Farley is a poet, writer and broadcaster from Liverpool. His poetry has received the Whitbread Poetry Award and his non-fiction book, *Edgelands*, co-authored with Michael Symmons Roberts, received the Royal Society of Literature's Jerwood Award. He is now a poetry professor at Lancaster University.

Adam Farrer is a writer and editor who edits the journal *The Real Story*. *Cold Fish Soup*, his first book, won the NorthBound Book Award 2021.

Harriet Fraser is a writer, poet, artist and visiting research fellow at Cumbria University. She is co-founder of the PLACE collective, a community of artists engaged with nature and rural landscapes.

Linda France has published ten poetry collections. *The Knucklebone Floor* (Smokestack 2022) won the Laurel Prize and *Startling* (New Writing North/Faber 2022) includes work from her Writing the Climate residency with New Writing North and Newcastle University.

Elizabeth Gaskell (1810-1865) was a novelist and biographer. She authored the best-known biography of Charlotte Brontë, *The Life of Charlotte Bro*ntë, as well as the well-known novel *North and South*, among others. Originally from London, she settled in Manchester.

Charlie Gere is Professor of Media Theory and History at Lancaster Institute for the Contemporary Arts at Lancaster University and author of *I Hate the Lake District* (Goldsmiths Press, 2019), *World's End* (Goldsmiths Press, 2021) and various books on art, philosophy and technology.

Caroline Gilfillan is a novelist, poet and short story writer. Her short stories have appeared in Mslexia and *The London Magazine*.

Sally Goldsmith is a writer and environmental campaigner, including in the fight for Sheffield's street trees. She has won many prizes for her poetry and broadcasts on BBC Radio 4. Her poetry collection, *Are We There Yet?* (Smith/Doorstop), was published in 2012.

John Gough, born in 1757 in Kendal, Westmorland, was a natural and scientific philosopher who oversaw influential investigations and experiments. Blind from the age of three after suffering from smallpox, Gough's achievements were remarkable. Using his sense of touch and scent he went on to identify every species of plant in the Lake District.

Born in Cumbria, **Katie Hale** is the author of a novel, *My Name is Monster* (Canongate, 2019), and two poetry pamphlets: *Breaking the Surface* (Flipped Eye, 2017) and *Assembly Instructions* (Southword Editions, 2019), which won the Munster Fool for Poetry Chapbook Competition. In 2019, she was awarded a MacDowell Fellowship, and was Poet in Residence at the Wordsworth Trust.

Sarah Hall, born in Carlisle, Cumbria, is a novelist and short story writer who lives in Cumbria. Her novels (including *Haweswater*, *The Electric Michelangelo*, *The Carhullan Army* and most recently, *Burntcoat*) have won or been listed in many awards, including the Booker Prize. She is a Fellow of the Royal Society of Literature.

Jack Threlfall Hartley is a writer and researcher of Old Norse-Icelandic literature and language, investigating some of the surprising ways this materialises in regional identity in twentieth-century Britain. Jack has previously worked for the manuscripts' institute in Reykjavík and does the odd bit of seasonal archaeology work, combining some of these themes in his writing and poetry. He is also a keen mountaineer.

Gerard Manley Hopkins (1884-1889) was a poet and Jesuit priest, who is remembered as one of the leading poets of the Victorian era.

Poet, playwright and broadcaster **Ian McMillan** was born in Barnsley. He has several poetry collections to his name and is well known as the presenter of BBC Radio 3's *The Verb* and for his work in schools and as Poet in Residence for Barnsley F.C.

Ted Hughes (1930-1998) was a poet, translator and children's writer. He was poet laureate in the UK from 1994 until his death. He is most well-known for his poetry. He was raised in the Calder Valley, and spent much of his life in Hebden Bridge.

Andrew Michael Hurley is a Lancastrian novelist and short story writer, a Lecturer in Creative Writing at Manchester Metropolitan University, and a former librarian. His first novel, *The Loney*, won the Costa Best First Novel Award in 2016.

Zaffar Kunial is a British poet born in Birmingham and living in Yorkshire. His award-winning work is widely published. In 2014 he was Poet-in-Residence at the Wordsworth Trust in Grasmere.

CONTRIBUTORS

Ann Lingard (Dr Ann Lackie) is a scientist who now runs a smallholding within sight of the Solway Firth, a novelist (with a special interest in the use of science in fiction), and writer of non-fiction. Her latest book is *The Fresh and the Salt: The Story of the Solway* (Birlinn 2020). Her personal blog is *Eliot and Entropy,* and she also blogs at *Solway Shore-walker* www.solwayshorewalker.co.uk

Karen Lloyd is the author of prizewinning nature books including *The Gathering Tide* and *The Blackbird Diaries.* She grew up in South Cumbria, and has lived there for most of her life. She has had poems commissioned by the BBC, and is the editor of this anthology.

Harriet Martineau (1802 – 1876) is known to many as the first female sociologist. After losing her hearing as a child, she studied avidly and was eventually able to support herself as a writer, working in a variety of genres. She spent significant portions of her life in Newcastle, Tynemouth and, later, Ambleside.

J.A. Mensah is a writer of prose and theatre and a Lecturer in English and Creative Writing at the University of York. *Castles from Cobwebs,* her first novel, won the inaugural NorthBound Book Award and was longlisted for the Desmond Elliott Prize 2021. Her plays have focused on human rights narratives and the testimonies of survivors.

Jake Morris-Campbell is an author, poet and critic with two published poetry pamphlets; he lectures in Creative Writing and English Literature.

Graham Mort lives in rural North Yorkshire and writes poetry and short fiction. His latest book of poems is *Black Shiver Moss* (Seren, 2017); his latest book of stories is *Like Fado* (Salt, 2020).

Helen Mort is a writer who has published two poetry collections, a novel and a short story collection. She has been shortlisted for the T.S Eliot and Costa prizes, and won the Fenton Aldeburgh prize. She is currently a senior lecturer at Manchester Metropolitan University.

Novelist, place writer, poet, journalist and critic **Benjamin Myers** was born in Durham. His work has been translated into several languages. His books include *The Perfect Golden Circle, The Offing, Under the Rock* and *The Gallows Pole, which won* the Walter Scott Prize. He has also won the Portico Prize for Literature and the Gordon Burn Prize.

Norman Nicholson (1914-1987) was a poet who focused on concerns local to Cumbria, where he lived. His poetry was characterised by a simplicity of language drawn from the everyday speech of people in his town.

Shirley Nicholson holds an MA from the Centre for New Writing, University of Manchester, and served on the advisory committee for Manchester-based Poets and Players. Her poems have appeared in various anthologies and magazines and been selected for the International Poems on the Move Competition in 2021 and 2022.

Ella Pontefract (1896-1945) was an author who wrote extensively on the subject of the Yorkshire Dales, producing six books on the subject. She lived in Yorkshire for the majority of her life.

Katrina Porteous is a poet, historian and broadcaster, specialising in work on the theme of nature and place. She has lived on the Northumberland coast since 1987. She is President of the Northumbrian Language Society and the Coble and Keelboat Society, and is an ambassador for New Networks for Nature.

Clare Proctor's poems have been published in magazines including *the North, Finished Creatures* and *Shooter* and in *the Handstand Press Anthology of New Cumbrian Writing.* She was runner-up in the Canterbury Festival Poet of the Year competition in 2018 and in the Ware Poetry competition in 2021.

Thomas de Quincey (1785 – 1859) was a writer, essayist and literary critic. Born in Manchester, he is best known for the autobiographical *Confessions of an English Opium-Eater*, chronicling his own addiction to Laudanum.

Kathleen Raine (1908–2003) was a poet, critic and founding member of the Temenos Academy, offering education in philosophy and the arts.

Laurence Rose is a writer and conservationist who has worked for the RSPB since 1983. His writing mainly focuses on the cultural aspects of nature and conservation. He is also a composer, having had pieces performed at concerts and festivals in the UK and the Netherlands.

Maggie Reed lives in West Malvern. She has been published in *The North magazine, Orbis and Three Drops from a Cauldron,* as well as numerous anthologies. She came *third* in *Settle Sessions Poetry Competition (2016)* and won *first prize in the Poem and a Pint competition (2019).* She tweets as @MaggieHow

Anita Sethi was born in Manchester, where her love of nature first flourished in wild urban spaces. Her first book, *I Belong Here: a Journey Along the Backbone of Britain* received outstanding reviews and was nominated for the Wainwright Prize for Nature Writing, the Portico Prize, Royal Society of Literature's Ondaatje Prize and Great Outdoors Award. Her writing has also appeared in anthologies and she has written for the *Guardian, Observer, i, Sunday Times, Telegraph, Vogue, TLS, BBC Wildlife* and more. www.anitasethi.com

Clare Shaw is a poet and creative writing tutor for literary organisations including the Poetry School, the Wordsworth Trust and the Arvon Foundation and is co-director of the Kendal Poetry Festival.

CONTRIBUTORS

Lemn Sissay is an author, poet and playwright who has published poetry collections, children's books and a memoir. He was the official poet of the London 2012 Olympics, and has been chancellor of the University of Manchester since 2015. He is also a successful broadcaster in both radio and television.

Michael Symmons Roberts is a writer from Preston, Lancashire. A poet, non-fiction writer and writer for the stage, he has been winner of the Whitbread Poetry Award, and been shortlisted for the T.S. Eliot prize. His collaborative work with composer James MacMillan – the opera *Clemency* – was nominated for an Olivier award.

Jane Routh is a poet living in Lancashire who has published five poetry collections to date. Her collections have been nominated for multiple poetry awards.

John Ruskin (1819–1900) was a prolific writer, philosopher and educator in the humanities, covering subjects from architecture and painting to literature and politics. Born in London, he travelled widely, living and working mostly in Oxford for many years before moving to the Lake District in 1872.

Lee Schofield is RSPB Site Manager at Haweswater in the Lake District National Park, and author of *Wild Fell: Fighting for Nature on a Lake District Hill Farm* (Doubleday, 2022). Follow him on Twitter @ leeinthelakes

Prudence Mary Scott (1926–2019) was a lifelong diarist and poet who moved to the Lake District in 1961. She brought up her four children in Windermere, mostly as a single parent, immersing them in nature.

Jane Smith lives in Cheshire and writes fiction and non-fiction, mainly on environmental themes. Website: www.janecsmith.com.

Jane Routh is a poet based in Lancashire. She has published five collections of poetry, and has had her work featured in the *Guardian*.

Robert Southey (1774 – 1843) was an English Romantic poet, who was poet laureate from 1813 until his death. As well as poetry, he also wrote histories, biographies, essays, travelogues, translations and more.

A southerner by birth, and a former museum archaeologist, **Anne Taylor** now lives and writes in Cumbria. "I always loved telling stories about ancient objects, seeing the human detail in a stone tool or piece of pottery; now I write about the local landscape, and the history in our place-names."

Jennifer Lee Tsai is the author of two poetry pamphlets, *Kismet* (ignitionpress, 2019), and *La Mystérique* (Guillemot Press, 2022). She won a Northern Writers Award in 2020 and is currently a doctoral candidate in Creative Writing at the University of Liverpool.

Tara Vallente is a journalist and writer based in the Lake District. Her work is a mixture of news, non-fiction and poetry.

Thomas West (1720 – 1779) was a Jesuit priest known for being among the first authors to write about and influence tourism in the Lake District through his 1778 *A Guide to the Lakes.*

Susie White is a writer, lecturer, photographer and gardener. She has published eight gardening books, is the garden columnist for *My Weekly* magazine, and her nature writing is regularly featured in the *Guardian.*

Elspeth Wilson is a creative writer and facilitator working across poetry and prose. She is particularly interested in embodiment, in different ways of looking at nature and how who we are impacts our relationship with the environment. Her work has been shortlisted for the Nan Shepherd Prize and the Penguin Write Now scheme.

Dorothy Wordsworth (1771-1855) was an author, diarist and poet. She was born in Cumberland and spent much of her life in the Lake District, where she lived with her brother, William Wordsworth.

William Wordsworth (1770-1850) was an English Romantic poet who is known for launching the romantic age of English Literature with a joint publication with Samuel Taylor Coleridge, titled *Lyrical Ballads.* He was born and spent much of his working life in the Lake District.

Po Yarwood's poems have been published in *The North, The Interpreter's House, Strix* and in several anthologies. Her pamphlets, *Image Junkie* (2017) and *Loop* (2021), are published by Wayleave Press.

Simon Zonenblick is a poet and nature writer from West Yorkshire. He has several poetry collections and a film to his name and contributes nature features to newspapers including the *Yorkshire Post.*

ACKNOWLEDGEMENTS

All contributions are copyright © by each individual author and are reproduced by kind permission of the author, except where noted below, or the author's works are in the public domain:

'Anthem of the North', © Lemn Sissay, was commissioned by the Great Exhibition of the North for National Poetry Day 2018, and is reproduced by kind permission of the author. 'The Magic Cattle Grid': Essay ©2022 Loren Cafferty, reproduced by permission of Loren Cafferty, first appeared as a podcast for Lancaster Litfest: Walking Solo 2020. Extract

ACKNOWLEDGEMENTS

from *Castles from Cobwebs*, Saraband © 2021 by J.A. Mensah. Extract from *The Stream Invites Us to Follow*, Saraband © 2021 Dick Capel. Extract from Cold Fish Soup, Saraband © 2022 by Adam Farrer. Extract from *Farewell Happy Fields* © 1973 by Kathleen Raine, reproduced by permission of Faber and Faber Ltd. 'Windscale' and 'Sea to the West' from *Collected Poems* by Norman Nicholson (Faber & Faber), reproduced by permission of David Higham Associates. 'An icy rain fell', © by Prudence Mary Scott, is reproduced by kind permission of Rebecca Scott. 'Seagulls' and 'Those Who Can Afford Time' © Jason Allen-Paisant, Thinking with Trees, Carcanet 2021, reproduced by kind permission of the author. 'Great Northern Diver', © Michael Symmons Roberts, reproduced by kind permission of the author. 'The Most Mancunian of Trees, by David Cooper: the author acknowledges that the research on the black poplar is being led by his friend and colleague, Christopher Hanley, to whom he extends his thanks. Extract from *The Electric Michelangelo*, © 2004 by Sarah Hall, reproduced by permission of Faber and Faber Ltd. 'Horses' © 1957 by Ted Hughes from *The Hawk in the Rain*, reproduced by permission of Faber and Faber Ltd. 'Spring Gentians' by Mark Cocker from *Ground Work* edited by Tim Dee. Published by Jonathan Cape. Copyright © Mark Cocker. Reproduced by permission of the author c/o Rogers, Coleridge & White Ltd., 20 Powis Mews, London W11 1JN. 'Black-backed Gull' © Paul Farley, reproduced by kind permission of the author. 'Sellafield' from *I Hate the Lake District*, © Charlie Gere, Goldsmiths Press, reproduced by kind permission of the author. Extract from *Fell*, © by Jenn Ashworth, reproduced with permission of Hodder and Stoughton Limited through PLSclear. 'Rain' from *Under the Rock: The Poetry of a Place* by Benjamin Myers (Elliott & Thompson, 2018) reproduced with permission of Ben Myers and Elliott & Thompson. 'Kneeling African: Dunham Massey' by Maxwell Ayamba, first published on the Black Health and the Humanities Blog, Black Health and Humanities Network, University of Bristol, reproduced by kind permission of the author. Extract from *The Moor: Lives, Landscape, Literature*, © 2014 by William Atkins, reproduced by permission of Faber and Faber Ltd. 'The Blue Lonnen' from *Two Countries*, © 2014 by Katrina Porteous, reproduced by permission of Bloodaxe Books. 'Tempest Avenue' from *To Fold the Evening Star: New And Selected Poems*, © Ian McMillan, reproduced by kind permission of Carcanet. 'Spotted Woodpeckers', © by Graham Mort, was previously published in *Black Shiver Moss* (Seren, 2017) and *Samara* (4Word, 2020), reproduced by kind permission of the author. 'The Ancient Land of Borsdane Wood'by Dani Cole was first published on the Manchester Mill, manchestermill.co.uk, reproduced by kind permission of the author and Manchester Mill. 'Mersey River'© by Jennifer

NORTH COUNTRY

Lee Tsai was originally published in *Kismet* (ignitionpress, 2019) and is reproduced by kind permission of the author. A longer version of 'A Trip to the Countryside', © by Anita Sethi, appeared in *Common People: An Anthology of Working Class Writers*, ed. Kit de Waal (Unbound, 2019), and this is reproduced by kind permission of the author. Extract from 'Clavicle Wood', © by Andrew Michael Hurley, an essay in Test Signal, ed. Nathan Connolly (Bloomsbury, 2021), reproduced by kind permission of the author. 'Bores on the Solway' © 2022 by Ann Lingard was first published in *Solway Shore-walker*. 'This Wild Garden', © 2022 by Victoria Bennett, is reproduced by kind permission of the author. 'Rain' and 'Puddle' from *Stanza Stones* (2013) © by Simon Armitage are reproduced by permission of Enitharmon Editions. 'Foxglove Country' by Zaffar Kunial. Copyright © Zaffar Kunial. Reproduced by permission of the author c/o Rogers, Coleridge & White Ltd., 20 Powis Mews, London W11 1JN. Parts of 'The Northern Hay Meadow' © by Lee Schofield were published in Wild Fell: Fighting for Nature on a Lake District Hill Farm (Transworld, 2022); this essay is reproduced by kind permission of the author. 'Spar Boxes, Northern England', from *Distance and Memory*, © by Peter Davidson, reproduced by permission of Carcanet Press Ltd. 'Kirkdale Cave, North Yorkshire, by Amy-Jane Beer; The Chevin, Otley, by Carey Davies; and Lordenshaw, Northumberland, by Susie White are all © by their respective authors and first appeared in the *Guardian* Country Diary. 'April' from *Green Noise*, Jean Sprackland, reproduced by permission of Morgan Green Creatives Ltd.

"I love the North."
JEANETTE WINTERSON
The Guardian, January 2018